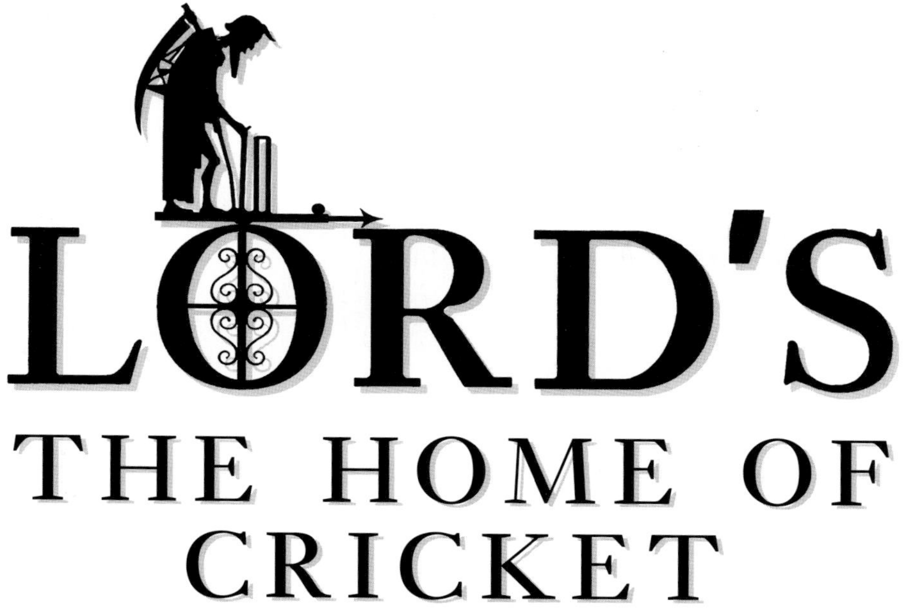

LORD'S
THE HOME OF CRICKET

'The pavilion sometimes seems the Valhalla

of the game, the home of the immortality of the

heroes of the past. Every cricketer would

give years of his life to have the honour of a century

at Lord's or of a superb bowling performance.'

Neville Cardus on Lord's

THE ILLUSTRATED HISTORY

Niall Edworthy

Virgin

Author Acknowledgements
I am indebted to a number of people for their help in putting this book together, but there are a few who deserve special thanks. At Lord's, Stephen Green, Gerald Howat, Chris Rea, Glenys Williams, Michael Wolton, and above all, Karen Marshall, could not have been more helpful. In James Bennett at Virgin Publishing I was lucky to have an editor of the very highest quality whose hard work, enthusiasm and thoroughness were greatly appreciated.

Publisher Acknowledgements
The publishers would like to thank the following for their help and enthusiasm: David Hamilton and Caroline Hutchinson at Link Licensing, Lynda Cole at Patrick Eagar Photography, Mark Goldsmith at Allsport, Oliver Frey and Keith Williams at Prima Creative Services, Richard Wilson and Steve Dobell.

First published in Great Britain in 1999 by Virgin Books
An imprint of Virgin Publishing Ltd
Thames Wharf Studios, Rainville Road, London W6 9HT

A catalogue record for the book is available from the British Library.

ISBN 1-85227-794-7

Design and repro by Prima Creative Services
Printed and bound by Butler and Tanner, Frome and London

Picture Credits:
© MCC: 13, 16, 17, 18, 19, 20, 23, 24, 30, 32, 33, 34, 35, 37, 42 top, 46, 47 top, 49, 51, 54, 60, 61, 62, 64, 65, 75, 78, 82, 85, 95, 96, 101, 114, 117, 119, 121, 124, 132, 198, 250 **© MCC courtesy of Bridgeman Art Library:** front cover, 7, 8, 9, 10, 11, 12, 14, 22, 25, 26-7, 28, 29, 36, 37 left, 38-39, 42 bottom, 43, 48, 50, 55, 58, 59, 66, 71, 86, 87, 88-89, 90, 92, 111, 219, 224 **© Hulton Getty:** 6, 94, 99 top, 102 bottom, 103, 108-109, 110, 126, 135 **© Allsport:** 40-41, 47 bottom, 52, 69, 70, 73, 76, 79, 80, 83, 84, 98-99, 100, 102 top, 104, 106, 107, 113, 115, 120, 122-123, 130, 136-137, 140, 145, 158, 163, 169, 176, 177, 178 bottom, 181, 186, 188-189, 193, 194, 195, 197 bottom, 200-201, 229, 230, 231, 232 top, 232 bottom, 233, 234, 235, 236, 241, 242, 243, 249 **© Mansell Collection/Time Inc./Katz:** 44, 45, 57, 74, 77, 91 **© Alpha/Sport and General:** 112, 139, 141, 142, 146, 148, 149, 150, 151, 152-153, 154-155, 156-157, 238, 246-247, 244, 246 bottom **© Patrick Eagar:** 2, 118, 129, 160, 162, 164, 165, 166, 167, 168, 170, 171, 172-173, 174, 175, 178 top, 179, 182, 183, 184, 185, 190-191, 192, 196, 197 top, 201, 202-203 top, 202-203 bottom, 204-205, 204 bottom, 206, 207, 208, 209, 210-211, 212-213, 214-215, 216-217, 218, 220, 222-223, 226, 248, 256

Front cover painting: 'England v. Australia Centenary Test Match' by Arthur Weaver (b.1918)

CONTENTS

1787–1870

THE FIRST CENTURY

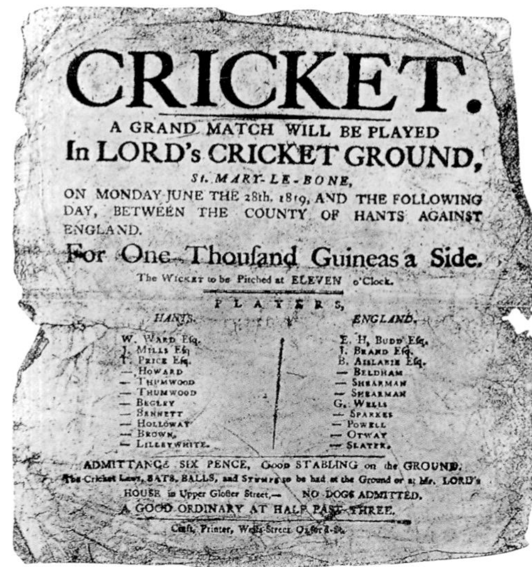

CRICKET.

A GRAND MATCH WILL BE PLAYED

In LORD's CRICKET GROUND,

St. MARY-LE-BONE,

ON MONDAY JUNE THE 28th, 1819, AND THE FOLLOWING DAY, BETWEEN THE COUNTY OF HANTS AGAINST ENGLAND.

For One Thouſand Guineas a Side.

The WICKET to be Pitched at ELEVEN o'Clock.

PLAYERS,

HANTS.	ENGLAND.
W. Ward Eſq.	E. H. Budd Eſq.
J. Mills Eſq	J. Brand Eſq.
T. Price Eſq.	B. Aislabie Eſq.
— Howard	— Beldham
— Thumwood	— Shearman
— Thumwood	— Shearman
— Begley	G. Wells
— Bennett	— Sparkes
— Holloway	— Powell
— Brown,	— Otway
— Lilleywhite.	— Slater.

ADMITTANCE SIX PENCE, Good STABLING on the GROUND.

The Cricket Laws, BATS, BALLS, and Stumps to be had at the Ground or at Mr. LORD's HOUSE in Upper Gloſter Street,— NO DOGS ADMITTED.

A GOOD ORDINARY AT HALF PAST THREE.

Craft, Printer, Wells-Street Oxford-St.

Handbill advertising an 1819 match between England and Hampshire at Lord's.

It has been said that if the French aristocracy had followed the example of their English cousins and played cricket with their people, then the 1789 Revolution might never have taken place and the whole course of Western European history would have been entirely different. Why chop off his Lordship's head with a guillotine when you can humiliate him with a cricket ball?

Cricket, the theory goes, provided England's labouring classes with the opportunity to feel that at least in some areas of life there was 'a level playing field'. The causes of the Revolution and the Terror that followed were, of course,

infinitely more complex, but there is more than a faint edge of truth to the notion of cricket having an equalising effect in a community. When word filtered through the shires or the squalid back streets of London that Bernard the blacksmith had clean bowled Lord Lymeswold for a duck, his Lordship's humiliation will have served the purpose of reminding the populace that the aristocracy were at least prepared to share a cricket field – if not their wealth – with the lower orders.

Two years before the French people stormed the Bastille and brought down the ancient regime, a group of England's pleasure-seeking aristocrats were concerned about finding a site in London where they could pursue their favourite new pastime. Two of their number, the Earl of Winchilsea and Charles Lennox, the future Duke of Richmond, employed Thomas Lord, an entrepreneurial Yorkshireman and fellow cricketer, to seek out a suitable field within a short carriage ride of their Mayfair homes. (On 14 July 1789, the day the Bastille was stormed, Winchilsea was twice bowled out for nought by Bullen in the Hampshire v. Kent match at Hambledon.) Little can Lord have known, when he took out a lease on a scruffy plot of land a mile or so to

CRICKET 18TH-CENTURY STYLE IN MARYLEBONE FIELDS.

the north-west of central London, that he had just founded what would become one of the most famous institutions in the British Empire and what today is still regarded as the spiritual home of cricket as well as the game's physical seat of power. The site he had found was the first of three homes for the Marylebone Cricket Club – all within half a mile of each other – before they settled once and for all, in 1814, on the plot of land that is the Lord's we know today.

Until the formation of MCC, Hambledon, a small village in Hampshire, had been the unofficial headquarters of English cricket. The club first began to attract interest from outside its immediate area from around 1756, when crowds from all over southern England flocked to see matches on the famous Broadhalfpenny Down ground.

A list of members drawn up by F.S. Ashley-Cooper in *The Hambledon Cricket Chronicle* suggests that out of 157 members eighteen were titled, while four were clergy, 27 were in the army or navy, six were MPs and the rest were sons of the more senior players and men from the local community. Hambledon was the most famous cricket club in England, but its lustre waned after it lost the patronage of several influential figures such as the Duke of Dorset and Sir Horatio Mann.

Organised cricket was a largely aristocratic initiative in its earliest years, and London was the aristocracy's playground. Hambledon, situated deep in the heart of the Hampshire countryside and reachable only by a network of meandering, pot-holed lanes, could not hope to compete with the geographical expediency and social attractions of Georgian London.

An upsurge in industry and commerce, meanwhile, brought unprecedented riches to an aspirational gentry and the arriviste mercantile classes. Hunting, shooting, cricket,

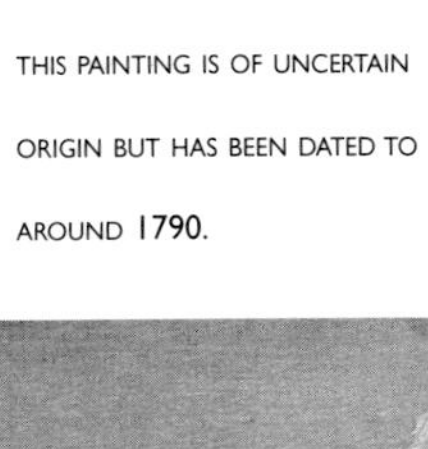

Entitled '*A Game of Cricket*', this painting is of uncertain origin but has been dated to around 1790.

WATERCOLOUR DRAWING BY GEORGE SHEPHEARD (1770-1842). IT SHOWS THE WELL-KNOWN HAMBLEDON PLAYERS WALKER, HARRIS AND BELDHAM.

card-playing and any form of gambling were the great activities of the day. No event, no matter how minor, could pass without a wager being placed on it. In 1743, for instance, punters could get odds of four to one on King George II being killed when he led his troops into battle against the French.

MCC evolved out of the White Conduit Club, an offshoot of another aristocratic club, the Je-ne-sais-quoi, which was also known as the Star and Garter Club and whose chairman was the Prince of Wales, the future George IV. The White Conduit was 'the acorn that blossomed into the gigantic oak known as the Marylebone Club', wrote the book collector A.D. Taylor in 1903 in *Annals of Lord's and History of the MCC*. The club originally played their matches on public fields in Islington close to what is now King's Cross station, but the members became unhappy with the constant intrusions of the local masses. The public order problem even prompted comment in The Times. In June 1785 the paper advised:

'It is recommended to the Lordling Cricketers who amuse themselves in White Conduit Fields, to procure an Act of Parliament for inclosing their play ground which will not only prevent them being incommoded, but protect themselves from a repetition of severe rebuke which they justly merit, and received on Saturday evening from some spirited citizens whom they insulted and attempted *vi et armis* to drive from their footpath, pretending it was within their bounds.'

The advice from London's leading newspaper did not go unheeded, and it was shortly after this that two of the club's most prominent members, Winchilsea and Lennox, instructed Lord, an employee of the club, to find a new private ground which could be enclosed to keep out the rougher elements of London's hoi polloi.

The first of MCC's three homes was established at Dorset Fields (now Dorset

Cricket in White Conduit Fields, Islington. Based on an engraving of 1787, this is one of six prints in a series entitled 'Manly Recreation'.

Square, situated between Marylebone and Baker Street stations) after Lord leased the land from the Portman Estate. The first match took place on 31 May 1787 between Essex and Middlesex, and the first MCC match against the White Conduit Club on 27 June the following year. Lord, a thrifty Yorkshireman, made the most of the new ground's popularity by erecting a fence and charging a small entrance fee to the public. Lord's quickly became a well-loved landmark in the capital, and not just for cricket-lovers, aristocrats and gamblers. Criminals found that rich pickings were to be had at the ground, as The Times reported in 1802:

'The pickpockets were so daring on Monday evening in the vicinity of Lord's Cricket Ground that they actually took the umbrellas of men and women by force, and even their watches and purses, threatening to stab those who made resistance. They were in gangs of between twenty and thirty and behaved in a manner the most audacious.'

After 21 years the lease on the original ground expired and the club was forced to relocate a mile or so up the road to North Bank – a stretch of open land which today can be seen just to the south of the current ground off the St John's Wood Road. The original ground at Dorset Fields was not abandoned immediately, and until 1811 matches were played on both sites by MCC and the newly formed St John's Wood Cricket Club. The following year, however, the itinerant club was on the move again – albeit just the distance of a good throw from the boundary – to the current site. The move was forced upon MCC by plans for the Grand Union Canal, which was designed to connect the Grand Junction Canal – the main artery from the industrial heartland of the Midlands – with the Thames docks. The proposed canal would split the ground in two, and so Lord, just as he had done before, tore up the best of his turf and had it replanted across the road.

Lord prepared the ground by building a small wooden pavilion, a string of huts and a

THOMAS LORD (1755–1832)

Thomas Lord, who started his career as a practice bowler and attendant to the gentlemen of London's prestigious White Conduit Club, was more businessman than cricket enthusiast. It was with an eye for a profit rather than a messianic urge to promote the game to which he owes his posthumous fame that he set about finding a plot of land which was later to become the headquarters of the cricketing world.

He was born into a Catholic family in the North Yorkshire market town of Thirsk in 1755 before his family moved to Norfolk and then to the capital. His father had been a gentleman farmer, who is thought to have had his land requisitioned following his participation in the Jacobite uprising of 1745, after which he was made to work as a labourer in the very fields he once owned.

The members of White Conduit Club, a private gentlemen's club in the West End, provided Lord with funds to lease a private ground. Lord, whose business activities included the sale of wine and spirits as well as property, found a site near Regent's Park – then on the outskirts of London – and he built a fence around the site and charged sixpence for admission.

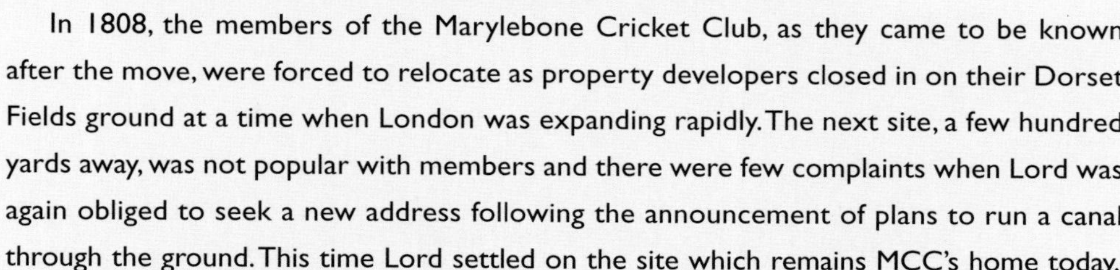

In 1808, the members of the Marylebone Cricket Club, as they came to be known after the move, were forced to relocate as property developers closed in on their Dorset Fields ground at a time when London was expanding rapidly. The next site, a few hundred yards away, was not popular with members and there were few complaints when Lord was again obliged to seek a new address following the announcement of plans to run a canal through the ground. This time Lord settled on the site which remains MCC's home today.

After a small wooden pavilion was built and a tavern had opened next to the ground, the new Lord's opened for business on 22 June 1814 with a match between MCC and Hertfordshire. In 1825 Lord was approached by property developers but William Ward, a prominent cricketer of the day, stepped in to buy Lord's interest for £5,000, thereby stopping a deal that would have spelt the end of the ground that still, proudly if ironically, bears the vendor's name.

Lord continued to live in the St John's Wood area for a while before retiring to West Meon in Hampshire, where he died and was buried in 1832 aged 76. His portrait hangs in the Long Room, and in 1953 he received the honour of having a train named after him by London Transport.

fence to enclose the rough playing area. A tavern had opened up next to the ground, and by 7 May 1814 Lord was able to place an advertisement in the *Morning Post* inviting back the cricketers: 'T. Lord respectfully informs the Noblemen and Gentlemen, Members of the Marylebone and St John's Wood Cricket Clubs that the New Ground is completely ready for playing on: that the first meeting will be on Monday 9th May and continue every Monday, Wednesday and Friday during the season.'

George
Earl of Winchilsea
& Nottingham.
1771.

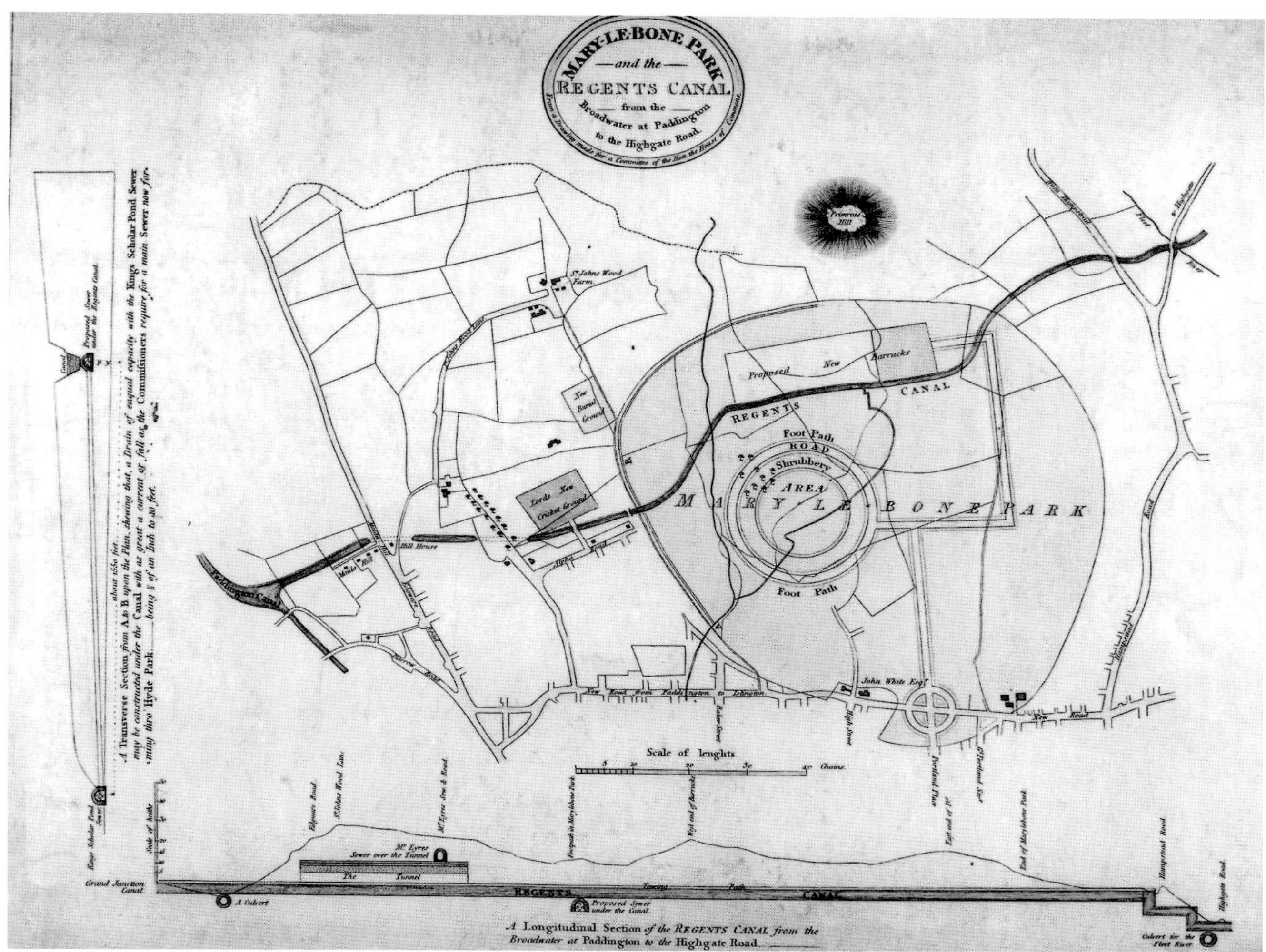

Above: Map showing the route of the Regent's Canal, the construction of which forced Lord to find a new ground.

Opposite: George, Earl of Winchilsea.

Four days before the ground was officially opened an alarming incident was reported in the capital's papers. 'A shocking incident took place on Thursday at New Lord's Cricket Ground public house, Marylebone Fields. The landlady of the house had occasion to use a small quantity of gunpowder, and whilst in the act of taking the same from a paper, containing a pound weight, a spark from the fire caught it, and it went off with a great explosion. The landlady, her sister, and four little girls were seriously burnt. The former are in a dangerous way.' (*The Press*, 1814.)

On 22 June 1814, in the first match at the ground which at the end of the century was to become one of the best-known landmarks in the British Empire, MCC beat Hertfordshire by an innings and 27 runs. The county were bowled out for just 79 and 55 (with only four players reaching double figures) and a Mr A. Schabner, opening the innings for MCC, had the distinction of scoring the first ever half-century on the ground. Lord Frederick Beauclerk, a colourful and cantankerous clergyman whose name would become synonymous with Lord's over the ensuing decades, took five wickets in Hertfordshire's first innings.

Lord's quickly established itself as London's centre of cricket. Players and spectators were joined by gamblers and bookmakers as the fixture list grew by the year. Single- and double-wicket competitions were a popular feature, especially with the betting fraternity. Although the aristocracy were the driving force – and supplied the money – behind the development of cricket at this time, the majority of the best players were ordinary men who were paid for

LORD FREDERICK BEAUCLERK (1773–1850)

Lord Frederick Beauclerk, who played in the very first match at the current Lord's ground, was one of the most influential, colourful and controversial figures in the early years of the Marylebone Cricket Club. The son of a peer and a parson by profession, Lord Frederick was a cricket fanatic as well as an inveterate gambler. But he was just as famous for his gamesmanship, vindictiveness and explosive temper, and by all accounts he seems to have had more enemies than friends by the time he died. A great all-rounder, who was appointed MCC President in 1826, he boasted that he made up to 600 guineas a year through betting on cricket matches, many of them games in which he played himself. Like so many clergymen of his era, he did not make the Church his priority, and it is significant that, although he was a well-known figure, in the evangelical mood of the mid-nineteenth century, *The Times* declined to publish an obituary following his death.

Lord Frederick, a descendant of Charles II and Nell Gwynne, was involved in one of organised cricket's first controversies when he banned from Lord's one of the leading professionals of the day, William Lambert. He accused the Surrey all-rounder of attempting to throw the result of a match between an England XI and a Nottingham XXII by not playing his hardest. He also took a dim view of batsmen using pads which, at the start of the nineteenth century, were no more than a thin piece of wooden board strapped to the front leg. Lord Frederick preferred the traditional and more manly use of a simple knee-high silk stocking, and although he had no objection to the use of pads for practice he is quoted as saying '... but how unfair for bowler if allowed in a match'.

Like many a gentleman cricketer of the day, Lord Frederick enjoyed intense rivalries with a number of his contemporaries, and honour – as well as the result of a sporting contest and the money placed on it – was often at stake in these long-running feuds. His rivalry with 'Squire' Osbaldeston was as legendary as his temper. Once, when bowling without any success at Tom Walker, 'Old Everlasting' of the Hambledon club, he threw his hat to the floor and jumped up and down screaming, 'You confounded old beast!'

Lord Frederick was regarded as the finest amateur batsman of his generation and he scored eight centuries at Lord's alone, on pitches which today would be regarded as unplayable. Disputes between teams up and down the country over the laws of the game were often referred to him as a leading member of the MCC at a time when it had emerged as the supreme, if unofficial, authority in the game. After his retirement he was often to be found at Lord's, sitting at the pavilion gate, a cigar in his mouth and small dog on his lap, muttering about the passing of cricket's finest days.

their services by the members of the leading clubs. They were professionals in everything but name and came from all over the South and the Midlands as the interest in cricket grew in the first part of the nineteeth century. One of the best-known 'professionals', many of whom were former Hambledon players, was William Lambert, whose powerful hitting made him one of the biggest crowd-pullers in the early days of Lord's. In 1817 he became the first man to score two centuries (107 not out and 157) in a match on the ground, when he was hired by Sussex to play against Epsom.

Lambert was closely associated with the Yorkshireman George Osbaldeston, known to everyone as 'the Squire', whose rivalry with other gentlemen cricketers of the day often extended beyond the field of play. Educated at Eton and Oxford, which he left without sitting his final exams, Osbaldeston, a short but powerfully built figure, quickly established his reputation as one of the finest sportsmen of his day. He was said to have once downed 98 pheasants with 100 shots, lost over £200,000 on the horses and at the age of 44 won a bet that he could ride 200 miles in under ten hours. In 1800 he won a bet of 200 guineas from Lord George Bentinck, who on handing over the money impugned the Squire's honour by exclaiming, 'This is robbery!' Osbaldeston, who played in the first ever match at Lord's, was furious and challenged Bentinck to a duel on Wormwood Scrubs. Accounts of the duel vary, some suggesting that Osbaldeston fired his pistol into the air, others claiming that his shot penetrated Bentinck's hat, missing his head by a matter of inches.

William Lambert, celebrated professional cricketer and gambler.

Betting often brought the game into disrepute with the more puritanical elements in society. By no means an exclusively upper-class pursuit, it often led to fighting in the crowds. In 1743 *The Gentleman's Magazine* was moved enough to describe cricket as 'a notorious breach of the laws, as it gives the most open encouragement to gambling'. Huge sums of money were often laid on the outcome of matches, and in 1786 £4,000 pounds was placed on a contest arranged by the Duke of York.

Bitter personal rivalries among members of the aristocracy and gentry were often the motivation behind cricket matches at Lord's – and elsewhere – in the early history of the game. In 1810 Osbaldeston, whose customary partner in double-wicket competitions was Lambert, challenged his old rival Lord Frederick Beauclerk to a match for 50 guineas. On the appointed day Osbaldeston, said to be the fastest bowler of his day as well as one of the biggest-hitting batsmen, was too ill to play, but he refused his adversary's request to postpone the match, insisting that Lambert would play against Lord Frederick and his partner T.C. Howard alone. Lambert won the contest by 14 runs after scoring a two-innings total of 80 and then bowling out Howard for 44 and his Lordship for 24. Lambert infuriated Lord Frederick by sending down a series of wide deliveries before bowling him with a straight one.

The rivalry between the two gentlemen continued for years. Osbaldeston later resigned his membership of MCC in a fit of bad temper, and when he eventually sought readmission having moved into one of the houses adjoining Lord's, the vengeful Beauclerk ensured that his request was not granted. Lambert's career at Lord's also came to a sad end when in 1817 he was 'warned off the turf', having been accused (by Beauclerk and others) of trying to throw the result of the England v. Nottinghamshire match by deliberately playing below his potential.

Like the single- and double-wicket competitions, most team matches (most of them eleven-a-side but some featuring as many as 22) were arranged on an informal basis, and it was not until the second part of the century that the fixture list assumed any kind of permanence. Teams played under the name of a club, village or county, but there was no competition structure nor any rules governing who might play for what team. A match would be arranged between two gentlemen, Lord's would be booked, paid players would be hired for the cause and battle would commence. However, three fixtures established early in the life of

CRICKET.

A GRAND MATCH
WILL BE PLAYED IN

LORD'S GROUND,

MARYLEBONE,

On MONDAY, JULY **31, 1848,** *& following Day.*

The Gentlemen against the Players.

PLAYERS.

Gentlemen.	Players.
Sir F. BATHURST	BOX
E. ELMHURST, Esq.	CLARK
N. FELIX, Esq.	DEAN
H. FELLOWES, Esq.	GUY
R. T. KING, Esq.	HILLYER
J. M. LEE, Esq.	LILLYWHITE
A. MYNN, Esq.	MARTINGALE
W. NICHOLSON, Esq.	PILCH
O. C. PELL, Esq.	W. PILCH
C. RIDDING, Esq.	PARR
G. YONGE, Esq.	WISDEN

MATCHES TO COME.

Wednesday, August 2nd, at Lord's—Harrow against Winchester
Thursday, August 3rd, at Lord's—Eton against Harrow
Friday, August 4th, at Lord's—Winchester against Eton

DARK'S newly-invented LEG GUARDS, also his TUBULAR and other INDIA-RUBBER GLOVES, SPIKED SOLES for CRICKET SHOES, & CRICKET BALLS, to be had of R. Dark, at the Tennis Court.

Cricket Bats and Stumps to be had of M. Dark, at the Manufactory on the Ground.

Admittance 6d............Stabling on the Ground..........Ordinary at 3 o'clock.

Morgan, Printer, 38, Church Street, adjoining the Marylebone Theatre.

Cricket.

A GRAND MATCH

WILL BE PLAYED IN

LORD'S GROUND

MARYLEBONE,

On THURSDAY, JULY, 28th. 1836.

AND FOLLOWING DAY.

The Gentlemen of Eton against the Gentlemen of Harrow

PLAYERS.

ETON	HARROW
ANSON, Esq	Hon. T. EDWARDS,
APTHORPE, Esq.	BENTINCK, Esq.
BALSTON, Esq.	DEFFELL, Esq.
BOUDIER, Esq.	DENISON, Esq.
ESSINGTON, Esq.	MASSEY, Esq.
HEATHCOTE, Esq.	MORRICE, Esq.
HUME, Esq.	NAPIER, Esq.
SAVILE, Esq.	NETHERCOTE, Esq.
SMITH, Esq.	PATERSON, Esq.
WITTS, Esq.	SURTEES, Esq.
YOUNG, Esq.	TORRE, Esq.

MATCH TO COME.

July, 29th, & 30th, The Gentlemen of Winchester against the Gentlemen of Eton.

Cricket Bats and Stumps may be had of M, DARK. on the Ground
Cricket Balls and the Laws of Cricket as revised by the Marylebone Club in 1835, to be had of J. DARK, at the Pavilion,

AN ORDINARY AT THREE O'CLOCK.
Admittance, 6d, Good Stabling on the Ground. No Dogs admitted.

MORGAN, Printer, 39, New Church Street, Portman Market.

Lord's conspired to provide some kind of continuity and helped cement the ground's status as the headquarters of English cricket. They were the annual clashes between the Gentlemen and the Players, the schoolboys of Eton and Harrow and the undergraduates of Oxford and Cambridge, although the latter two matches did not become permanent fixtures until the 1820s. These were not only fiercely fought sporting occasions, they were also great social events which would attract huge crowds until the 1950s.

The amateur Gentlemen were generally no match for the paid Players, although they did have four outstanding players in Lord Beauclerk, Ward, E.H. Budd and Squire Osbaldeston. Budd, who scored the first ever century at Lord's for his own eleven against a team raised by Osbaldeston, was a great all-rounder and one of the most powerful hitters of the day. But such was the superiority of the Players that the Gentlemen were forced to recruit several of their number in order to create an even contest and allow the bookmakers to quote attractive odds. In many of the early matches it was not uncommon for the Gentlemen to field sixteen players against eleven, and in the famous contest of 1837, which came to be known as the 'Barn Door match', the Players were forced to defend wickets twice the ordinary size but still managed to beat the amateurs by an innings. In 1829 the Gentlemen's victory over the Players was achieved almost entirely through the efforts of two of the day's leading 'professionals', Lillywhite and Broadridge, who took nineteen wickets between them, the twentieth wicket being a run-out.

The first recorded match between Eton and Harrow took place in 1805. Lord Byron played in the match and batted with a runner because of his club foot. He scored 7 and 2. It was not until 1822 that the contest between the young adversaries, many of them the sons of MCC members, became an annual fixture.

At the end of the eighteenth century, cricket was still some way from establishing itself as a genteel, civilised pastime, and masters at the country's leading public schools sought to ban their pupils from playing it. Early matches between the schools were arranged by the boys themselves and they often gave rise to scenes of violence. In 1792 Westminster boys smashed windows on their way to a cricket match and were fired at by a furious local resident. Four years later the entire Eton team was flogged by the headmaster, Dr Keate, after flouting his ban on cricket by playing a match against Westminster. Originally the public school games were a three-way affair, with Winchester also playing annual matches against Eton and Harrow at Lord's. However, after parents complained about their boys being led into temptation by the bright lights of London, Winchester's headmaster, Dr Moberley, a future Bishop of Salisbury, put an end to his

William Lillywhite, an early exponent of the round-arm style of bowling.

Opposite: Benjamin Aislabie, first Secretary of MCC.

school's involvement in the fixtures in 1854. To this day Winchester calls its eleven the Lord's XI.

1825 was a momentous year in the history of Lord's. A fire swept through the pavilion, reducing it and all the early records of MCC to ashes, symbolically bringing to an end the first 'age' of the ground and ushering in a new era in which MCC would establish itself as the supreme authority of cricket for the next 160 years, with Lord's as its bastion. This was also the year that Lord sold out his interest to William Ward and MCC took on their first professionals to provide practice for their members. The fire started at half past one in the morning of 29 July, not long after the match between Eton and Harrow. The following report appeared in *The Times* the next day:

'In about an hour and a half after the commencement of the fire, the whole pavilion was reduced to a heap of ruins, saving only the foundation which is about three feet high of brickwork. So strong was the fire, that the wooden rails round the building were partly destroyed. There was a very valuable wine cellar well-stocked in the pavilion, belonging to the gentlemen of the various clubs who frequently play in the ground, which shared the same with the building. Happily no houses were near enough to the spot to be in the least danger, but some of the trees on the adjoining grounds were scorched.'

Records show that it was around the time of the fire that MCC was starting to cast itself as cricket's official legislator and judge, as well as the guardian of its spirit and values. Lord's was already the game's elite venue and points of contention between clubs throughout the country were often referred to MCC for clarification. Before the mid-1820s, however, the club was not much more than a loose collection of gentlemen with a love for cricket but little inclination towards administration and law-making. Admittedly the club's early records were destroyed in the pavilion blaze, but it does not appear MCC had made any concerted effort previously to establish itself as the game's governing body.

In 1818 a dispute between two Midlands clubs was dealt with by Lord Frederick Beauclerk and not by MCC as a body, suggesting that the club's supreme authority in the running of the game had yet to be firmly established. In his book on the origins of the game, *English Cricket*, Christopher Brookes records a report which appeared in the *Leicester Journal* in July 1818. 'The rule of play in dispute between Oakham and Melton Mowbray Cricket Clubs having been referred to the Marylebone Club, a decision was last week communicated by Lord F. Beauclerk that the umpire at the bowler's end should have decided whether the striker were out or not without reference to the other umpire, and consequently the Oakham Club won the game.'

The report tells us two things about MCC at this time. Firstly, it shows that decisions on the laws of the game were still dealt with on a very informal basis, with leading figures of the day such as Lord Frederick, rather than a committee, laying down the right way to play the game. Secondly, it indicates that the country's burgeoning band of cricketers were looking for some kind of official leadership. The rapid expansion of cricket in the first part of the nineteenth century, which saw the game spread out in all directions from London and the south-east of England, created an obvious need for a central authority to impose itself. It was about this time that MCC, which began its life with no greater ambitions than to provide its aristocratic members with a pleasant diversion from life's more serious business, finally rose to the challenge and established itself as the unquestioned power in the game until 1969.

The first step in this direction came in 1822, when Benjamin Aislabie, an obese and jovial London wine merchant, was appointed the

M.C.C.
SUBSCRIBERS TO MATCHES.

club's first Secretary, albeit only in an honorary capacity. Aislabie's huge girth was legendary, and his country home in Kent was referred to by teasing friends as the Elephant and Castle. But it was not just his twenty-stone physique which made him such a large presence at Lord's. Aislabie had a talent for administration that many of his more leisure-minded contemporaries lacked, and even before his appointment as Secretary he was busy keeping the club's books and subscriptions in order. Aislabie, who kept the post until his death in 1842 at the age of 68, was not a great cricketer but he played as important a role in the evolution of MCC as anyone in this defining period of the club's – and the sport's – history. Aislabie, who wrote a number of cricket poems and songs, was a larger-than-life character, and played for MCC against Rugby School in 1841 – an event recalled in the fiction of *Tom Brown's Schooldays*.

Thomas Lord may have been a great cricket lover, but his commercial instincts were even stronger. In 1825 he placed the future of the ground in doubt when, after being approached by property developers, he in turn approached the Eyre Estate, who held the freehold to the site, with a plan to build a belt of houses. The developments, adding considerable value to the lease, would have severely limited the playing area. The ground was saved from almost certain extinction by William Ward, a director of the

THE 'GRAND JUBILEE MATCH' COMMEMORATING THE 50TH ANNIVERSARY OF MCC IN 1837.

Bank of England and a future Member of Parliament, who bought out Lord for £5,000. Ward was also one of the most famous batsmen of the day, and his 278 for MCC against Norfolk in 1820 was a ground record that stood for over 100 years before it was broken by P. Holmes' 315 not out for Yorkshire against Middlesex in 1925. But Ward, who famously used the same four-pound bat for 50 years, suffered a slump in his fortunes and ten years later was forced to sell on the lease of the ground to James Dark, an entrepreneur who had been brought up locally.

The ground remained under Dark's ownership for the next thirty years, during which time he made a number of notable improvements. At the time of his take-over the ground was no more than a country field. The pavilion was a cottage bordered by a few shrubs, while sheep grazed on the pitch when matches were not in progress to keep the outfield in reasonable order. At one end of the ground there were two ponds and a hillock which gave way to a small 'valley'. One of the ponds was so deep that a member of the groundstaff, Stevie Slatter, was able to teach himself to swim. The state of the Lord's ground remained a cause for grumbling among members and visiting players for many decades to come. Not until 1864 did MCC appoint their first groundsman to take over from the sheep the responsibility of maintaining a decent playing surface.

Dark, according to MCC minutes of 1850, resolved a long-standing complaint of members when he had the field drained 'at his sole expense'. All financial and administrative matters were dealt with by Dark, who received annual subscriptions from members and entrance fees from the public. Dark arranged the annual fixtures list and was responsible for the maintenance of the ground, and only in 1866, nearly 80 years after MCC's foundation, did the ownership of Lord's pass to the club's members.

THE OLD PAVILION IN 1889, SHORTLY BEFORE IT WAS DEMOLISHED TO MAKE WAY FOR THE CURRENT BUILDING.

OPPOSITE: PORTRAIT OF GEORGE PARR, WHO LED TOURS TO THE UNITED STATES AND AUSTRALIA.

BELOW: JULIUS CAESAR.

A new pavilion, replacing the one destroyed by the 1825 fire, was ready for use by May of the following season. This building, although it was extended in 1865, would remain largely unchanged until 1889, when construction of the present pavilion got under way.

In 1837, the year Queen Victoria acceded to the throne, MCC celebrated its golden jubilee with a game between the North and the South which the southerners won by five wickets. It was dominated by the great Sussex bowler William Lillywhite, who took fourteen wickets in a low-scoring match (the highest innings total was the South's 70 for 5 to clinch victory). To the huge Lord's crowd, English cricket must have appeared to be in a state of happy order. But behind the scenes powerful tensions were emerging between amateurs and professionals and between northern and southern players.

The middle third of the nineteenth century was to be a tumultuous period in the development of cricket. By the start of the 1870s the authority of the old amateur order as represented by MCC had been vigorously challenged and shaken by the professional cricketer, who rose to prominence on the back of a nationwide upsurge of interest in the game. Long before the turn of the century the structure of the game we recognise today, both at domestic and international level, was firmly in place. And despite the best efforts – or lack of them – of its more apathetic and reactionary members, MCC emerged intact as the supreme authority in the game.

In June 1844 a report in *The Times* of a match involving many of the leading players of the day, including Alfred Mynn and Nicholas Wanostrocht (also known as Felix), suggested that all was well enough with the state of English cricket. 'The match between the gentlemen of England and the gentlemen of Kent was one of the most astonishing in the annals of cricket. It commenced on Monday at Lord's in the presence of one of the most distinguished assemblages we ever remember to have seen upon a similar occasion. The brilliancy of the scene, too, was very considerably enhanced by some extremely large marquees which have been erected for the fancy fair and promenade, which is to take place on Thursday for the benefit of the ship-wrecked mariners.' Kent were the outright favourites with the many bookmakers who descended on Lord's at the start of the day, but 'greatly to the surprise of all the spectators' England won by six wickets.

The significant decline in the status of amateur cricket is reflected in the bare fact that during the 1850s the Gentlemen lost nine of their annual matches against the Players at Lord's. The Players, meanwhile, were growing in strength and the period saw the emergence of a clutch of great players such as Julius Caesar, William Caffyn, H.H. Stephenson and John Jackson. Caesar, whose family once put on a match in which twelve Caesars figured in the scorebook, was one of the most powerful hitters of the day. Jackson, an intimidating fast bowler, travelled across the Atlantic with George Parr's team in 1859 as well as to Australia on the tour of 1864. Known as 'the Foghorn' owing to his habit of blowing his nose each time he took a wicket, Jackson would eventually die a homeless pauper. Caffyn was one of the great all-rounders of the time and, like Jackson, toured Australia in 1864 and stayed there for seven years, working as a coach in Melbourne and Sydney.

THE ALL-ENGLAND XI, BY FELIX, SCHOOLMASTER, PORTRAIT PAINTER AND CRICKETER. THE PLAYERS FEATURED FROM LEFT TO RIGHT ARE GUY, PARR, MARTINGELL, A MYNN ESQ., W. DENISON ESQ., DEAN, CLARKE, FELIX, O.C. PELL ESQ., HILLYER, LILLYWHITE, DORRINTON, PILCH AND SEWELL.

If the reputation of amateur cricket had declined by the 1850s, it had positively nosedived in the decade that followed, taking with it the status of Lord's as the country's most prestigious venue. The only matches which continued to keep their fascination for the public were the traditional fixtures, Gentlemen v. Players, Eton v. Harrow and the Varsity match. But these contests were as much fashionable occasions, which had become part of the social 'season', as they were sporting encounters.

Lord's became a dispiriting place for those who remembered the earlier days.

Edward Rutter, a member of the MCC Committee at various times between 1873 and 1903, believed the club was close to extinction during this time. In his *Cricket Memories*, he recalled: 'The reader will be surprised to hear that the matches in the fifties and sixties were mostly of no interest except to the players themselves … Lord's was a heavy clay and badly drained and the outfielding was always rough and treacherous. There were no boundaries – except the pavilion – no stands or fixed seats of any kind, nothing but the small old pavilion and a line of loose benches running part of the way round the ground, and these were but little occupied save at the most important matches.' Rutter laid the blame for the deterioration of Lord's squarely on the MCC Committee, whom he described as 'deplorably lethargic and out of date'.

Great improvements in transport during the middle third of the century meant that many more games were possible between teams from further afield. MCC, however, failed to respond to the new developments around the country and the club developed a reputation for being reactionary, aloof and impervious to the changes sweeping through cricket at the professional level. Another factor behind the downturn in attendances at this time was an increase in the cost of admission, which alienated many ordinary spectators even if it did succeed in keeping out the more undesirable elements of the London public.

The same apathy which cost MCC some of their respect at this time also led them to lose control of their famous ground – albeit only for a brief period. The survival of Lord's was placed in jeopardy again in 1860 when the Eyre Estate sold the freehold at a public auction. Curiously, MCC members refused to enter the bidding, and for six years the ground's ownership passed into the hands of Isaac Moses. When Moses sold the ground to MCC in 1866 for £18,333 six shillings and eightpence, he had made a tidy profit of over £10,000. The members were indebted to Mr William Nicholson, an old Harrovian and a future MP, for putting up the money.

A frequent criticism that contemporaries directed at Lord's concerned the quality of the wicket and the outfield. The heavy clay and the poor drainage system led to low-scoring matches and prolonged stoppages in play. Other grounds, like The Oval and Trent Bridge, offered better conditions and more exciting, high-scoring games. Such was the poor quality of the Lord's playing surface in 1859 that Surrey even refused to play there.

Lord's remained a defiant bastion of amateurism at a time when the growing band of professionals throughout the country were becoming increasingly frustrated by what they saw as the conservatism of MCC. By the middle of the century the club had about ten professionals of their own, whose main task, when they were not playing in matches, was to bowl to the club's members. A number of boys were also on the books to act as fielders. Class distinctions in Victorian society were reflected in cricket: generally gentlemen preferred to bat while bowling was the great strength of the professionals. The legendary Kent batsman Fuller Pilch, who played for the Players against the Gentlemen 24 times between 1827 and 1849, was the most notable exception to this general rule. Pilch, who became the 'Champion of England' after a single-wicket competition in 1833, was one of the first proponents of front-foot play and was one of the stars of William Clarke's All England XI.

John Wisden, feared fast bowler and founder of the famous almanack.

The tension between the country's professionals and the gentlemen at Lord's was manifested in a long-running argument which began in the late 1820s. The professionals wanted a new round-arm style of bowling to be accepted, but MCC claimed it was potentially dangerous and amounted to throwing, even though the delivery was made with a straight arm. The dispute became the focus of the professionals' wider grievances towards the amateurs, and in 1835 MCC were forced to accept the change in their rules as umpires around the country proved to be virtually powerless to impose the club's will. William Lillywhite, the deadliest bowler of the day, was at the forefront of the stand against MCC, and it was his revolutionary use of overarm bowling that sparked a further row with the law-makers at Lord's. In 1845 MCC widened the split between the amateurs and professionals by banning the rebel bowlers from any matches in which the club was involved. Not all members of MCC agreed with the club's haughty attitude towards the professionals, and many argued that the two groups should bury their differences and play alongside each other in a county format. But the dispute rumbled on for the next nineteen years until overarm bowling was finally accepted as a legitimate part of the game in 1864.

It was during this period that the professionals forged ahead with their own form of the game and the great touring teams were established. In 1846 a team calling itself the 'All England XI' was founded by William Clarke, who despite being one of the leading bowlers of his day was not selected to represent the Players until he was in his 48th year. Clarke's aim was to establish a profitable form of cricket that was independent of MCC, and his All England XI were a kind of Harlem Globetrotters of their day. They were made up largely of paid professionals,

although the famous amateurs Mynn and Felix also represented the side. (Felix, a Camberwell schoolmaster of Flemish origin, is credited with inventing the first batting gloves.) The team travelled the country attracting great crowds and playing against teams who would often field 16, 18, 20 or 22 players so as to have any chance of beating the visiting stars. The leading players of the day jumped at the chance of regular employment with the team, but life on the road with the All England XI was hard. The team went as far afield as Truro and Dublin, often travelling overnight to fulfil a punishing schedule of fixtures. One of the stars of the team, Richard Daft, recalled in his book *Kings of Cricket* that the All England XI '... used to play six days a week for five months except on Sunday and when it was wet.' Clarke's team may have thrilled cricket-lovers up and down the country, but Clarke himself, a bricklayer by trade, had a reputation for being authoritarian and miserly, and in 1852 a breakaway team, calling itself the United England XI, was formed by John Wisden and Jem Dean.

Wisden, whose name has been immortalised by the famous almanack he founded in 1864, cut a slight figure at just five feet four inches and seven stones, but he was one of the fastest and most feared bowlers of his day and was known as the 'Little Wonder'. His most notable feat on the field came at Lord's in 1850, when he took ten wickets in the second innings for the North against the South – all of them bowled. Following the death of his old adversary Clarke in 1856, Wisden teamed up with George Parr, the new captain of the All England XI, for a tour of the United States and Canada, having merged the best players from each side. In his book *Cricket*, published in 1891, W.G. Grace confirms the excitement generated by clashes between the two teams:

'Undoubtedly the contests of the year were the All England XI v. The United XI, and the

WATERCOLOUR OF LORD'S, 1851, BY FELIX.

A MAN OF ENERGY AND VISION: R.A. FITZGERALD, MCC SECRETARY 1863-76.

North v. South, at Lord's, especially the former. When the two famous Elevens met reputation was at stake. It was the match of the year... and crowds testified to it by turning out in thousands.'

On 27 July 1858 the All England XI met the United England XI in a benefit match for Parr which attracted 6,000 spectators to Lord's. *The Times* reported the appearance of a special guest at the match: 'The ground was especially honoured by the presence of the French ambassador, the Duke of Malakhoff, who met with a most enthusiastic reception. The points of the game were explained to his Excellency, who seemed much to appreciate them, and he enrolled his name as a patron.'

A further breakaway took place in 1865 when the United England XI split into two after the northern professionals refused to play alongside their southern counterparts. Behind the conflict lay simmering tensions over selection and pay at a time when there were more professional cricketers than there was work to go round. The selection of Surrey's H.H. Stephenson ahead of Parr to captain a touring team to Australia in 1861 increased the tensions between the two camps, and four years later the mutual distrust exploded into open conflict. In August 1866 *The Times* took up the cause of the 'Gentlemen' at Lord's, whose authority, they claimed, had been undermined by the greed and vanity of the insurgent northerners. An article in the paper read:

'... The cause of this unfortunate position of things is to be found in the too prosperous conditions of the players. So long as they can earn more money by playing matches against Twenty-Two's than by appearing at Lord's – so long as they can be "mistered" in public houses, and stared at in railway stations, they will care very little for being absent from the Metropolitan Ground. But they are wrong. They may be certain that the "Gentlemen" will not give way in this struggle.'

During the difficult period of the 1850s and 1860s there were loosely two factions within MCC at loggerheads over the future of the game: the conservatives and the progressives. The former hung on doggedly to the traditions of amateurism, while the latter called for reform. One of the most vociferous progressives was R.A. 'Bob' Fitzgerald, Secretary between 1863 and 1876, who saw early on that the future of cricket lay with the counties. His attempt to woo Middlesex to play their matches at Lord's failed, though the county finally accepted MCC's invitation in 1877. Fitzgerald had realised how out-of-date the MCC Committee had become, and was keen to liven it up by the introduction of some young fresh blood. This was provided by C.E. Green and Edward Rutter, who according to Rutter found the older members so supercilious that Green declared he would never serve on the committee again.

The row with MCC led to talk of an independent 'Parliament' being set up as an alternative authority, but the 'Gentlemen' rode out the turbulence and soon the rebels found themselves ostracised not just from the polite society of MCC but also from their own county clubs. One man who was happy that MCC got its way was the most famous gentleman cricketer of them all, W.G. Grace. In his book *Cricket*, he wrote:

'In the early part of 1864 an agitation was set going in one of the leading newspapers which had for its aim the formation of a "cricket Parliament" to depose the Marylebone club from its position as the authority on the game; but it met with little countenance, and the old club, which had now played on its present ground for fifty years, was allowed to carry on the work which it, and it alone, seemed to be able to do with firmness and impartiality.'

The days of the professional elevens were numbered as county cricket emerged from the chaos of in-fighting to establish itself as the principal form of the domestic game. By 1880 the All England XI, the United North XI and the United South XI had ceased to exist, their magic spell over the public having long since vanished.

County cricket offered a happy compromise between the amateur and professional disciplines, and the popularity it began to enjoy in the 1860s owed much to the foresight of the clubs' administrators, who recognised a middle way for cricket to progress. At the heart of the debate lay a clash of understandings about the purpose of sport which reflected class differences in Victorian society. For the professional player, cricket was a skill by which a

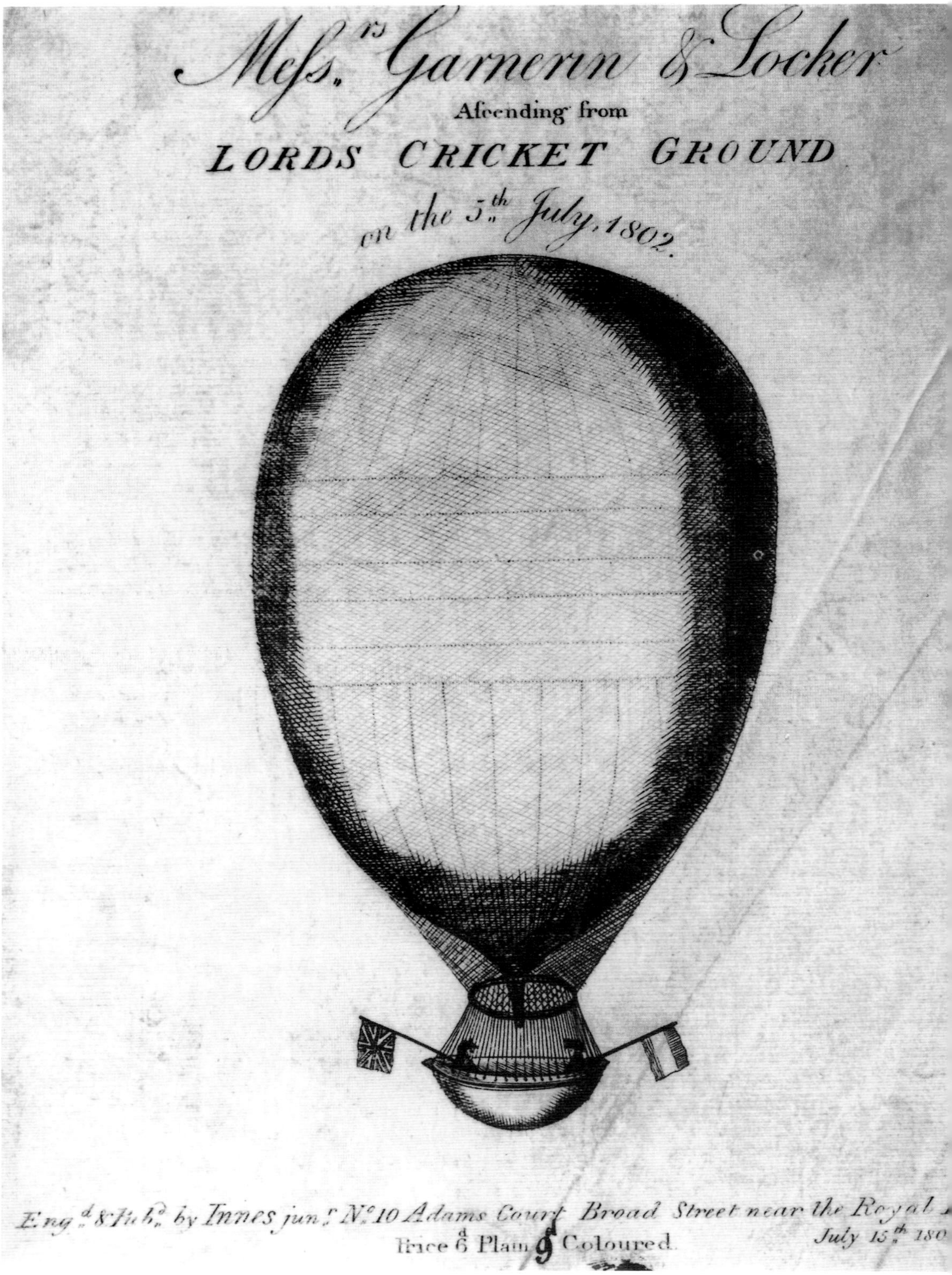

Mess.rs Garnerin & Locker
Afcending from
LORDS CRICKET GROUND
on the 5th July, 1802.

Eng.d & Pub.d by Innes jun.r No 10 Adams Court Broad Street near the Royal
Price 6d Plain 9d Coloured
July 15th 180

reasonable living might be earned for about half the year. This bare economic attitude towards the game stood at odds with the amateur conception, which saw cricket as a pleasurable pursuit embodying a set of noble values in the public school, Empire-building tradition. County cricket, in encouraging the two to play alongside each other, headed off a major schism in the game and allowed the 'Gentlemen' of Lord's to re-establish their authority over the game.

Engraving of the encampment of Iowa Indians at Lord's in 1844.

The Eton v. Harrow match was also making the newspaper headlines for all the wrong reasons around this time. The behaviour of the rival spectators was so rowdy at the 1873 match that MCC was forced to issue the following statement: 'The Committee regret that notwithstanding all their efforts to prevent a scene of confusion at the termination of the Schools' match, their efforts were frustrated by the unseemly conduct of some persons on the ground. Such scenes as those witnessed on Saturday would not occur if the partisans of both schools were to assist the authorities in checking the immoderate expression of feeling at the conclusion of the match. The Committee appeal to the old and young members of the two schools to assist them in future in preventing a repetition of such disorder, which must inevitably end in a discontinuance of the match.'

The Times, however, felt that the trouble had been blown out of proportion, its correspondent declaring: 'People who were not at Lord's, but who read the accounts of the match in Monday's papers, must have thought that there was something like a very free fight between Eton and Harrow going on ... Now, we who write were on the top of the Pavilion, just beyond the centre, during the whole of the row, and we can fairly say that we did not see one single blow struck in anger throughout.'

Cricket matches were not the only spectacles to be staged at Lord's in the nineteenth century. In 1802 a large crowd turned out to watch a hot-air balloon ascent by

CELEBRATING THE AUSTRALIAN ABORIGINALS' TOUR OF ENGLAND IN 1868.

AUSTRALIAN ABORIGINAL CRICKETERS

Frenchman Monsieur Garnerin and in 1844 the London public was treated to an exhibition which included dancing and archery performed by the Red Indians of the Iowa tribe. Other entertainments at the ground included canary shows, pigeon flying and hopping races, while the tennis courts, bowling green and billiards tables all attracted the leading players of the day.

In 1868 Lord's welcomed a team of Australian Aboriginals, the first party from Down Under to tour Britain. The team was coached by Charles Lawrence, a former all-rounder with Middlesex and Surrey, and on a gruelling tour they played no fewer than 47 matches, winning 14 and drawing 19. Most of the tour party were from the now extinct

Werrumbrook tribe, and the novelty of their appearance was a cause of fascination to the Victorian public. Shortly after their arrival in England, *The Times* described the tourists:

'Their hair and beards are long and wiry; their skins vary in shades of blackness, and most of them have broadly expanded nostrils, but they are all of the true Australian type. Having been brought up in the bush to agricultural pursuits under European settlers, they are perfectly civilised, and are quite familiar with the English language. As most of their native names are polysyllabic, and not very euphonious, each has adopted a soubriquet under which he will doubtlessly be recognised in this country.'

Those 'soubriquets' were Dick-a-dick, Mosquito, Johnny Cuzens, Bullocky, Twopenny, Charlie Dumas, Tiger, Johnny Mullagh, Red Cap, King Cole, Sundown and Jim Crow. King Cole, who was said to be the best player in the party, fell ill early in the tour and died. The players, who took to the field sporting different coloured scarves, would entertain the crowd during intervals with demonstrations of boomerang and spear throwing. One such exhibition, as *The Times* reported in September, had a near fatal outcome. 'At an exhibition of native Australian sports by the aboriginal cricketers, at Bootle near Liverpool, on Saturday, a boomerang, thrown by Mullagh, was carried by the wind among the audience. It struck a gentleman on the head, the brim of the hat saving the face from severe laceration. As it was, the boomerang cut through the hat and inflicted a severe wound across the brow. Surgical aid was at once procured, and the gentleman was able to return home.'

Six years later, another huge crowd turned out at Lord's to see a team of American cricketers take on MCC, as well as a baseball exhibition by two of the United States' leading teams, which saw the Bostons trounce the Philadelphian Athletics 24–7. In the cricket match, the Americans more than held their own against the most famous cricket club in the world, scoring 107 to MCC's 105 before rain the following day saved the members from a potentially embarrassing defeat.

1868 also witnessed the appearance at Lord's of a supremely confident nineteen-year-old whose heroics over the next three decades did more than anything else to transform cricket into a national sport with a huge following up and down the country. The young man scored 134 out of a total of 201 for the Gentlemen v. Players on a dreadful wicket and then took ten wickets for 81 runs. W.G. Grace had arrived.

The LAWS of the NOBLE GAME of CRICKET,
as Eftablifhed at the Star and Garter Pall-Mall by a Committee of Noblemen & Gentlemen.

THE BALL.

THE BAT.

THE STUMPS.

THE BOWLING CREASE.

THE POPPING CREASE.

THE PARTY which goes from home,

THE BOWLER.

THE STRIKER. is out,

The WICKET KEEPER

THE UMPIRES

BETS.

THE END.

THE LAWS AS REVISED BY MCC IN 1809.

1870–1900

THE AGE OF GRACE

The last three decades of the nineteenth century saw cricket transformed from a popular pastime into a national institution. It was during this period that the County Championship evolved into the format we recognise today and international cricket began with the first ever Test in 1877 when England played Australia at Melbourne. Though it was not until the 1890s that the matches became known as 'Tests', from the outset the encounters between the two countries were fiercely contested and generated huge public interest on both sides of the globe. The Melbourne Test alerted English cricket to the emerging challenge from the southern hemisphere, but it was not until the following year when Australia thrashed MCC on home soil that the reputation of Australian cricket was firmly established and cricket's most ancient rivalry had begun in earnest. In their early encounters the two founding countries of

View of the pavilion, c.1874, by Henry Barraud (1811-74).

THE ASHES, KEPT IN PRIDE OF PLACE IN THE MUSEUM AT LORD'S.

international cricket were evenly matched, and of the 56 Tests played before the new century, England won 26 and Australia 20.

The establishment of formal competitions at international and county level, coupled with the coverage they began to receive in the nation's newspapers, played a major part in the boom of interest in cricket at this time. Sports, though, are nothing without their heroes, and in W.G. Grace cricket found a figure who did more than anyone else - and more than any competition or institution – to popularise it. Grace, who bestrode the game like a colossus for four decades, became a national icon, as recognisable and talked about as Mr Gladstone or the Prince of Wales. His remarkable feats on the field as well as his unmistakable appearance and extravagant personality made him a legend in his own lifetime. Though the period produced other great cricketers and other great characters, such as Lord Harris, Prince Ranjitsinhji, C.B. Fry, A.C. MacLaren and Arthur Shrewsbury, it is no exaggeration to say that, without Grace, cricket would never have achieved the heights of popularity that it did at this time, and that given the competition from other emerging organised sports such as football, rugby and tennis, it might never have taken a permanent foothold in the national consciousness.

W. G. GRACE, THE GREAT CRICKETER.

After a fallow period in the middle of the century, amateur cricket reasserted itself from 1870 onwards, and the traditional matches between Eton and Harrow and between Oxford and Cambridge, as well as a variety of MCC matches, attracted massive crowds to Lord's. During this time Lord's remained the axis around which the developing cricketing world revolved. The authority of MCC was firmly re-established and Lord's became the scene of great social gatherings as cricket's popularity boomed. The traditional fixtures involving England's most famous universities and public schools became major events in the English social season, drawing full houses of extravagantly dressed spectators of whom the vast majority came to be seen rather than to see. It is worth noting that during the Edwardian period and even for several years after the First World War these fixtures were considered – at least by the newspapers and the paying public – to be as important as Test matches. (As late as 1921 *The Times* devoted a whole page to a preview of the Eton v. Harrow match, with individual profiles of every player.) On these occasions, Lord's would be surrounded by hundreds of horse-drawn carriages, and as sumptuous picnics were laid out around the perimeter of the pitch, men in top hats and tails and women in bonnets and flowing dresses carrying dainty parasols would stroll elegantly about the ground.

One of the best descriptions of these social events comes from E.V. Lucas, who in 1898 wrote of the University match: 'When Blue meets Blue, the student of Lord's types is a little bewildered. His eyes are dazzled by the unfamiliar presence of fair ladies, who swarm around the ring, and in the interval, all over the ground, like such a cloud of butterflies as one comes upon suddenly in a clear space in a wood on a hot August day. But none the less the types are there, hidden away among summer fashions, pressed out from their

A BREAK IN PLAY: LORD'S ON A GENTLEMEN V. PLAYERS DAY, 1895. GRACE IS SEEN WALKING THE WICKET.

accustomed places by this brightly hued, cheering, invading host. Where is the churl who would grumble at the presence of Beauty's Daughters at a cricket match? Let them come forward and be rebuked. True, they have hats that shut out yards of the pitch; true, their heads are so restless that it little avails him who sits behind to crane his neck either way; true, their use of the sunshade shows a lack of imaginative sympathy; true, they talk frivolously of the most serious deeds ever performed on the green spots of the earth …'

On 27 May 1878 4,000 spectators were at Lord's to experience a major shock to English cricket when an MCC team including Grace was beaten by nine wickets in less than a day by an Australian side that no one had been taking very seriously. The great fast bowler Fred Spofforth took 10 for 20 and the *Daily Telegraph* reported: 'The MCC suffered today a humiliating and unexpected defeat at the hands of the touring Australian team, losing by nine wickets after only four and a half hours' play. After their innings defeat in their first match by Nottingham, the Australians have shown their mettle, bowling England out twice for an aggregate of 52 runs, and while no Australian batsman scored more than 10 runs, they finished easy victors.'

The tour firmly established the Australians, or the 'Colonials' as they were often referred

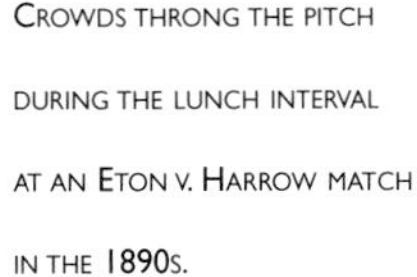

Crowds throng the pitch during the lunch interval at an Eton v. Harrow match in the 1890s.

to at the time, as a force for the English to reckon with. Such was their impact that, following their departure from Liverpool, *The Times* felt moved to write a leading column praising their achievements. The paper said: 'Yesterday, it will be seen, the Australian cricketers started on their homeward journey from Liverpool, visiting the United States on their way, and hoping, no doubt, to win fresh laurels there. The summer is over, the equinox is near, the days are shortening, the weather is breaking, and warned by the signs of coming winter, our visitors from the Antipodes, like other birds of passage, have taken their flight. They may be congratulated on the complete success of their visit. If they have not been uniformly victorious, if they have succumbed now and again to the teams which the mother country could array against them, they have at any rate shown that the national game is as well understood and as diligently practised in Australia as it is at home, and that the mysteries of batting, bowling and fielding are not the exclusive privilege of a small island in the northern hemisphere ...'

The author of the article was clearly unfamiliar with the meteorological conditions Down Under, for he added: 'Australia is not perhaps naturally so favourable a home for the game as England, but the success of the

Australian cricketers is a proof that they have learnt to neutralise the disadvantages of climate by assiduous practice and skilful generalship ...'

Lord's was also busy behind the scenes in 1878, and MCC finally clarified the distinction between the amateur and the professional player. On 2 November a resolution was passed which prohibited gentlemen cricketers from making any money from the game, ruling: 'That no gentleman ought to make a profit by his services in cricket, and that for the future, no cricketer who takes more than his expenses in any match shall be qualified to play for the Gentlemen v. Players at Lord's: but that if any gentleman feels difficulty in joining in the match without pecuniary assistance, he shall not be debarred from playing as a gentleman by having his actual expenses defrayed.'

On 22 July the following summer Grace had the first of his several testimonial matches in a contest between an Over Thirty XI and an

Under Thirty XI. He was just 31 years old but his expanding waistline, combined with a dip in form, had led many to believe that he was no longer the great player that he had been. Donors including the Prince of Wales and several leading noblemen contributed to a total of £1,500 for Grace, who was also presented with a bronze and marble clock. The testimonial turned out to be somewhat premature, as two decades later the great man would still be playing for England.

In 1880 the first ever 'Test' in England was played, and in 1882 the Australians returned to defeat the home team in just two days at the Oval. This prompted the famous mock obituary in the *Sporting Times*, mourning the death of English cricket and noting that 'the body will be cremated and the ashes taken to Australia'. Six months later an England team under the Hon. Ivo Bligh went to Australia, where they were presented with a small four-inch terracotta urn full of ashes. After the Third Test some Melbourne women had burnt one of the match stumps, and thus was born one of the most famous trophies, and almost certainly the smallest, in world sport.

In 1884 Lord's staged its first ever Test match, seven years after the first official contest against Australia in Melbourne and four years after the first Test was played in England at The Oval. Lord Harris was the captain and 13,456 spectators paid to see the first day's play. The highlight of the match, which England won comfortably by an innings and five runs, was an innings by A.G. Steel, whose 148 was the first Test hundred made on the ground. It came in England's first innings 379 as all but two of their batsmen reached double figures in reply to Australia's 229 – a total boosted by a last-wicket partnership of 69 between H.J. Scott and H.F.

ABOVE: FAMOUS ENGLISH CRICKETERS, 1880, FROM *THE BOY'S OWN PAPER*.

OPPOSITE TOP: F.R. SPOFFORTH, THE GREAT AUSTRALIAN BOWLER.

OPPOSITE BOTTOM: THE SECOND AUSTRALIAN TEAM TO TOUR ENGLAND, IN 1880.

LORD HARRIS (1851–1932)

Lord Harris (of Belmont, Seringapatam and Mysore) was one of the most influential figures in English cricket, inspiring, like his fellow peer, a mixture of fear and respect in all who crossed his path in his rich and varied life. 'A true English gentleman' is a recurring epithet in descriptions of him, although his high-minded principles and appetite for confrontation did not endear him to everyone. Gubby Allen described him as a 'tyrant as well as a great administrator'.

The fourth Lord Harris was born in the West Indies and educated at Eton and Oxford. He captained Kent between 1875 and 1889 as well as his country before embarking on a highly successful political career which saw him appointed Under-Secretary for India and later Governor of Bombay. Cricket, though, remained his greatest passion and shortly before his death he declared: 'My whole life has pivoted on Lord's.' As a tribute to his contributions to the life of MCC and English cricket as a whole, the club erected a memorial to him and gave his name to the gardens behind the pavilion. He played in just four Tests, captaining the side on each occasion, and was said to be an attractive batsman to watch as well as a superb fielder.

In 1879 he was involved in a riot that created a crisis in England's relations with Australia. Spectators in Sydney stormed the field during a match between New South Wales and MCC after a home player had been given out by the English umpire, G. Coulthard. The New South Wales captain, D. Gregory, who captained Australia in the first ever Test match against England at Melbourne in 1877, came on to the field to protest. Harris refused his request to change the umpire, sparking a violent pitch invasion. MCC players were assaulted by the furious mob, and Harris was hit with a stick while trying to protect the umpire. The events placed future tours between the two countries in jeopardy, but the crisis was finally resolved when Harris himself agreed to field a team to play Australia in the first Test on home soil in 1880.

During his political career in India, Lord Harris played a major part in developing cricket in that country. It was his influence that helped launch the sparkling career of Prince Ranjitsinhji in English cricket, but on a matter of principle (not racism) he tried to block the player's selection for England after the Indian had impressed for Cambridge University and Sussex. He was unsuccessful in his attempt, however, as it was the committee of the host venue who chose the team in those days, and the Old Trafford committee got their way.

Lord Harris's strong principles about qualification were not confined to the national team; he was equally adamant that domestic players could represent only the county in which they had either been born or had lived for a sufficient period of time. When he discovered that the great Gloucestershire and England batsman Wally Hammond was born in Kent, Harris objected and the player was forced out of the county game for a short period. When he sought to prevent another player from representing a county where he wasn't born, he was confronted by an angry Lord Deerhurst, the President of Worcestershire, who said to him: 'May I congratulate you, my Lord, on having buggered the career of another young cricketer.' Harris was equally zealous in his witch-hunt against bowlers with suspect actions, and in 1885 he instructed the committee at Kent not to play matches against Lancashire while they continued to field two bowlers whom he, and others, considered to be 'chuckers'.

In 1895 Lord Harris was nominated President of MCC, and he was the most powerful figure on the Committee for years, forming a close and influential alliance with Sir Francis Lacey, the Club's Secretary between 1898 and 1926. The walking embodiment of Victorian and Edwardian imperialism, Harris never lost his love of cricket, and played for MCC v. Indian Gymkhana at Lord's in 1929 at the age of 79. On his 80th birthday he exhorted the younger generation to play as much cricket as they could, saying: 'You do well to love it, for it is freer from anything sordid, anything dishonourable, than any game in the world. To play it keenly, honourably, generously, self-sacrificingly is a moral lesson in itself, and the class-room is God's air and sunshine.' When Sir Donald Bradman was asked, on the occasion of his own 87th birthday, if he had any advice for young cricketers, he recited the above passage.

Boyle. (Scott was finally caught by his own captain, W.L. Murdoch, who was fielding as a substitute for the injured Grace.) The Australian captain objected to the width of Steel's bat, but on subsequent examination the England batsman was cleared of any sharp practice. G. Ulyett was England's hero with the ball, taking 7 for 36 in Australia's second innings and forcing the retirement of J.M. Blackman who bravely, if unwisely, took to the crease without wearing any gloves. Ulyett's task was inadvertently made easier by the great Australian bowler Fred Spofforth, whose follow-through during England's innings had created a rough patch which Ulyett exploited to the full.

In 1886 a team of Indian cricketers played their first match in England when the Parsees

ARTHUR SHREWSBURY (1856–1903)

Shrewsbury was the best professional batsman of his day, and it should be said from the outset that his first home was not Lord's but Trent Bridge, where he scored the majority of his 26,000 runs for Nottinghamshire in a career that started in 1875 and ended in 1903 at the age of 47. But in his 23 Tests and as an automatic choice for the Players in the annual fixtures against the Gentlemen he also made a lasting impression at headquarters. He first appeared at Lord's in 1873 at the age of seventeen for the Colts of England against MCC. In 1886 his 164 on the ground against a formidable Australian bowling attack that included the great Fred Spofforth as well as Palmer, Giffen, Garret and Evans ranks as one of the most outstanding performances in the early years of Test cricket, and in later years he claimed it was his finest innings. Lord's was the scene of all his greatest innings outside Trent Bridge, and he returned there in 1893 to torment the Australians with innings of 106 and 81. Patient and circumspect rather than cavalier, Shrewsbury was truly 'professional' in his approach to batting, and his constant use of the pad as a second line of defence was often cited as a reason why the lbw laws should be changed. He was thought of mainly as a batsman to save rather than to win a match, and his back-foot play was said to be second to no one of his generation. He was known to say when walking out to bat after lunch, 'Bring me a cup of tea at tea-time.' He was also a great footballer and missed the whole of the 1888 English cricket season when he remained in Australia to coach the game.

Shrewsbury took his own life in May of 1903, amid mounting worries about his health, despite assurances by his doctors that he was suffering from nothing life-threatening. He shot himself with a revolver, first in the chest, which proved unsuccessful, and then in the temple. He was still somewhere near the peak of his powers in the season before his death, topping the Nottinghamshire averages with a mean score of just over 52.

LEFT: THE PARSEES, THE FIRST TEAM FROM INDIA TO TOUR ENGLAND, IN 1886.

BELOW: ARTHUR SHREWSBURY, ONE OF THE GREAT 'PROFESSIONAL' BATSMEN OF THE DAY.

met MCC at Lord's. The tourists lost the match by an innings against a strong side including Grace, but the occasion marked the beginnings of India's emergence as a major cricket-playing nation. Tours by teams from abroad were becoming more common and the following year a team from Canada arrived and held a powerful MCC side to a draw.

The Australians were also in England that year, and it was at Lord's that the home side beat them by an innings and 106 runs to take an unassailable 2–0 lead in the series and retain the Ashes. Nottinghamshire's Arthur Shrewsbury, the outstanding professional batsman of the era, hit 164, the highest score against the Australians in England. Though 'Test' matches were barely ten years old, their popularity among the public was enormous. *The Daily Telegraph* reported: 'Something like 20,000 visitors patronised the second day's play in the second match between England and Australia at Lord's, 15,663 paying at the gates. The play was again of a highly interesting character, and as far as the Englishmen were concerned, very satisfactory, but the Australians' batting fell short of anticipation.'

Later in the summer, Grace, representing an England XI against the 'Colonials', scored the first run to be recorded on the new telegraph

scoreboard, which updated the scores as the runs were made.

In 1887, while Queen Victoria was celebrating her Golden Jubilee, Lord's commemorated its centenary with a match on 14 June between an MCC side and an England XI. The national side won by a massive innings and 117 runs, Shrewsbury and Stoddart both passing the 150 mark, but the result was of little importance to the nation's cricket writers, who used the occasion to praise the Club for its contribution to the development of the organised game.

The Times led the tributes, saying: 'Rarely has a club attained such longevity and then found itself in the zenith of its fame as that which the Marylebone Club are celebrating this week at Lord's ... though, at its outset the records of the Marylebone Club are so bare as to leave its earliest doings almost in a cloud, it is certain that, once well established, it has always held the indisputable position it now so deservedly occupies. It must be remembered that the laws which governed the game a hundred years ago were in a very crude state. If for nothing else, the early attention to and careful revision of these laws by the Marylebone Club would alone entitle them to the respect of all lovers of the game ... To enumerate the long roll of exploits with which the name of the Marylebone Club is associated would be to give the history of cricket since it has become indisputably the national game ... It is now without doubt the ambition of all cricketers to appear in a match at Lord's ...'

Later that year MCC delved into the property market and bought a stretch of land to the north-east of the playing area known as Henderson's Nursery, where the best pineapples and tulips were said to be grown. It

THIS COMPOSITE PAINTING BY H. BARRABLE AND R. PONSONBY STAPLES PORTRAYS AN IMAGINARY MATCH BETWEEN ENGLAND AND AUSTRALIA IN THE MCC'S CENTENARY YEAR, 1887. NOTABLE CRICKETERS FEATURED INCLUDE W.G. GRACE, F.R. SPOFFORTH AND T.W. GARRETT, WATCHED BY THE PRINCE AND PRINCESS OF WALES AND THE ACTRESS LILLIE LANGTRY.

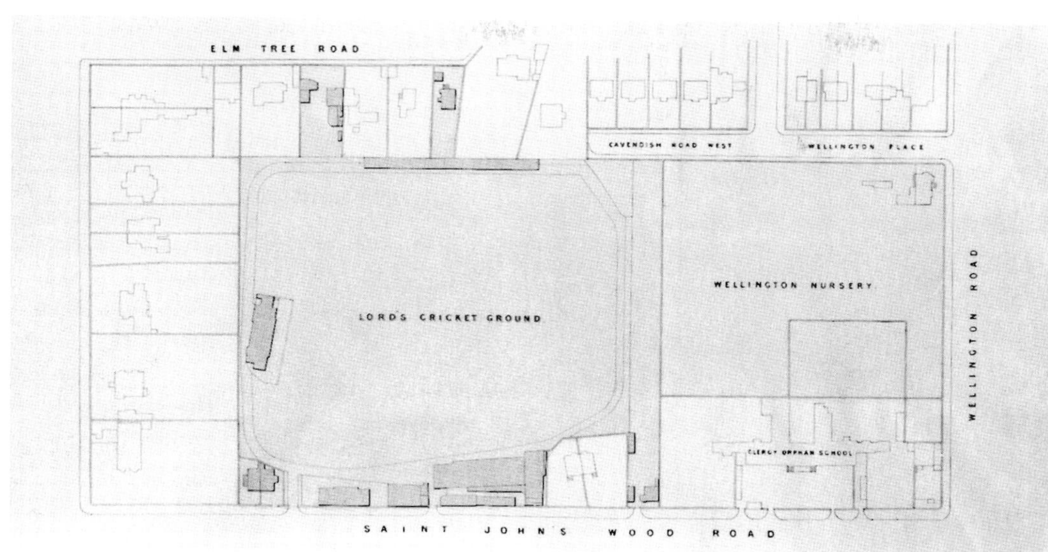

Original plan of Lord's drawn up in 1889 when the current pavilion was constructed.

was thus that the famous Nursery End came to assume its name.

The following summer Australia ended a run of seven successive defeats by England when they won at Lord's by 61 runs to record only their second ever victory over the English on their own turf (although they went on to lose the series). The *Daily Telegraph* reporter tried his best not to downplay the Australian achievement when he wrote: 'Without wishing to detract from the merits of their win, it must be said that the Australians secured a great advantage by winning the toss and batting first on an easy wicket. A sage authority said previous to the start that, considering the surroundings, the wicket and the weather, it was, in effect, tossing for the match. And so it proved ...'

On May Day 1889 the MCC Committee made a number of momentous decisions at their annual general meeting. First they voted in favour of the construction of a new pavilion at a cost of £13,000. In September 1889 Sir Spencer Ponsonby-Fane laid the foundation stone for the pavilion, which was designed by the architect F.T. Verity, who also played a part in the design of the Royal Albert Hall. The red-brick pavilion, an outstanding example of *fin de siècle* architecture, opened the following year and has remained largely unchanged to this day.

The Committee also overcame the objections of Surrey and passed a number of major rule changes. Henceforth, they decided, overs would be made up of five balls and not four (though the six-ball over would remain in Australia), while bowlers would be able to change ends as often as they liked as long as they did not bowl two overs in succession.

On 1 June 1891 MCC recorded a remarkable victory over Nottinghamshire when the county were dismissed in an hour and five minutes for

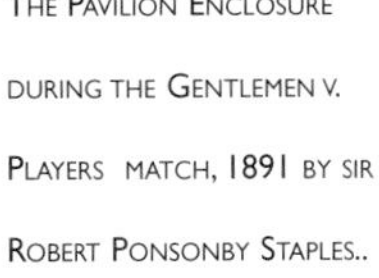

The Pavilion Enclosure during the Gentlemen v. Players match, 1891 by Sir Robert Ponsonby Staples..

just 21 – the lowest score at Lord's since the MCC were so famously routed for 19 in 1878 by the Australians. The *Daily Telegraph* reported: 'The wicket was treacherous, bright sunshine having followed the heavy rains last week, while the visitors, who were put into bat, were without Shrewsbury and Mr Dixon. Yet their display was a very poor one. Only 15 were scored with the bat, the top score being made by opening bat C.W. Wright, who was an hour at the wicket for his five.'

One of the greatest threats to the survival of Lord's during its early history was the demands of the capital's transport system. The shortage of space in central London made the wide open acres of Lord's an attractive target for property developers and transport planners. If canals were the main threat in the early part of the century, then railways had become the new menace towards its end. In 1888 the Great Central Railway sponsored a Bill to the Houses of Parliament which proposed to build a line straight through the cricket ground. By then Lord's had become something of a national treasure, and a vigorous campaign by MCC and other cricket-

The current pavilion, designed by Thomas Verity and opened in 1890.

A.E. STODDART (1863–1915)

Andrew Stoddart, one of the best batsmen of his generation, was a prominent figure at Lord's, where he played for Middlesex, England and MCC. After taking up cricket at the late age of 22, he made his reputation playing for the powerful Hampstead club in north London before joining Middlesex, where he shone with the bat between 1886 and 1900 (he missed the 1888 season after taking up an invitation to play rugby in Australia and New Zealand). It was for Hampstead that he made 485 against the Stoics, which at the time was the highest score on record. His highest first-class score came in his last season at Middlesex, when he hit 221 against Somerset at Lord's. He toured Australia four times and became a household name in the country with consistently high scoring there. He captained the side to a 3–2 triumph in 1894–95 and again in 1897-98, when England were crushed 4–0. Stoddart, who represented England at rugby on ten occasions and captained the side against Wales in 1890, was one of the finest stroke-makers of his day, famous for his ability to perform on all types of wicket.

Stoddart was also a fine rugby player, and is credited with helping to modernise the game. His drop goal against the winds of a violent gale for Middlesex against Yorkshire gave the London county victory by a goal to four tries and led to a major overhaul of Rugby Union's points system. Until then a goal counted for more than any amount of tries.

At the end of an outstanding career Stoddart's name was added to the extraordinarily long list of cricketers who have taken their own lives when he shot himself in the head. At the inquest into his death, his wife said that he had fallen into bad health and depression and had suffered a nervous breakdown. According to various newspaper reports he had also lost a lot of money following the outbreak of war and had become 'increasingly moody'.

lovers created enough trouble for the Bill to be dropped. In 1891 the Club pre-empted further trouble by buying the Clergy Female Orphan School near the south-west corner of the ground from another railway company, who retained the right to tunnel underneath the area.

The University match in 1893 saw the first of several 'follow-on' controversies which led to angry scenes in the 1896 fixture and brought about a major rule change in 1900. Upward of 20,000 spectators were packed into Lord's, all immaculately turned out for one of the great events of the social calendar, but many among the distinguished gathering were moved to voice their disapproval when Cambridge's bowlers deliberately bowled wides and no-balls to ensure that Oxford would not follow on. Two weeks later another full house at Lord's was in happier mood when Shrewsbury became the first batsman to score 1,000 runs in Tests against Australia in his innings of 106 and 81. In the same match Stoddart, captaining for the injured Grace, made the first ever declaration in a Test under new rules introduced by MCC.

The late nineteenth century was a busy time for cricket's legislators at Lord's. Unable to settle their differences among themselves over the structure of a county championship which had been running in some form or other since the mid-1860s, the leading clubs (Yorkshire, Lancashire, Nottinghamshire, Middlesex, Surrey, Gloucestershire, Sussex and Kent) turned to MCC for guidance, effectively acknowledging once and for all that the committee men at Lord's held the supreme authority in the administration of the game. In a significant landmark in the history of cricket, MCC spelt out the meaning of the phrase 'first-class' and laid down the ground rules for the County Championship. This was what they concluded:

'Cricketing counties shall be considered as belonging to the first class or not. There is no necessity for any further subdivision. First-class counties are those whose matches with one another, the MCC and Ground, with the Universities, with the Australians and other such Elevens as shall be adjudged 'first-class matches' by the MCC Committee, are used in compilation of first-class batting or bowling averages. There shall be no limit to the number of first-class counties. The MCC Committee may bring new counties into the list, may remove existing ones from it, or may do both. The list for 1895 is as follows: Derbyshire, Essex, Gloucestershire, Hampshire, Kent, Lancashire, Leicestershire, Middlesex, Nottinghamshire, Somersetshire, Surrey, Sussex, Warwickshire and Yorkshire.

'After the close of each cricket season the Committee of the MCC shall decide the County Championship. It shall be competed for by first-class counties. No county shall be eligible unless it shall have played at least eight out-and-home matches with other counties; provided that if no play can take place owing to weather or other unavoidable causes, such match shall be reckoned as unfinished. One point shall be reckoned for each win; one point shall be deducted for each loss; unfinished games shall not be reckoned. The county which, during the season, shall have, in finished matches, obtained the greatest proportionate number of points shall be reckoned the Champion county.'

Surrey became the first champions under the new guidelines, but it was Lord Hawke's Yorkshire who emerged as the dominant county between 1895 and 1914. During that time, the Tykes won the championship eight times, while Kent won it four times, Surrey three times, Lancashire twice and Nottinghamshire and Warwickshire once each.

MCC also assumed the authority to organise home Test matches and tours abroad; Warner led the first tour under the auspices of

Portrait of the formidable Lord Hawke, by Shirley Slocombe 1903.

LORD HAWKE (1860–1938)

Martin Bladen, better known as the seventh Lord Hawke, was a Yorkshireman first and an Englishman second, but he made a lasting contribution to the national game in his connections with MCC. He was a powerful, outspoken character who inspired respect before affection, and his name will be for ever associated with Yorkshire. He steered the county to eight championship titles during his 27-year captaincy and served as the club's President for 40 years.

Though not an outstanding cricketer (his 16,749 first-class runs came at a modest average of 20.15), he was an inspirational captain and a good administrator. Educated at Eton and Oxford, like so many of the dominant figures in English cricket in Victorian and Edwardian times, he became a Test selector and sat on the MCC Committee for years before becoming the Club's President during the First World War and later its Treasurer for six years.

He established himself as a distinguished ambassador for the sport when he led touring teams to India, the United States, New Zealand, Canada, West Indies and Argentina. Lord Hawke was famous for his tough discipline and he once sent off the famous all-rounder Robert Peel for being drunk during Yorkshire's match against Middlesex in Sheffield in 1897. He also had the courage to give the formidable W.G. Grace a dressing down for talking too much in the field.

It is unfortunate that he became best known to later generations for his famous declaration: 'Pray heaven no professional may captain England!' Ironically, he did more than anyone in his day to improve the lot of the professional cricketer. At Yorkshire he introduced a pay system which ensured the county's players received money throughout the year rather than just in the season, and he also instituted a fund for the players when they retired. His loyalty to Yorkshire overrode all other considerations, and in 1893 he came in for heavy criticism when he refused to release Stanley Jackson, a future knight and MCC President, for the Test match against Australia at Old Trafford.

Lord Hawke was a man who seemed to arouse a variety of feelings in his contemporaries. The tributes paid to him after his death shortly before the Second World War invariably contained muffled criticism as well as fulsome praise. Sir Pelham Warner, who came to replace Lord Hawke as the dominant figure at Lord's, considered the great Yorkshireman to be too old-fashioned and not receptive to new ideas. Warner also expressed regret that despite the fact that Hawke had travelled widely and done much for Dominion and Colonial cricket, he was not always keen to welcome Australian touring teams.

W.G. GRACE (1848–1915)

No history of Lord's would be complete without a tribute to Dr William Gilbert Grace. Although he played his county cricket for Gloucestershire, his name will for ever be associated with the home of English cricket, where he played for MCC, England and the Gentlemen as well as in a number of one-off matches.

The imposing gates bearing his name at the main entrance to the ground were erected in 1923 as a monument to his astonishing achievements. The charming simplicity of the inscription on the memorial highlights the inadequacy of words in describing the man who did more than anyone else to establish cricket as a national game. It reads:

> TO THE MEMORY OF WILLIAM GILBERT GRACE THE GREAT CRICKETER 1848–1915
> THESE GATES WERE ERECTED BY THE MCC AND OTHER FRIENDS AND ADMIRERS

Grace became one of the most famous figures in English society, and his gradually expanding bulk and the extravagance of his beard made him an unmistakable figure throughout the country. His outrageous talent was matched only by his colossal personality.

Born in Bristol, the fourth of five brothers, Grace was a beardless nine-year-old when he first played for West Gloucestershire CC, for whom at the age of eleven he hit his first half-century against Clifton. At fifteen he played against William Clarke's famous All England XI and a year later he made his first appearance at Lord's. By the end of his career Grace had amassed a mighty 54,896 runs (12,690 of them at Lord's) in first-class cricket over a period when the rough pitches made batting an infinitely more difficult exercise than it later became. (Only four batsmen have scored more: Hobbs, Woolley, Hendren and Mead.) One of his most celebrated innings was the 134 he hit for the Gentlemen against the Players at Lord's on a wicket so poor that one witness to it, Frederick Gale, was moved to write: 'I have no hesitation in saying that in nine cricket grounds out of ten within twenty miles of London, whether village cricket green or county club ground, a local club could find a better wicket, in spite of drought, and in spite of their poverty, than Marylebone club supplied.'

Although they cannot convey the great character of the man, the bare facts of his career are astounding. In addition to being comfortably the greatest batsman of his generation – to many, of all time – Grace was also a great bowler. He took a total of 2,876 first-class wickets at an average of 17.92 with his slow-medium leg breaks, and in 1877 he took seventeen wickets for Gloucestershire against Nottinghamshire at Cheltenham. In 1876 he hit his highest first-class score of 344 for MCC against Kent at Canterbury. The innings was the first recorded triple century, and the bat he used was later displayed in the Long Room at Lord's. He also scored two triple centuries for Gloucestershire (318 not out against Yorkshire at Cheltenham, also in 1876, and 301 against Sussex at Bristol in 1896). In total he scored 126 centuries, including 152 on his England debut in the first Test against the Australians on English soil at The Oval in 1880. (Two of his brothers, Dr E.M. and G.F., also played in the match, which England won by five wickets.)

In 1873 he became the first player to score 1,000 runs and take 100 wickets in a season – a feat he repeated for the next five seasons and again in 1885 and 1886. He

carried his bat through seventeen innings – a record he shares with C.J.B. Wood. In 1886 he showed his ability to adapt to all circumstances when he made 34 in three and a half hours against the Australians at The Oval. He made his first-class debut in 1865 and played his last game 43 years later, when he was 60. Only Lord Harris, at 60 years and five months, can beat him for longevity in the first-class game. He was captain of his county between 1871 and 1898 and skippered England in thirteen Tests against Australia, losing just three times.

Grace, however, never became President of MCC, nor even a Committee Member. In the 1997/98 *Cricket Yearbook*, Gerald Howat, historian and award-winning biographer, explained: 'As for MCC, its highest accolade was never even remotely possible for someone who could not lay claim to a public-school upbringing or an Oxbridge degree nor be a scion of the aristocracy. What Grace did achieve was to pave the way for the Victorian middle classes –men of the professions and commerce – to enter the ranks of MCC. He himself was the quintessential Victorian middle class persona in his commitment to work and play, his entrepreneurial approach to money, his competitiveness and his paternal authoritarianism.'

Grace has come to symbolise all that is supposedly noble about cricket, but the truth, according to his numerous biographers, was that he was neither averse to exploiting the game for a profit nor unimpeachable in his adherence to the spirit of its values. He was supposedly an amateur playing purely for the love of the game, but he compiled a fortune from cricket which made him a virtual millionaire at today's values. He played a number of testimonials and exhibition matches, and such was his cost to the organisers that grounds would often have to double their admission fees to cover his payments. In 1891 he kept for himself twenty per cent of the money paid by the Australian organisers for England's tour Down Under.

Many of his antics would have landed him in hot water with today's authorities at Lord's. On the 1873–74 tour of Australia he was involved in a string of heated rows over pitches and umpires. When he returned in 1891-92 there were further disputes, again mostly about umpiring, and during the tour he even led his players from the pitch, declaring it unplayable. He was known to put off fielders by shouting as they went for a catch, and in the famous 1882 match against the Australians at The Oval (after which the mock obituary of English cricket appeared), he tried to run out one of the tourists when he was prodding the wicket between deliveries. He also practised what today would be called sledging by talking basso profundo with his fellow fielders as the batsman wound up to receive from the bowler.

But despite his less than immaculate cricketing manners, Grace became a legend long before his death. The eulogy of the Bishop of Hereford, as recorded in *A History of Cricket* (1926) by H.S. Altham – a prominent figure at Lord's himself – captures the awe in which Grace was held in late Victorian and Edwardian society. 'Had Grace been born in ancient Greece, the *Iliad* would have been a different book. Had he lived in the Middle Ages, he would have been a crusader … As he was born when the world was older, he was the best known of all Englishmen and the king of that game least spoilt by any form of vice!'

OPPOSITE: A FAMILIAR IMAGE OF W.G. GRACE, PAINTED IN 1890 BY A. J. S. WORTLEY.

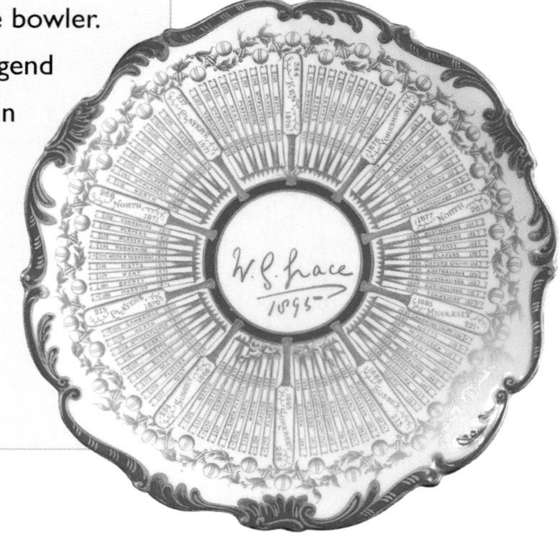

PLATE SHOWING W G GRACE'S CAPS, 1866-88

AN UNIDENTIFIED PAINTING OF A GENTLEMEN V. PLAYERS GAME AT LORD'S.

MCC in 1903-04. In the early years of the Tests against Australia, the entire organisation of the match, down to selecting the actual team, was done by the host venue. For years, Lord's, The Oval and Old Trafford were the only Test venues, but mounting complaints from other counties, in particular Nottinghamshire, Warwickshire and Yorkshire, saw Test match authority pass into the increasingly powerful hands of MCC.

Lord Hawke, captain of Yorkshire and later a highly influential figure at Lord's, was the most vociferous critic of the Test scene. He frequently drew criticism from the rest of the country when he refused to release his players for Test matches in protest that no international matches were played in his beloved county. His campaign to expand the Test match circuit reached a head in 1898 when a resolution, at the behest of the counties, was passed by MCC. It stated: 'The MCC should appoint a Board to govern future Test matches between England and Australia at home.' It was afterwards agreed 'that such Board be composed of the President of the MCC, five of the club committee, and one representative from six of the first-class counties selected by the MCC to send a representative. The President of the MCC to have the casting vote.'

The new Board of Control met before the end of the year and decided that Australia's next tour would involve five Tests and that Nottinghamshire and Yorkshire would provide the additional venues. The Board also established a three-man panel of selectors which would be composed of W.G. Grace, Lord Hawke and H.W. Bainbridge, the captain of Warwickshire. The MCC's supreme authority over all domestic and international cricket was completed five years later when it was agreed that responsibility for the organisation of England tours should be theirs. Until then, touring teams had been privately raised by a leading cricketer of the day.

During the 1890s MCC tackled some of the most contentious rules of the game, introducing new laws governing the follow-on, declarations and the especially controversial issue of 'throwing'. But its attempt to change the lbw rules, which were heavily in favour of the batsman and were more than partly responsible for some of the massive totals of the era, ended in failure. It was proposed in 1898 that a batsman would be considered out if the ball struck him on the pad and would have hit the stumps even if it was pitched outside the line. The motion was passed by MCC, but not by the two-thirds majority required, and the law remained unchanged until 1937.

W.G. Grace, by now 47 years old and touching 20 stone on the scales, added to his legend in 1895 by becoming the first batsman to score 1,000 runs in the month of May. He completed the total on the very last day of the month with an innings that saw him occupy the crease for almost the whole day at the headquarters of cricket. 'The opening day's play at Lord's was notable for the climax of what has been another remarkable performance from "the Champion", W.G. Grace,' reported the *Daily Telegraph*. He achieved the milestone when he reached 153 in his 169 by crashing a boundary to leg during Gloucestershire's match against Middlesex, sparking scenes of wild celebrations among the 7,000-strong crowd. 'The majority of spectators were aware of the achievement, and all round the ground they rose from their seats and cheered heartily,' added the *Telegraph*. The bearded doctor achieved his feat in just 21 days at an average of 112, hitting two centuries as well as 288 and a 257.

'A Close Run':
Eton v. Harrow in the 1880s.

PRINCE RANJITSINHJI (1872–1933)

Kumar Shri Ranjitsinhji, or Jam Saheb of Nawanagar, was an Indian potentate of considerable wealth who played for England and became one of the leading figures of English 'high society' at the turn of the century. The charismatic prince was an endless source of fascination to the English public during a period when Anglo-Indian relations were under constant strain. No one, though, thought it strange that he should represent England – except Lord Harris, that formidable figure of English cricket who discovered the young prodigy during his Imperial service in India. Ironically it was his Lordship – a strong believer that even at county level players should only represent the place of their birth – who launched Ranji's career with Cambridge University and Sussex. For the majority of the late Victorian public, however, Ranji's wish to play for England was seen as proof that the British Empire was a happier family than its critics suggested.

Unlike a number of the great players of his age, Ranji, ever modest and cheerful, was well liked by his contemporaries. At Cambridge, where he arrived at the age of just sixteen, he transformed himself, by hours of intensive coaching and practice, from a raw talent into one of the most elegant batsmen of his generation. In his first season with Sussex, where he struck up a great friendship as well as cricketing partnership with the incomparable C.B. Fry, Ranji scored 1,700 runs and delighted crowds all over the country with his magical strokeplay.

Despite being dogged by chronic asthma, Ranji continued to perform marvels with the bat until well into the next century, though his best years were 1899 to 1901. In 1896 his exclusion from the England side, at the insistence of Lord Harris, sparked a national outcry, but when the Old Trafford selectors chose him for the next match against the Australians he did not disappoint his admiring public, scoring 62 and 154 not out. At the end of that summer, only his second in county cricket, he was being compared to Grace after scoring 2,780 runs to surpass the great man's record aggregate for a season which had stood for 26 years. In doing so he matched Grace's record of scoring ten centuries in a season. Ranji, constantly trying to improve his game through hours of net practice, continued to shatter the records, scoring 3,159 runs in 1899 and 3,065 the following year.

Ranji led a double life; in England he was every inch the English gentleman, in India every bit the Indian prince. His close friend Sir Home Gordon wrote of him: 'When we all met him, the Jam Saheb was thoroughly western, apart from due assumption of his dignity as an Indian prince when occasion arose. But I have been told that out there he had phases of going entirely native, not speaking English for weeks and subsisting then solely on rice with some condiments in the curries.'

Though he found time to write *The Jubilee Book of Cricket*, a classic of cricket literature, Ranji devoted much of his later life to political affairs and served as an Indian representative at the League of Nations before his death in 1933.

(A few days earlier, left-armer Fred 'Nutty' Martin also found his way into record books when he took four wickets in four balls for MCC v. Derbyshire at Lord's.)

Two weeks later it was announced by MCC that another testimonial match would be played in Grace's honour, with all proceeds going to his already swelling coffers. *The Times* applauded the announcement, saying: 'Not only has there never been a cricketer who as batsman, bowler, field, and captain, is comparable to Mr W.G. Grace, but while other great cricketers commonly disappear after ten years, or fifteen at the most, he has filled the foremost place for more than thirty years, and during the present season, at forty-seven years of age, has proved himself a more formidable batsman than ever. It is very natural that this should have touched the imagination of England, and that a characteristic expression should be given to a universal feeling ... The Greeks used to crown their Olympic victor – we can at least make ours comfortable.'

New records continued to be established at Lord's the following year in two memorable encounters involving the Australians. The first occasion was reported thus 'By a Spectator' in the *Daily Telegraph*: 'Few of the 12,000 spectators who today witnessed the cricket at Lord's will forget the incidents attending one of the most sensational afternoons ever spent on the famous enclosure at St John's Wood.' The MCC wreaked revenge for their crushing defeat at the hands of the tourists 18 years earlier when they were bowled out for 19. On this occasion the visitors, fresh from handsome wins over Yorkshire and Lancashire among others, were bowled out for one fewer. England had made a respectable 219 on a rain-affected wicket. The Australians had reached 18 for 3 in reply when Grace put on Dick Pougher and not another run was added to the total as the Australians collapsed in extraordinary fashion, Pougher taking 5 for 0.

Two weeks later, the Australians returned to Lord's for the First Test against England. An evenly contested match ended in a six-wicket

G.L. Jessop (1874-1955), one of the most powerful hitters of all time.

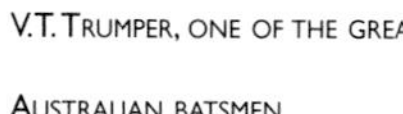

V.T. TRUMPER, ONE OF THE GREAT AUSTRALIAN BATSMEN.

Spectators at the Eton v. Harrow match, 1889 by Albert Ludovici jr.

win for England and was memorable for a number of reasons. This was the match when a short-pitched ball allegedly went for four byes having passed straight through Grace's famously luxuriant beard. Grace went on to make his 1,000th run in Test cricket. The Australians, who made just 53 in the first innings, seemed on their way to a heavy innings defeat before the great all-rounder Albert Trott and Sydney Gregory put on the highest partnership in Test cricket. The *Daily Telegraph* reported: 'Before they were parted, these young Colonists, who had no idea what it was to be beaten, put on 221 runs for the fourth wicket. Trott, with a duck's egg yesterday, played a brilliant innings, against the same bowling, of 143; Gregory, toiling by his side through the burden and heat of the day, found himself with 103 runs to his credit …'

On 14 July 1897 the great crowd-pleaser and all-rounder Gilbert Jessop played one of the most memorable of his many remarkable innings in the Gentlemen's 78-run defeat by the Players. There were 9,000 spectators at Lord's to see 'the Croucher,' striking a half-century in just 23 minutes, hitting a formidable bowling attack of Richardson, Hearne and Hayward 'as though they had been harmless bowlers of a college eleven', according to the *Daily Telegraph* reporter. 'It was an extraordinary innings. One can scarcely think of another batsman who could have played it. He lashed out at nearly every ball. Long hops, half volleys and yorkers were treated in an impartial manner that fairly delighted the onlookers.'

As a tribute to Grace, the second annual Gentlemen v. Players match in 1898 was scheduled for 20 July to coincide with the great man's 50th birthday. Over 20,000 spectators had turned up, but many had left long before the end after the star of the show, who was already carrying a foot injury, was struck a painful blow on the hand in his first innings 43 and failed to appear in the top order of the second. Moreover, much of the excitement of the match had ebbed away as the professionals seemed on course for a crushing win. But in a dramatic finale to the contest Grace emerged from the Pavilion when seven wickets had fallen and despite his badly damaged hand he almost pulled off a remarkable escape before the Players clinched victory with just two minutes remaining.

The *Manchester Guardian*, which has boasted some of the game's greatest cricket writers down the years, including the peerless Neville Cardus and John Arlott, began its report of the match as follows: 'The week which is past has been in a cricketing sense the greatest week of all the year. We have had Mr Grace's jubilee match at Lord's, a match which finished in so gloriously exciting a fashion four minutes from time on Wednesday night. The game in itself would lend distinction to any season, and it will certainly live in cricket annals as a memorable encounter – memorable because of the man to whom it was, as it were, dedicated, and memorable, too, because of the play itself. Many cricketers, we are sure, would have given a good deal to see the play during those three hours on Wednesday. No one doubted when the Gentlemen began their second innings that the match would be a draw.'

The following year Middlesex grabbed the headlines in an extraordinary County Championship encounter against Kent at Lord's. The powerful Middlesex batting line-up had collapsed to 55 for 9 before the Anglo-Australian Bill Roche and the amateur Richard Nicholls came together for the last wicket. Over the next two and half hours the pair established a new first-class record of 230 for a tenth-wicket partnership, Nicholls hitting 154 and Roche 74 to set up a highly improbable 118-run win for Middlesex.

Lord's was the only venue to produce a result in the first five-match Test series against the Australians that summer. The tourists won by ten wickets, thanks largely to two young batsmen, Clem Hill and Victor Trumper, who both scored 135. Trumper, widely regarded as the greatest Australian batsman after Don Bradman, had become a household name in cricket circles at the end of a highly successful tour in which he scored over 1,500 runs, including an unbeaten 300 against Sussex at Hove.

The final year of the century also saw the appearance at Lord's of the author Sir Arthur Conan Doyle, who took 7 for 61 for MCC against Cambridgeshire. Doyle, who carried his bat for just 32 runs against Leicestershire at Lord's two years later, was a keen cricket follower, and it is said that the Nottinghamshire player Shacklock was the inspiration behind the name of his most celebrated character, Sherlock Holmes. Doyle was also a regular feature at the annual Authors v. Actors match, played at Lord's, which began at the turn of the century. P.G. Wodehouse and A.A. Milne, said to be a top-class fielder, were key figures for the Authors, while the great Hollywood actor C. Aubrey Smith captained the thespians. Smith is the only player to have captained England on his only appearance for his country – against South Africa in Port Elizabeth on the 1888/9 tour.

1900–1914

THE GOLDEN AGE

OPPOSITE: A VERY EARLY PHOTOGRAPH, ORIGINALLY CAPTIONED 'AMONG THE BRAKES', CAPTURES THE ATMOSPHERE OF SOCIETY MATCHES AT LORD'S AT THE BEGINNING OF THE TWENTIETH CENTURY.

Cricket was never more popular than it was in the twenty or so years before the outbreak of the First World War. The organisation of county and Test cricket into established formats was just one of several reasons for the upsurge of national interest in the game. First-class cricket at new or improved grounds arrived in the heart of many of England's biggest cities and towns. Matches started to be extensively covered in the national and local newspapers, helping to create the cult of the sportsman as national hero. The *Daily Mail*, *Daily Express* and *Daily Mirror* were all established by the first few years of the new century, and sport was reported in depth in all of them as well as in the 'qualities' such as *The Times* and the *Daily Telegraph*. W.G. Grace was cricket's first superstar, but by the turn of the century there were a score of highly individual cricketers who had also become household names.

Neville Cardus wrote of the period: 'Between 1890 and 1914 the history of English cricket can only be discussed in terms of Men, each a character and law unto himself, each playing the game in a way vividly his own.' At the same time local and community cricket clubs were springing up in their hundreds. 'Never, before or since, were there so many active cricketers in England,' wrote the celebrated sports writer and broadcaster John Arlott.

The period has come to be regarded as the Golden Age of cricket, in which some of the most illustrious names lifted the game to new levels of popularity. This was the age of the remarkable all-round sportsman C.B. Fry, Ranjitsinhji the Indian prince, the feared and fearful Archie MacLaren and, towards its end, Jack Hobbs, the most prolific run-scorer in the history of first-class cricket. An astonishingly gifted generation of batsmen – in a period when the laws of the game greatly favoured bat over ball – also witnessed the talents of J.T. Tyldesley, Arthur Shrewsbury, Tom Hayward, George Gunn and the Foster family of Worcestershire (or Fostershire, as it came to be known after seven brothers of that family all appeared for the county).

Such was the dominance of the batsman at this time that in 1910 MCC again tried, without success, to pass a resolution to change the lbw law so that a player could be given out to a ball which was deemed to be hitting the stumps whether or not it had pitched in line. This was also the age that saw the emergence of some of the greatest all-rounders in history in Jessop, Barnes, Hirst and Rhodes. Cricket was also

S. F. BARNES (1873–1967)

S.F. Barnes, a blunt, acerbic and outspoken character, was the most feared bowler of his day and one of the greatest in the history of the game. He cut an intimidating presence both on and off the pitch and was one of the few professionals of his time publicly to express his objection to the distinction between amateurs and professionals.

During the 1912 Triangular tournament involving England, Australia and South Africa Barnes took eleven wickets at Lord's, inspiring England to a crushing innings and 62-run win over the South Africans. In his report of the match for *The Times*, E.B. Noel described him in action: 'A fine figure of a man, whether in rest or action; a run-up to the wicket lithe and "springy", in which not a step is wasted; a beautiful action with the arm right over the head, and then the ball is made to go away or to come back; and there is always that inexorable length, the life off the pitch, and the subtle changes of pace. It is the perfection of the bowler's art, and there is no question that Barnes is the greatest bowler of this generation.'

Barnes made his name at Lancashire after catching the eye of county captain Archie MacLaren, who plucked him from league side Burnley. It was also the Lancashire and England captain who persuaded sceptical selectors that the young bowler should travel on the tour of Australia in 1901–02, even though Barnes had taken just nine wickets in a handful of appearances for his county. His selection caused general amazement, but within a few years the Australian captain Monty Noble was hailing him as the greatest bowler in the world, while Pelham Warner said he was the most difficult he had ever faced.

On the voyage out to Australia that year the ship ran into a heavy sea and MacLaren, not everyone's first choice as a drinking companion himself, was heard to remark: 'Well, at least if we go down we'll take that bugger Barnes with us.' Barnes was a revelation on tour, and in the first two Tests he took seventeen wickets before a knee injury sidelined him for the remainder of the rubber. On the triumphant tour Down Under ten years later, when England won the series 4–0, Barnes was again the pick of the English bowlers and returned home with another 34 Australian wickets to his name.

His performances against the South Africans were even more remarkable. In 1913 he took seventeen wickets against them in the Second Test at Johannesburg – the record for wickets in a Test until Jim Laker took nineteen against the Australians at Old Trafford in 1956. On that tour Barnes took 49 wickets in four Tests (all on matting wickets) at an average of just under 11. In all, he took 189 Test wickets at an average of 16.43. Representing the minor county Staffordshire, Barnes was still performing heroics at the age of 48, when he finished the 1924 season with 73 wickets at an average of 7.17.

Barnes, who played league cricket until well into his fifties, had little time for the social conventions of the day, which dictated that a professional addressed an amateur as 'Sir', and that the two 'groups' within the same team used separate dressing-rooms, ate at separate tables and entered the field of play by separate gates. Amateurs, though often immeasurably richer than their team-mates, had their travelling and food expenses paid for, while the professional was forced to pay for these costs out of his own pocket. Barnes frequently let his 'gentlemen' colleagues know exactly what he thought of these distinctions, and his disaffection with first-class cricket led him to abandon it and spend the later years of his career in the relative obscurity of league cricket with Smethwick in the Birmingham and District League. His rebellious attitude won him few friends among the amateur fraternity and because he did not have a first-class county after leaving Lancashire, his test appearances were limited to 27.

enjoying a boom in talent on the other side of the world, as Australia's great batsmen, Victor Trumper and Clem Hill, and her outstanding captains, Joe Darling and Warwick Armstrong, lifted the standard and profile of the game to unprecedented heights. In theory, England were the stronger of the two countries, and their touring side of 1911–12, which won 4–0 in Australia, has been described as the most powerful team ever to leave English shores. But the Australians more than held their own, and though each country won four series during the period, overall Australia won 15 matches to England's 14.

The basic structures of organised cricket, as well as Rugby Union and football, were all in place by the late nineteenth century. Governing bodies and annual competitions were established, rules were laid down, there were stadiums and grounds in towns and cities all over England, and crowds descended in their tens of thousands up and down the country to see a new breed of heroes in action. Cricket, more than any other sport, seemed to provide the perfect expression for the Edwardian emphasis on elegance and manliness. Of all the many sports to flourish in the late Victorian and Edwardian period, cricket was the one most readily accepted by the upper classes. As Cardus explained: 'In the 90s cricket was looked upon as the gentleman's game; tennis was not yet popular with men of proper late-Victorian masculinity; it was for what was then known as the "masher", with his straw boater and his designs on the "fair sex". Golf was more for the middle-aged; while football was deemed mainly "low" unless it was possible to play for the Corinthians.'

The first Gentlemen v. Players match of the new century was one of the most remarkable in the history of the fixture. On the second day R.E. Foster, the 'English Trumper' according to Jessop, became the first man to score two centuries in the 95 years of the match. In doing so, Foster, who was also a brilliant footballer, equalled Grace's record of scoring two hundreds in a game for a third time. The result of the match seemed a foregone conclusion as the Gentlemen set the Players 501 (467 of them to be scored on the last day) thanks to Foster's heroics. Incredibly, the Players reached their target – in the last over, with two wickets to spare – Abel hitting 98 and Hayward 111, while Brown, having recovered from sunstroke sustained in the field the day before, made 163.

Reporters of the match the following year were back in their cramped quarters in the Grand Stand following a row with MCC about their accommodation. A few days earlier at the University match the gentlemen of the press had been moved to another part of the ground to accommodate their swelling numbers. The reporters, who had long complained about their working conditions at the ground, were not happy with the new arrangements and clearly tried to force MCC's hand by reporting the matter in their accounts of the game. Ernest Ward of *The Times* wrote on the first day of the University match: 'With regard to the cricket, we are able to give only a few general observations. The Marylebone Club executive have recently shown much hostility to the Press at Lord's; and yesterday the cricket reporters were exiled from the Grand Stand to a position in the north-east corner of the ground, from which it was impossible to secure an accurate idea of the play. Our representative's application to the Secretary of the Club for a place where the game could be followed was met with a curt refusal.' The complaints, which continued in the following day's papers, appeared to work. A week later the press were back in their customary Grand Stand position and the next year a new press box was built.

R.E. Foster, of the famous Worcestershire family.

Kumar Shri Ranjitsinhji, or Ranji, caricatured by Spy.

Wisden's editor Sydney Pardon joined the criticism of MCC, writing: 'It was an ungracious and uncalled-for act to shift the Press representatives from the Grand Stand to the roof of the ground bowlers' house in the corner of the ground. Happily the protest in the newspapers was so loud and unanimous that the MCC bowed before the storm ... I cannot see why the MCC should be so reluctant to build a proper Press box, commanding an end-on view of the game ... It is hardly the thing for the first cricket club in the world thus to lag behind the counties in so simple a matter.'

Until the emergence of Grace, the traditional Gentlemen v. Players fixture had become something of a farce. The professional players were always too strong for the amateurs, who often had to be given some form of handicap to make the contests reasonably even. The public had tired of the spectacle, and gamblers stayed away as the inevitability of the outcome made for poor odds. But the quality of the fixture improved immeasurably as towards the end of the century Grace led a revival in the standard of the amateurs' play, which was maintained by an Edwardian generation of brilliant gentlemen cricketers.

In 1903 the fixture provided one of the most magnificent batting displays ever seen at Lord's by three of the stars of the era. On the final day the Gentlemen followed on 293 runs behind, and they suffered an early setback when Pelham Warner, the future England captain, MCC stalwart and cricket historian, was out for 27. Ranji joined his Sussex colleague and close friend C.B. Fry for the second wicket and made a characteristically wristy and graceful 60 to keep the amateurs in with a faint chance of saving the match. When he was out, the domineering, blustering figure of Archie McLaren joined Fry and, in a breathtaking display of strokeplay, the pair took the score to 500, MacLaren hitting 168 not out and Fry 232 not out in a partnership of 309. 'Never has such batsmanship been seen as this for opulence and prerogative,' wrote Neville Cardus. 'It occurred a year after the Coronation of Edward VII; and it was indeed Coronation cricket.'

The centenary Gentlemen v. Players match of 1906 was remarkable for the domination of ball over bat. All but one of the 40 wickets fell to four fast bowlers: Knox, Brearley, Lees and Fielder, the latter taking all ten wickets in the Gentlemen's first innings. Reggie Spooner hit a hundred for the Gentlemen in the second innings and Jessop lifted the total to 321 with a trademark quick-fire 79. Knox then demolished the Players with seven wickets in the last innings to seal a highly memorable 45-run win for the amateurs.

But while the Gentlemen v. Players fixture held its own as a sporting encounter, the Eton v. Harrow and Oxford v. Cambridge fixtures

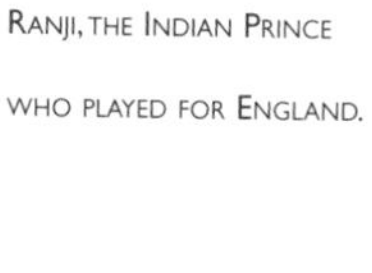

Ranji, the Indian Prince who played for England.

C.B. FRY, A MAN OF MANY TALENTS.

C. B. FRY (1872–1956)

C.B. Fry was an extraordinarily talented man who won Blues at Oxford in cricket, football and athletics and only missed out on one in rugby through injury. He set the world long jump record while at university, played football for the Corinthians, appeared in an FA Cup final, starred for the Barbarians at rugby and still found time to be a fine boxer. He was a distinguished Classics scholar, stood as Liberal candidate for Brighton (losing only narrowly after polling 20,000 votes) and represented India at the League of Nations alongside his Sussex and England colleague Prince Ranjitsinhji. It is sobering to consider how much Fry might have achieved had he chosen to concentrate his gifts in just one or two areas.

Such was his fame as an all-round talent that he was even invited by Hitler to come to Germany to help with the development of the Nazi youth programme. He also wrote a number of books, and in his autobiography, *Life Worth Living*, Fry revealed how he came close to being crowned King of Albania after a delegation from the mountainous Mediterranean country came to England to find an English country gentleman with an annual income of £10,000.

Fry scored over 30,000 runs in his career at an average of just over 50. He played for England 26 times between 1899 and 1912, despite never touring Australia. In 1901 he hit six consecutive hundreds – a record matched only by Don Bradman and Mike Procter – and amassed an astonishing 3,147 runs for the season. His 232 for Gentlemen v. Players in 1903 was the highest score ever in the fixture. The legitimacy of his bowling action was called into question throughout his career, and he once offered to bowl in a wooden splint to prove that his arm was straight at the point of delivery.

No one was more aware of his outrageous talents than Fry himself, and he was not the most popular cricketer of his day. Neville Cardus believed Fry was misunderstood, even though he admitted he was somewhat 'at the mercy of an impulsive, highly strung temperament'. In his obituary of Fry in *Wisden*, Cardus wrote: 'He sometimes, in his heyday, got on the wrong side of the crowd by his complete absorption in himself, which was mistaken for posing or egoism. He would stand classically poised after making an on-drive, contemplating the direction and grandeur of it. The game of cricket has seen no sight more Grecian than the one presented by Fry in the pride and handsomeness of his young manhood.'

A.C. MacLaren: a controversial figure.

A. C. MACLAREN (1871–1944)

Described by Cardus as 'magnificent in his ambition and reckless in his sovereignty', Archie MacLaren was an aggressive batsman and personality, universally admired as a cricketer but little liked by his contemporaries. His long first-class career for Lancashire stretched from 1890 to 1923, during which he played for England 35 times and captained the side on 22 occasions.

MacLaren's 424 for Lancashire against Somerset in 1895 surpassed Grace's 344 and remained the highest first-class score made in England until Brian Lara's 501 not out for Warwickshire against Durham at Edgbaston in 1994. He was always short of money, and though he was an amateur he constantly relied on handouts from Lancashire, who appointed him captain when he was only 22 years old. He was educated at Harrow (for whom he scored 55 and 67 against Eton at the age of fifteen) and later taught in a preparatory school near his Alma Mater. After their father lost much of his fortune MacLaren's younger brothers were unable to follow in his footsteps at Harrow. MacLaren's blustering and overbearing manner rankled with many of his contemporaries, who felt that his haughty air was born out of a sense of social insecurity. One of them, George Lyttelton, described him as 'an extremely stupid, prejudiced and pig-headed man'.

Despite his unquestioned skill as a batsman, MacLaren met with little success as England captain. Under his leadership England lost three successive series against the Australians at the turn of the century and he was overlooked for the post for the 1903–04 tour. MCC opted instead for Pelham Warner even though the young Middlesex player had yet to represent his country. Incensed, MacLaren refused to travel with the party as a mere player, but MCC's judgement was proved right as England returned with the Ashes after winning a thrilling series 3–2. MacLaren captained the side once again in the 1909 home series against Australia, but he proved no more successful as England lost two of the first three Tests. In his defence it should be said that he was not helped by the constant shuffling of the team by selectors who chose a total of 24 players during the series. The Third Test proved to be his last.

In the Gentlemen v. Players match of 1903 MacLaren featured in one of the great partnerships witnessed at Lord's when he and C.B. Fry put on 309 for the third wicket in under three hours.

In the summer of 1921, as his long, controversial career was reaching its end, he boasted that he could raise a team to beat a seemingly invincible Australian side. It sounded like the vain and foolish declaration of a man embittered by past failures and perceived snubs to his qualities as a leader. He was granted his wish when he was allowed to raise an England XI against the tourists at Eastbourne at the end of August. When England were dismissed for just 43 in their first innings, MacLaren appeared to have given his critics a stick with which to beat him. However, in the second innings they amassed 326, G.A. Faulkner scoring 153, and then bowled out the previously unbeaten tourists for 167 to clinch a famous win by 26 runs.

were considered by many to have been wrecked by the 'Society' aspect of the occasions. Not least among the critics were the hard-bitten reporters of the *Manchester Guardian*, who saw in the posers and social peacocks of the events the perfect opportunity to bash MCC. In 1898 the correspondent at the Eton v. Harrow match observed: 'Very pleasing it is to see the portly respectabilities from the City, sunburnt colonels from the East,

OPPOSITE: JESSOP POSES FOR THE CAMERA.

G.L. JESSOP (1874–1955)

Known as 'the Croucher', owing to his hunched stance from which he would explode on to the ball, G.L. Jessop was one of the biggest hitters and fastest scorers that cricket has ever seen. During his career, which began in 1894 and ended at the outbreak of the First World War, he was the great crowd-puller of his day and one of the most famous men in England. In *A History of Cricket*, H.S. Altham and E.W. Swanton described the phenomenon: 'As a hitter, Jessop stands alone; others such as C.I. Thornton and Bonnor may have driven the ball farther and higher but no cricketer that has ever lived hit it so often, so fast, and with such a bewildering variety of strokes. His very stance like a panther's crouch bespoke aggression.'

His legendary 104 in 77 minutes, to seal a highly improbable win over Australia at The Oval in 1902, ranks as one of the greatest innings of all time. England had only narrowly avoided the follow-on and slumped to 48 for 5 in their second innings on a wicket made sodden by heavy overnight rain. What followed in the next one hour and a quarter established Jessop as a legend and inspired Neville Cardus to wax lyrical: 'This innings by Jessop had immortal longings in it; it will never be forgotten. The vision, the undying chivalry of it, belong not only to cricket, but to the unwritten saga of the English people ...' Not until Ian Botham launched himself into the Australians in 1981 would such a paean again be written in honour of an English cricketer.

Jessop was an all-rounder, but was chosen for his first Test in 1899 purely as a fast bowler. He was also one of the most feared fielders of the day. However, he was considered by many in authority to be an extravagant luxury and his Test appearances were limited to just eighteen.

The power of his hitting and the speed of his scoring were truly breathtaking. In 1900, playing for his native Gloucestershire against the first West Indies side to tour England, Jessop hit 157 in exactly an hour. The sheer exhilaration of Jessop's hitting left the tourists in a state of nervous awe. The West Indians, it seemed, had never seen anything like it (nor probably had the English crowd) and, according to contemporary accounts, several of them fell to the ground and began laughing uncontrollably as ball after ball sailed towards or over the boundary.

Against Yorkshire at Harrogate he hit the fastest first-class century on record in just 40 minutes, his 101 containing six sixes and twelve fours. Only Percy Fender, whose 100 for Surrey against Northamptonshire in 1920 arrived in just 35 minutes, has since topped his achievement.

Of the 53 centuries he hit in his career five were double centuries – and all were scored at well over a run a minute. He scored 286 for Gloucestershire against Sussex in 1903 in just 175 minutes, 240 against the same opposition four years later in 200 minutes, 234 against Somerset in 1905 in 155 minutes, 233 for an England XI against Yorkshire in 150 minutes, and 206 for Gloucestershire against Nottinghamshire in 1904 in 150 minutes.

Jessop read Classics at Cambridge, where he won a Blue as a hockey goalkeeper and ran the 100 yards in a lightning 10.2 seconds. He originally planned to enter the priesthood, but instead became a teacher. During the First World War he served as a captain with the Manchester Regiment before being invalided out with a damaged heart in 1918.

Mr G. L. Jessop.

A. Chevallier Tayler
1905

OPPOSITE: GILBERT L. JESSOP, THE GREAT ALL-ROUNDER.

A.E. TROTT (1872–1914)

Albert Trott, the younger brother of the celebrated Australian captain Harry Trott, was chiefly a bowler, but also a hard-hitting batsman and a great fielder. He made his name in the 1894–95 home series against England, but to general astonishment he was left out of the Australian tour party to England the following year. Disillusioned, he decided to come to England, where he joined the Lord's groundstaff and forced his way into the Middlesex side. He even played two matches for England against South Africa in 1898. He quickly became a favourite with the Lord's crowd, and in 1899 he achieved everlasting fame when, playing for MCC against his compatriots, he became the only man to hit a six over the Lord's pavilion.

Trott's best years for Middlesex came in 1899 and 1900, when he he took over 200 wickets and scored 1,000 runs in each season. His deteriorating health, though, began to affect his cricket and he retired in his mid-thirties and slid into near poverty.

On 31 July 1914, just five days before the outbreak of the First World War, Trott was found dead in bed by his landlady, with a wound to the temple and a gun lying beside him. He had been ill for several years, spending much of the last days of his 42-year life in St Mary's Hospital, Paddington, and had added his name to the curiously long list of cricketers who have committed suicide.

The Times said of Trott: 'As he was an Australian he had no opportunity of Test match cricket in his English days. As a batsman he was a great deal more than a mere hard hitter, though he loved "having a go". In the last year or two he had been a first-class umpire and had proved himself a most capable one.'

England v. South Africa at Lord's, July 1907.

and rosy-cheeked squires shaking each other warmly by the hand and recalling their school days in story after story. The fashionable world has taken the match under its expansive wing; Royalty has often honoured it by being present; and the ladies, as perhaps is only natural, have made it the occasion for a display of dress which almost rivals that in the Ascot enclosures on Cup day. To keen cricketers this seems a degradation of a great match. As Lord Granby wrote last year in an indignant letter to *The Times*, cricket becomes "subsidiary to carriages, corsets and chatter"'.

Lord's was the scene of a major controversy in the summer of 1907, and the provocative figure of Archie MacLaren was the principal character in the drama. MacLaren, the captain of Lancashire, had taken his side to Lord's for the counties' penultimate game of the season. Heavy rain made only two hours' play possible in the three days, but it was time enough to create a row that would be talked about for months to come. When the umpires abandoned play on the second day, hundreds of angry spectators, protesting about not getting their money back, made their way on

SIR STANLEY JACKSON (1870–1947)

Born into a Yorkshire family who had made their money in the leather trade, F.S. Jackson was the walking embodiment of Edwardian imperialism, distinguishing himself in business, politics and on the battlefield. At Harrow he was fagmaster to Winston Churchill. He served in the army during the Boer War and reached the rank of colonel by the age of 30. He was later appointed Governor of Bengal and survived an assassination attempt by an Indian girl who fired five rounds at him. He commanded a West Yorkshire regiment, served on the Privy Council, sat in Parliament as a Unionist and was later knighted in recognition of his multiple contributions to British public life.

Jackson was 22 when he played the first of his twenty Tests for England against Australia in 1893. He scored 91 and followed it with a century in his second Test appearance. He captained England against Australia in 1905 in his last international series, winning the toss in all five matches. That summer he twice reached three figures, thus becoming the first man to score five centuries against Australia, and ended the rubber at the top of England's batting and bowling averages. Despite never captaining Yorkshire (this was the era of Lord Hawke) he proved an inspired leader as England won the series 2–0.

Jackson, an Edwardian gentleman to his toes, was the best amateur all-rounder of his day. He was the very picture of sartorial elegance and never took the field without his light blue silk Cambridge sash wrapped neatly around the top of his immaculately pressed flannels. After a highly distinguished playing career he retired from first-class cricket in 1907 to devote himself to a life in politics and cricket administration. He proved to be an energetic and dedicated Committee Member of MCC, and in 1921 he was appointed the Club's President.

Chalk drawing of A.E. Trott, one of a series by Albert Chevallier Tayler.

Opposite: An illuminated match card celebrating the centenary of the first match played at the current Lord's ground.

to the pitch, damaging the sodden wicket in the process.

MacLaren then issued a statement, in which he declared: 'Owing to the pitch having been deliberately torn up by the public, I, as captain of the Lancashire eleven, cannot see my way to continue the game, the groundsman bearing me out that the wicket could not be again put right.' Lancashire did not even bother to turn up for the third day, when the pitch, after some heavy rolling, was considered fit for play. MacLaren's actions were roundly condemned in the press as well as by some of the most influential cricketing figures of the day, including Grace.

It may be difficult for modern cricket followers to understand how a school match could be capable of making headlines in the national press. However, the Eton v. Harrow match continued to hold a strong fascination for the upper reaches of English society, and in July 1910 a young Eton pupil, Robert St Leger Fowler,

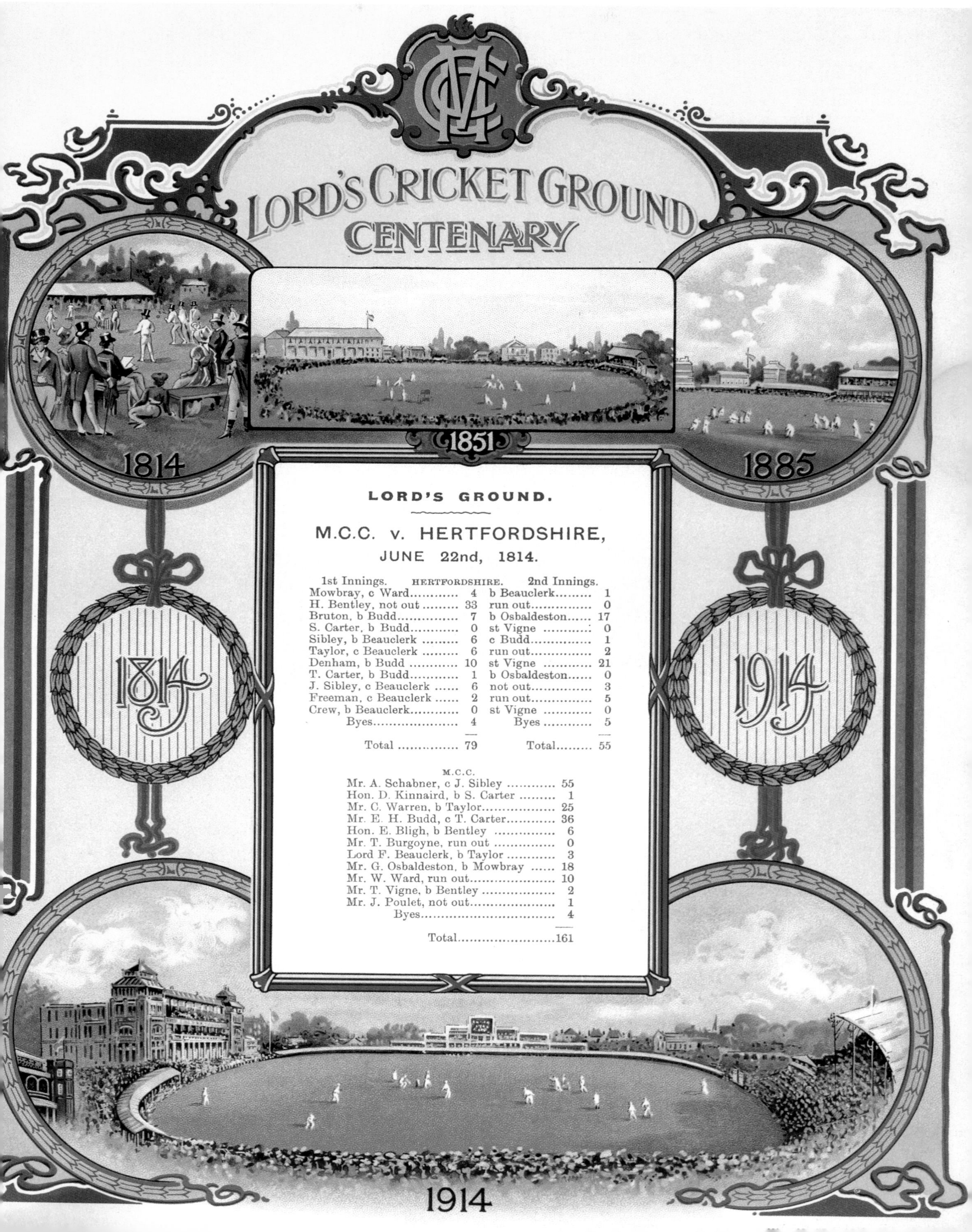

LORD'S CRICKET GROUND CENTENARY

1814

1851

1885

LORD'S GROUND.

M.C.C. v. HERTFORDSHIRE,

JUNE 22nd, 1814.

HERTFORDSHIRE.

1st Innings.		2nd Innings.	
Mowbray, c Ward	4	b Beauclerk	1
H. Bentley, not out	33	run out	0
Bruton, b Budd	7	b Osbaldeston	17
S. Carter, b Budd	0	st Vigne	0
Sibley, b Beauclerk	6	c Budd	1
Taylor, c Beauclerk	6	run out	2
Denham, b Budd	10	st Vigne	21
T. Carter, b Budd	1	b Osbaldeston	0
J. Sibley, c Beauclerk	6	not out	3
Freeman, c Beauclerk	2	run out	5
Crew, b Beauclerk	0	st Vigne	0
Byes	4	Byes	5
Total	79	Total	55

M.C.C.

Mr. A. Schabner, c J. Sibley	55
Hon. D. Kinnaird, b S. Carter	1
Mr. C. Warren, b Taylor	25
Mr. E. H. Budd, c T. Carter	36
Hon. E. Bligh, b Bentley	6
Mr. T. Burgoyne, run out	0
Lord F. Beauclerk, b Taylor	3
Mr. G. Osbaldeston, b Mowbray	18
Mr. W. Ward, run out	10
Mr. T. Vigne, b Bentley	2
Mr. J. Poulet, not out	1
Byes	4
Total	161

1814

1914

1914

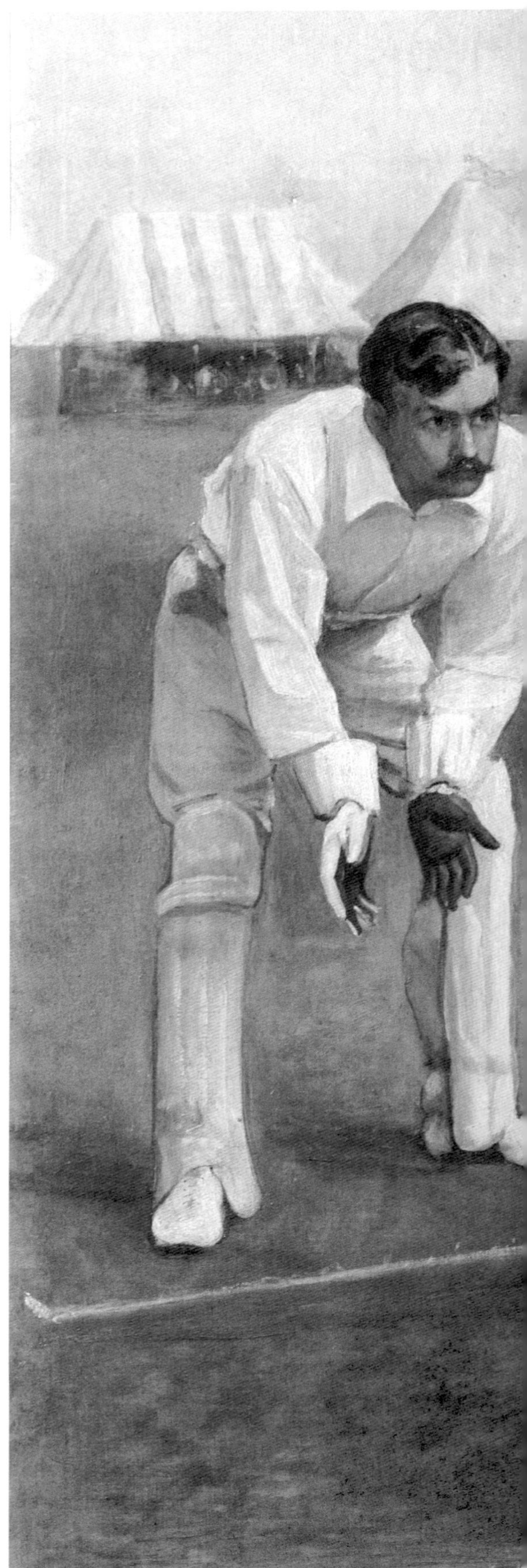

A PAINTING FROM AROUND 1900, PORTRAYING A.E. STODDART BATTING IN AN I ZINGARI CAP, WITH GREGOR MACGREGOR KEEPING WICKET. THE ARTIST IS UNKNOWN.

caused a sensation in one of the most talked-about matches ever to be played at Lord's.

The *Daily Telegraph* began its report of the annual fixture as follows: 'One can never tell what will occur at cricket, but the limit of the game's possibilities must have been nearly reached at Lord's this evening, Eton winning by nine runs having recovered from a seemingly impossible position. Following on 165 behind, Eton lost their ninth wicket soon after four o'clock when they were only four runs ahead. Yet at six o'clock their victory was an accomplished fact. This will go down as Fowler's match, such was the Eton captain's all-round play today ...'

Fowler top-scored in a paltry first-innings total of 67 as the Eton batsmen struggled against the 'googlies' of Alexander (later Field Marshal Earl Alexander of Tunis). In *The Golden Age of Cricket* George Plumptre recounts that the wife of Pelham Warner was so appalled by the quality of Eton's batting that she stood up and declared, 'I shall not send my boy to Eton as they cannot play cricket,' and promptly stormed out of the ground. (Mrs Warner did send her children to the school in the end.) In the follow-on Fowler, with a rapid 64, ensured that Harrow would have to bat again and, thanks to Manners, who made an unbeaten 40 and featured in a last-wicket partnership of 50, Harrow were set 55 to win. Fowler chose to bowl himself, and in an increasingly raucous atmosphere he took six wickets as Harrow crashed to 21 for 6. Fowler added two more to his tally as Eton won the match by nine runs, sparking scenes of hysterical jubilation among the crowd. 'In the whole history of cricket there has been nothing more sensational,' the match report in *Wisden* declared. Fowler's first-class career was limited by his career in the army, and he died at the age of 34.

On 24 June 1914, six weeks before the start of the First World War, the most illustrious names in cricket gathered at Lord's

ABOVE: W.G. GRACE BY HENRY SCOTT TUKE (1858-1929).

OPPOSITE: GRACE IN 1883. HE PLAYED HIS LAST GAME OF FIRST-CLASS CRICKET SOME 15 YEARS LATER.

to celebrate the centenary year of the current ground. Among their number were Grace, his mighty beard now streaked with white, Fry, Jackson, Jessop, Hobbs, Hirst, Lord Harris, Bosanquet and Stoddart. Other guests of distinction included Prince Albert of Schleswig-Holstein, the Duke of Devonshire, Lord Chesterfield, the Duke of Rutland and Lord Desborough. With hindsight, the gathering assumes a poignancy that would have escaped the hallowed greats of English cricket, blissfully unaware of the horrors that were about to be unleashed by the outbreak of hostilities with Germany. The Great War, that emphatic full stop at the end of a particular chapter in world history, also marked the end of the Golden Age of English cricket. Like the society in which it had played so prominent a part in the preceding 20 or 30 years, cricket would never be the same again.

In his after-dinner speech Lord Hawke, the MCC President, gave a wide-ranging assessment of the state of the game and the part that MCC and Lord's had played in its development. The *Manchester Guardian* reported his address as follows: 'Lord Hawke spoke of the progress of the club in the past century. "Lord's," he said, "has become the Parliament House for arranging not only our home fixtures but all the fixtures of our overseas dominions." Cricket, Lord Hawke claimed, was the true democracy. He would not admit that the cricket was losing ground today. It was true that twenty years ago cricket had not to face the rivalry of golf and lawn tennis, but twenty years ago there were only eight first-class counties, whereas now there are sixteen. This showed that the national game was progressing and still enjoyed a fair share of public support. Lord Hawke deplored the rage for averages. We live in an age of selfishness, he said, in which batsmen, perhaps, play for their own scores. "How I hate these averages! If newspapers would give averages only once a month or once a season they would do more to help cricket than by publishing correspondence on the decline of cricket."'

County cricket only continued for a few weeks after war was declared on 4 August 1914. Amid mounting criticism from the public, and following a letter to *The Sportsman* by Grace, urging MCC to call a halt to the championship, play was stopped by September and first-class cricket remained suspended for the duration of the conflict.

1914–1945

WAR TO WAR CRICKET

Lord's was put to a variety of military uses during the First World War, and at various points during the conflict the ground housed units from several regiments, including the Royal Army Medical Corps and the Royal Artillery. Despite the suspension of first-class cricket, some matches were played at Lord's from 1916 as the public, so hostile to the notion of recreation at the outbreak of the war, saw the benefits of diverting attention away from the rapidly mounting atrocities across the Channel.

In 1916 the ground staged a baseball match between Canadians and Americans, the proceeds of which went to the families of Canadian war dead. In 1917 two charity matches were played at the ground: an English Army XI v. an Australian Army XI and a Combined Army and Navy XI v. a Combined Australian and South African Forces side. The following year Lord's hosted two further matches for charity, both of them between an England XI and a Dominion XI. The crowds on both occasions were swelled by clusters of wounded soldiers or those on leave, while a further reminder of the far grimmer conflict being waged less than 100 miles away could be seen in the scorecard of the second match, on which only one name out of 22 was not preceded by a military title. In his book *Double Century*, celebrating 200 years of MCC history, Tony Lewis cites an article in *The Spectator* putting the match in its context: 'We seem to see beyond the smooth turf and the group of white figures, and the still crowds where the great game is being played, to those fields in France and Flanders, in Italy and in Mesopotamia, and the spaces of the seas where the greatest and ghastly game is being played in which many also who wielded bat or ball at Lord's have played their last ball and closed a noble innings.'

Four great cricketers, Grace, Trumper, Trott and Stoddart, died during the war years, while countless other first-class players were killed in action. Grace died of a stroke in his garden in Kent in 1915. In its obituary the *Daily Telegraph* wrote: 'Out! and another master player retires

LORD'S DURING THE ENGLAND V AUSTRALIA TEST MATCH OF 1938, BY CHARLES CUNDALL.

THE MAIN GATES JUST BEFORE THE START OF PLAY IN THE SECOND TEST, 27 JUNE 1930.

from the wicket to the great Pavilion, never to take the field again. Dr W.G. Grace is dead and with him dies the finest all-round cricketer that ever donned flannels. For once there is no danger of overpraise. Giants of the game there still are; giants there were long before Grace's schoolboy name began to be known at Lord's more than half a century ago. But there has never been but one "W.G.'"

After a five-and-a-half-year break, first-class cricket returned to Lord's in the summer of 1919, and any fears that the war had killed off public interest in the game were quickly dispelled as huge crowds poured into grounds up and down the country. After years of bloodshed, bereavement and deprivation, the English people, it seemed, wanted to rediscover how to enjoy themselves. Helped by cheap admission and high unemployment, gates were often double what they had been in the first part of the century, and as many as 30,000 would squeeze into Lord's in the early years of the decade.

Oddly, this surge of interest in cricket – and other sports – which was comparable to the boom at the turn of the century, took place despite an understandable deterioration in the standard of first-class and Test cricket. Lack of practice had made English cricketers imperfect. In 1920–21 England were thrashed 5–0 by Australia on their first tour since 1911–12, and although they showed some improvement the following summer, when they lost the return rubber 3–0, it was not until 1926 that they finally overcame their old adversaries and ended a run of eleven defeats in thirteen matches. The more pessimistic commentators predicted the end of the sport as a national game, but the English public did not appear to be listening.

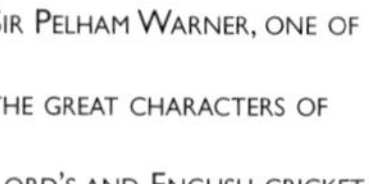

Sir Pelham Warner, one of the great characters of Lord's and English cricket.

SIR PELHAM WARNER (1873–1963)

He was slightly frail in stature and prone to ill health but no figure looms larger in the history of Lord's than that of Sir Pelham Warner. As captain of Middlesex and England and later national team manager, Test selector, MCC Deputy Secretary, long-serving Committee Member and finally the Club's President in 1950–51, 'Plum' was more bound up in the history of the ground than anyone before or since. Despite being a qualified barrister, he never took a brief, instead devoting his whole life to cricket, whether playing, administrating or writing about it. When he died, his ashes were scattered beneath the stand that bears his name along the boundary where he scored his first four as a sixteen-year-old playing for Rugby against Marlborough.

The eighteenth child of the Attorney-General of Trinidad, Warner got his first experience of the ground that would become the focus of his life in 1887, at the age of fourteen, shortly after stepping off a boat from the Caribbean. The match that day was MCC v. Sussex, and Warner watched the great figure of W.G. Grace 'with undisguised admiration, not to say awe'. Two years later he made his first appearance there as a player, scoring 3 and 16 for Rugby. After Oxford he made his debut for Middlesex in 1894, beginning a lifelong association with the county. Warner scored 60 first-class centuries, 32 of them at Lord's, during a first-class career that saw him amass 29,028 runs, with a highest score of 244 for the Rest of England against Warwickshire. As a captain he was said to be a shrewd tactician and good motivator of men. As a batsman he was neat and resourceful rather than powerful, as comfortable against pace as he was against spin.

On his Test debut on the tour of South Africa in 1898–99 he carried his bat for 132, and in 1903–04 he led the first England tour to Australia under the auspices of MCC, when the tourists clinched a 3–2 victory thanks largely to the 'googlies' of B.J. Bosanquet. The following year Warner led a tour to South Africa before returning to Australia in 1911-12 at the head of what many believe was the strongest team ever to leave England's shores. England won the series 4-1, but illness restricted Warner's appearances on the field. On his return from Down Under he was invited to join the MCC Committee at the young age of 31 (he would remain in some post at the Club until shortly before his death). In spite of his poor health, which invalided him out of what he describes as 'The First German War' and which dogged him throughout his life, he was one of the best travelled cricketers of his day, also featuring on tours to the West Indies, United States, Canada and even Portugal.

Warner retired from the first-class game in 1920, at the end of a season which culminated in his being chaired from the field after guiding Middlesex to the County Championship. Thereafter he devoted his considerable energies to writing and administration. He grew to be the most dominant figure in the MCC, and after the death of the autocratic Lord Harris he presided over a more genial and no less efficient period in the club's history. He wrote or co-wrote eighteen books in a highly successful career as a writer, which began in 1921 as cricket correspondent on the *Morning Post* – the same year that he founded *The Cricketer* magazine.

Perhaps the most controversial episode in his distinguished career came in the notorious 1932–33 Bodyline tour to Australia, which caused uproar on both sides of the globe and led to a full diplomatic crisis in Anglo-Australian relations. Warner's role in the affair has been questioned by many critics who claim that as manager of the tour and chairman of selectors, as well as a member of the MCC Committee for over two decades, he should have exerted his authority more forcibly over captain Douglas Jardine, whose strategy of intimidatory bowling so incensed the Australians and appalled so many of his fellow countrymen. Instead he kept out of the trouble, despite going into print before and after the tour to state that he wholly disapproved of bodyline tactics.

His silence during the furore, together with the absence from the archives of Warner's tour report and correspondence with MCC, has led to accusations of a cover-up as well as to questions about his leadership qualities. In his 1983 book *Lord's*, Geoffrey Moorhouse wrote of the supposed 'conspiracy of silence': 'It seems remarkable that an epic ... which excited so many passions, which achieved so much publicity, which has been analysed almost to the point of tedium, is so devoid of first-hand observation about the behaviour and utterances of the man who had chosen the English team, who was actually managing it on the battlefield, who was to be knighted four years later for his services to cricket.'

With his impeccable manners and gentle if patrician outlook on life, Warner was one of the last old-style 'Gentlemen' of English cricket. One of his many quaint habits was that throughout his life he would always insist on showing his MCC pass each time he entered Lord's, despite being better known to the gate attendants than anyone else. Although he was whole-hearted in his support for the professional cricketer, he was adamant that the distinction between Gentlemen and Players should never be removed. It was ironic that Warner, who always wore a top hat and tails on the day of the University match, died on the day in 1963 when MCC decided to do away with the distinction. His old-fashioned habits once led to an amusing exchange with the famous writer and broadcaster John Arlott. The pair were appearing as guest speakers at the launch of an exhibition of cricket memorabilia, and during his address Warner expressed his disapproval of the modern tendency among broadcasters to refer to players by their first names. When his turn came to speak, the gruff and formidable Arlott rose to the bait, retorting: 'For my part, I shall continue to speak of Denis Compton as though he were my friend and not my groom.'

In 1937 Warner, who was fond of describing MCC as 'a private club with a public function', was knighted for his services to cricket. He distinguished himself during the Second World War by working tirelessly to keep Lord's running despite acute shortages of supplies and money. On his 80th birthday in 1953 MCC held a lavish dinner in his honour in the Long Room, the floodlit scoreboard outside showing 80 not out.

The press gave even wider coverage to the game than they had done before the war, and the first radio broadcasts of matches were transmitted, bringing live cricket into people's homes for the first time. In 1938 the BBC made the first live television broadcast of cricket.

Despite the changes in society brought about by the war, Lord's had lost none of its charismatic hold over the imagination of the English public. Indeed, with every passing year the eulogies to the home of cricket grew ever more plentiful and fulsome. The status of Lord's as one of the country's great institutions – rather than just a great cricketing institution – had been firmly established by the construction in 1890 of the current pavilion in all its imposing red-brick grandeur. But the daunting facade of F.T. Verity's design – as well as the isolation and exclusivity of its inhabitants – is perhaps responsible for creating occasional impressions of it as a cold, haughty, undemocratic and elitist place.

In 1926 the writer of an anonymous piece in *The Guardian* felt as if he had been transported back to a bygone era on his visit to Lord's. He wrote: 'Those who are not of the elect survey the pavilion at Lord's during a Test match and rub their eyes, wondering whether the world really has moved on; whether Whig and Tory are labels out of date, and whether the old gentlemen in the sacred seats really are types of the modern world or guests from some distant cricket era returned to see the great old game. One sees there more of the England of Palmerston than anywhere else in the modern world.'

In all the thousands of references to Lord's down the years, it is virtually impossible to find one which does not carry a strong feeling either in support or in criticism of the place. The author of a leading article in *The Times* three years later formed an entirely different impression of the ground, identifying the spectators of every class, age and, increasingly, gender as the ground's most valuable and

Sutcliffe faces for England against Australia in 1926, the year England regained the Ashes.

Spectators queue for the first day of the Eton v Harrow match, 1928.

PUBLIC SCHOOL CRICKET – HARROW BAT AGAINST ETON IN THE 1927 MATCH.

unique asset. 'As befits the citizens of a world centre, the Lord's crowd is catholic in its sympathies ... London without Lord's could hardly be considered London. Mr Lord builded better than he knew. It will not be thought a disproportionate reward that his name should belong at once to the household and to the world, and should be immortal.'

But it was not just the hordes of spectators that made Lord's such a busy place between the wars. As the headquarters of domestic and international cricket, Lord's saw a huge increase in its administrative duties during this period. MCC was responsible for the running of the English game from top to bottom. The Club chose the Test side, ran the County Championship, organised teams for tours at home and abroad. As the legislators, judges and jurors of the laws of the game, MCC was obliged to deal with bagfuls of correspondence from around the rapidly expanding cricket world. All-India, New Zealand and the West Indies were all granted Test match status at this time, and MCC set up the Imperial Conference to handle the new raft of responsibilities that came with the new arrivals.

Lord's effectively became cricket's Houses of Parliament, with the Secretary its leader and the Committee its cabinet, while the dozens of of sub-committees behind the scenes sat regularly to deal with much of the routine business of governing the sport, just as select committees do in Westminster. MCC, which

had begun its life as a gentlemen's convivial club dedicated solely to the pursuit of cricket-related pleasure, had become an all-powerful governing body charged, whether they liked it or not, with the duty to ensure the welfare of the game and preside over its every last detail. The growing importance of the Club's role in public life was reflected in the knighthood bestowed on F.E. Lacey, whose energy and dedication did much to promote the welfare of the game during his long reign as Secretary between 1898 and 1926. Lacey was the first person to be knighted for services to sport.

Middlesex became County Champions in 1920, clinching the title on the last day of the season at Lord's with victory over Surrey and their ninth successive win. The dramatic finale to the season provided a fitting end to the first-class career of the great Pelham Warner, captain of his county and his country during his near 30-year playing career. Warner was chaired from the field by his team-mates as the capacity crowd swarmed on to the pitch.

Colonel Philip Trevor CBE of the *Daily Telegraph* reported the event as follows: 'Middlesex won a magnificent victory over Surrey at Lord's today, and with it they won the Championship for the second time in their history after a gap of 17 years. The end came at 22 minutes past six, with victory by 55 runs. The crowd surged over the field, and gathered in front of the pavilion, loudly calling for "Warner", the Middlesex captain, a wonderful

Pelham Warner is chaired from the field after Middlesex clinch the County Championship, 31 August 1920.

Above: The R101 airship emerges from low cloud over Lord's as England battle with Australia on 27 June 1930.

Right: Selling souvenir cricket balls at Lord's, 1921.

Opposite: Crowds wait patiently outside the main gates at Lord's, June 1935.

Sir Jack Hobbs, one-time holder of the highest score at Lord's, pictured at the Oval in 1930.

servant of both club and country, who came out to address them from the balcony.

'This was Plum Warner's last match, and what a reward it was for his admirable captaincy and untiring zeal on behalf of the county. And what a climax for Middlesex, who had won eight matches in succession in August and had to win this one, Lancashire having beaten Worcester, if they were to win the title.'

Following his retirement as a player, Warner turned his gifted hands to writing, and in 1921 he launched *The Cricketer* magazine. In one of its earliest editions, the magazine criticised the club, which would later appoint him its President, for failing to adapt to the massive growth in public interest in the game. 'The arrangements made at Lord's for coping with the great crowd, which everybody who has followed cricket at all closely during the last few years knew would assemble for the Test match, were very bad indeed. There was a most frightful crush outside the ground on the first day, ticket-holders and those who had no tickets being inextricably mixed up. It is not pleasant to see women fainting in a crowd, and the authorities at Lord's cannot escape criticism ... The interest in cricket today is greater than it has ever been, and the MCC must in their own interests move with the times.'

In 1926 Lord's witnessed one of the greatest innings ever seen at the ground when Jack Hobbs hit an unbeaten 316 not out for Surrey against Middlesex. He was just under seven hours at the crease, scoring his runs at roughly a hundred per session to surpass the highest innings at Lord's, set the summer before by P. Holmes, who hit 315 not out for Yorkshire against Middlesex. 'The great batsman,' reported *Wisden*, 'who obtained his runs mainly on the on side, placed the ball with marvellous skill and did not appear to give a chance.' Hobbs's innings remained the highest score on the ground until 1990, when Graham Gooch hit 333 for England against India.

Against a backdrop of unquenchable public enthusiasm for cricket, England's fortunes steadily improved as the decade wore on and in 1926 they regained the Ashes after a fourteen-year wait with the only victory of the series in the Fifth Test at The Oval amid scenes of great jubilation.

The Second Test at Lord's drew record crowds, and over 10,000 people were turned away on the Saturday of the match. Batsman dominated bowler throughout the match, as was the case during the entire series. Bardsley hit 193 in Australia's first innings of 383, becoming the third man to carry his bat through a whole Test innings and recording the highest Test score at Lord's (a record which Bradman would smash four years later). On the second morning of the match the players woke up to headlines in the newspapers claiming that the wicket had been tampered with. But an urgent inspection of the wicket by the umpires revealed that a hose-pipe had not been properly turned off and had leaked into the middle of the wicket and not, luckily, into either end. Had it done so, and the playing surface had been ruined, the umpires would almost certainly have been forced to abandon the match. Hobbs hit a flawless 119, but England were unable to force the pace on a wicket giving little encouragement to the bowler, and the match petered out into a draw.

At the end of June 1928 Lord's played host as the West Indies were beaten by an innings and 58 runs in their first ever Test match. A couple of weeks earlier the tourists had caused a sensation at Lord's by beating Middlesex, one of the strongest counties of the day, thanks almost entirely to the astonishing efforts of the great Learie Constantine.

'The West Indies beat Middlesex at Lord's this evening by three wickets, a result the outcome

'Patsy' Hendren faces Australia in the Second Test at Lord's, 1930.

of some of the most amazing cricket I or anyone else has ever witnessed,' reported Colonel Philip Trevor in the *Daily Telegraph*. 'L.N. Constantine won the match for his side by almost unbelievable batting and bowling, and I am sure I have never seen so signal an instance of a one-man victory. The spectators went wild with delight when he was in action, and at the end they crowded round the pavilion and cheered him to the echo.'

At the start of play on the last day Middlesex were 168 runs ahead with eight wickets in hand before Constantine, a fast bowler, removed six of them for eleven runs in 6.1 overs as the county collapsed to 136 all out. That still left West Indies the daunting task of getting 259 runs at a run a minute, and when they lost half their batsmen for 79 they appeared to be facing heavy defeat. But

The great Don Bradman hits to leg.

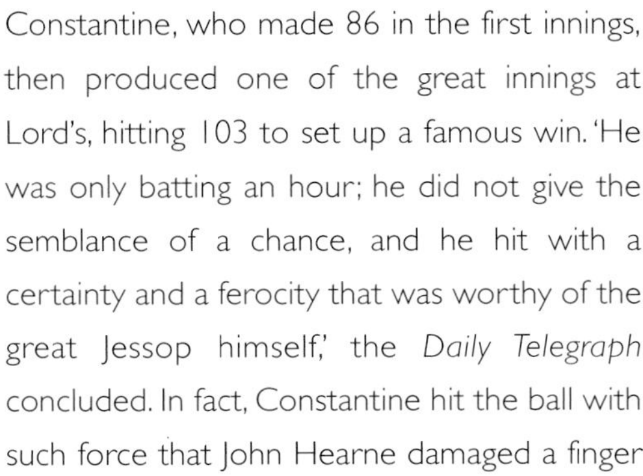

Constantine, who made 86 in the first innings, then produced one of the great innings at Lord's, hitting 103 to set up a famous win. 'He was only batting an hour; he did not give the semblance of a chance, and he hit with a certainty and a ferocity that was worthy of the great Jessop himself,' the *Daily Telegraph* concluded. In fact, Constantine hit the ball with such force that John Hearne damaged a finger badly while trying to stop one of his fulminating drives and played no further cricket that season.

The 1930s was a decade memorable mainly for one great batsman and one great bally-hoo: Don Bradman and the Bodyline controversy. Bradman had begun tormenting English bowlers in the late 1920s, and riding on the

Police disperse crowds who had failed to gain admission to Lord's for the 1934 England v Australia Test.

back of his tidal wave of runs Australia swept to a sequence of victories over England, winning every series of the decade apart from the Bodyline series of 1932–33. England had a brilliant batsman of their own in Walter Hammond, who on the 1928–29 tour had plundered the Australian attack for 905 runs – including an innings of 251 at Sydney – for a series average of 113.12.

Inspired by Bradman, Australia won the 1930 series in England by two Tests to one. In the Second Test at Lord's the records tumbled.

England were without two of their key players, Larwood and Sutcliffe, but they seemed to manage well enough as they reached 425 in their first innings. The great Kent left-hander Woolley, going in with Hobbs at the top of the order in place of Sutcliffe, gave England a flying start. But the highlight of the day was provided by the debut performance of K.S. Duleepsinhji, the nephew of the great Prince Ranjitsinhji, who compiled a beautifully crafted 173 with a wristy elegance that would have delighted his uncle. English hopes of a positive result, however, were quickly extinguished the next day when Ponsford and captain Woodfull, who went on to make 155, raced to 162 for the first wicket. But their onslaught was as nothing compared with the havoc wreaked by Bradman, who cracked an unbeaten 155 in 165 minutes. 'Only at Manchester have I seen a more heart-breaking wicket than this,' wrote H.S. Altham in *A History of Cricket*, 'and never such a ruthlessly efficient innings as Bradman's, both in the evening when he leapt at the bowling like a tiger and on the Monday when he set out to wear it down once more.' Bradman went on to make 254, comfortably surpassing Bardsley's 193 in 1926 for the highest Test score ever recorded in England. Australia declared on a massive 729 for 6, having caused a minor panic in the scorebox, where the operators were forced to post an improvised seven as the creators of the original telegraph had not allowed for the possibility of a total in excess of 699. The Australian total was the highest ever score in Ashes history, surpassing the 636 England made at Sydney on the 1928–29 tour. Chapman and Allen shone in the second innings, but not even the most die-hard and optimistic of patriots entertained hopes of an England triumph. For a brief spell on the final day a truly remarkable upset seemed possible when England sent back Ponsford, Kippax and Bradman as the Australians slumped to 22 for 3, but Woodfull and McCabe arrested the slide and steered the tourists past the 72 runs needed for victory.

At the start of the 1931 season the *Daily Telegraph*, along with the rest of the national

ETON BOYS ARRIVING FOR THE ANNUAL FIXTURE AGAINST HARROW, 1928.

PORTRAIT OF D.R. JARDINE BY HERBERT OLIVIER, WHICH HANGS IN THE LONG ROOM.

newspapers, was reporting more extraordinary events at Lord's. New Zealand, in England for their first ever Test match, shocked English cricket with an overwhelming victory over a powerful MCC side at the start of a highly successful tour. The Daily Telegraph reported: 'We forgot that the chill grey of an English Maytime continued to mock our cricket fields as we sat absolutely still and stared ... Not since 1878, when the Australians dismissed them for 19, have the MCC been humiliated on their own ground so thoroughly.'

New Zealand went on to perform so creditably in their one scheduled Test at Lord's, which finished in a draw, that two further matches were hastily arranged. England won by an innings at The Oval, and the rain-wrecked Third Test at Old Trafford was drawn. At Lord's the New Zealanders had threatened an upset when England subsided to 190 for 7 in reply to the tourists' 224 at the close of the first day. When play resumed, Allen and Ames produced a stirring counter-attack as they put on 246 in 165 minutes for the eighth wicket to give England a lead of 230. Centuries by Dempster and Page and 96 from Blunt put New Zealand back in control, and when England stumbled to 146 for 5 by stumps on the final day, the mother country of cricket was forced to concede that her colonial offspring were growing up faster than expected.

Above: England captain Jardine facing India's L. Amar Singh in the Lord's test, 1932.

Opposite: England fast bowler Harold Larwood, a central figure in the Bodyline controversy.

The traditional Eton v. Harrow and Oxford v. Cambridge fixtures, particularly the former, continued to form an important part of the English social calendar up until the Second World War. The most eloquent description of a day at Lord's on such an occasion is supplied by Neville Cardus. Writing in *The Guardian* in 1932, he gives an amusing account of his experience at the Eton v. Harrow match. 'At lunch the colours of the ladies' gowns during the promenade over the field put me in mind of a transcendental seed merchant's catalogue ... Just before the tea interval the terraces were jammed, and all the perfumes of Araby filled the air. There surely has never been a time when women dressed so charmingly. But the men – with their preposterous collars and waistcoats and toppers and spats! Even boys were wearing monocles. Beau Brummel himself would look emasculate and rather feeble minded dressed in this tailor's dummy fashion.'

SPECTATORS
NOT ALLOWED
PLAYING AREA

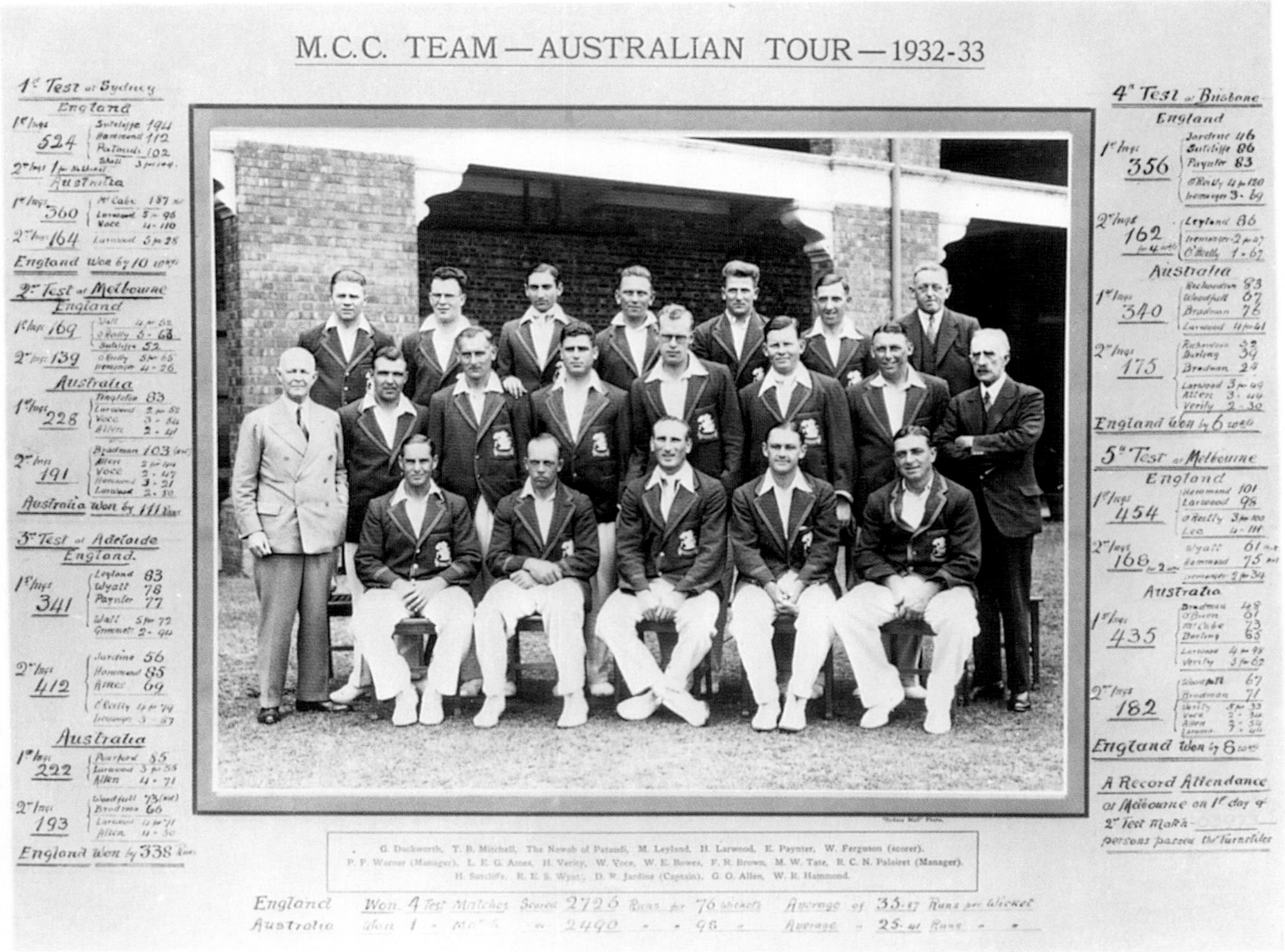
M.C.C. TEAM—AUSTRALIAN TOUR—1932-33
G. Duckworth, T. B. Mitchell, The Nawab of Pataudi, M. Leyland, H. Larwood, E. Paynter, W. Ferguson (scorer).
P. F. Warner (Manager), L. E. G. Ames, H. Verity, W. Voce, W. E. Bowes, F. R. Brown, M. W. Tate, R. C. N. Palairet (Manager).
H. Sutcliffe, R. E. S. Wyatt, D. R. Jardine (Captain), G. O. Allen, W. R. Hammond.
England Won 4 Test Matches Scored 2726 Runs for 76 wickets Average of 35.87 Runs per Wicket

THE MCC PARTY FOR THE STORMY 1932/3 TOUR OF AUSTRALIA.

All-India, the fifth nation to be granted Test match status, made her first official tour to England that summer. Political in-fighting was a constant problem for the All-India side and would not be resolved until India's independence from Britain and the simultaneous partitioning of Pakistan in 1947. However, there was no doubting the natural talent of the new tourists, who won eight matches and lost one before their single Test, at Lord's, which was lost by 158 runs. '... altogether the team, without setting the Thames on fire, gave the English public much pleasurable entertainment,' wrote Altham in *A History of Cricket.* The tourists, though, were not so successful on their return to England four years later, when they won only four of their 28 first-class matches and were outplayed in the three-match Test series, which England won 2–0. It was not the happiest tour party to visit England, and the feuding spilled into the open when Amar Nath was sent home by the captain, the Maharaj of Vizianagram. In the rain-affected Test at Lord's England trailed the Indians by 13 runs in the first innings, but the tourists were skittled for 93 in their second innings and England cantered home by nine wickets.

The notorious Bodyline tour of 1932–33 may have taken place 12,000 miles away, but as the headquarters of international cricket Lord's was central to the drama of those few months. The aggressive bowling tactics employed by England captain Douglas Jardine in a bid to negate the threat of Don Bradman sparked one of the most acrimonious disputes in the history of sport. The events of those few stormy months led to a strain in Anglo-Australian relations that extended well beyond the world of cricket and had an impact that reverberated through the game for years to come. Even today, the controversy prompts a surge of blood in the heart of every cricket-loving Englishman or Australian.

There was nothing in the laws to prevent England's bowlers from spearing short balls to a predominantly leg-sided field, forcing the batsman to protect himself and give a possible catch to the semicircle of fielders surrounding him. Jardine's alleged crime was to have corrupted the soul of the game. Many Englishmen took the side of the old enemy in the debate, but many others complained that the 'green caps' were nothing more than bad losers, beaten by a better side with better tactics. The Australians, the critics said, did not respond with similar tactics simply because they did not have the bowling firepower to do so. Moreover, it was claimed, the tactics had been employed for years.

The scandal did not explode until the Third Test at Adelaide when, with the series tied at 1–1, Jardine put his well-prepared plan of attack into action. All hell was let loose and telegrams from either side of the world fizzed down the wires as MCC and the Australian cricket authorities clashed over an issue that was seen to go right to the very heart of the game's traditional values.

AUSTRALIA'S WOODFULL DUCKS A BALL FROM LARWOOD IN THE FOURTH TEST AT BRISBANE, 1933.

In England's warm-up games to the Test matches, the Australians were given prior warning of the bombardment that would follow. Shortly before the First Test at Sydney, the newpapers reported that Jardine was sending five 'storm troops': Larwood, Allen, Voce, Tate and Bowes. The theory that speed rather than spin might be more effective against such giants as Bradman was borne out in the early matches: Bradman scored 103 runs in six innings; Woodfull 48 in four, including a duck. The *Telegraph* reported that 'such meagre figures were not anticipated even in our wildest dreams. The moral effect of this devastation must be tremendous.'

However, when two of their batsmen were injured in the barrage of short-pitched balls that rained down on them at Adelaide, the Australians were furious and decided to take action. Woodfull, the genial Australian captain, was one of the players to be struck, and he had strong words for Pelham Warner when England's tour manager went into the dressing-room to apologise for England's intimidatory policy. 'I don't want to speak to you, Mr Warner,' said the man known as 'The Great Unbowlable'. 'Of the two teams out there, one is playing cricket, the other is making no effort to play the game.' Warner allegedly returned to the England changing-room in tears.

The Australian Board of Control dispatched its now famous telegram to MCC which read: 'Bodyline bowling has reached such proportions as to menace the best interests of the game, making protection of the body by the batsman the main consideration. This is causing intensely bitter feeling between the players, as well as injury. In our opinion it is unsportsmanlike. Unless stopped at once, it is likely to upset the friendly relations existing between Australia and England.' The author of the telegram was not simply referring to the relations between the cricketing representatives of those two countries. The public outrage on both sides of the world was considerable.

One strange aspect of the whole saga was the silence of Warner, the MCC tour manager. Before England's departure he had condemned the principle of bodyline tactics in print, but once the short-pitched balls and telegrams started flying, Warner was not so much ducking the danger as not even appearing at the wicket. The arguing was left to Jardine, MCC and the Australians, and all records of Warner's correspondence with MCC during the controversy are nowhere to be found in the archives at Lord's. For a time it looked as if the tour might not continue, amid calls for the Australians to sever all links with the mother country. But continue it did, albeit in a hostile and fractious atmosphere.

The MCC Committee assembled for an emergency meeting to consider its response to the Australian Board's complaint, and they dispatched the following unequivocal conclusion: 'We, Marylebone Cricket Club, deplore your cable. We deprecate your opinion that there has been unsportsmanlike play. We have the fullest confidence in captain, team and managers and are convinced that they would do nothing to infringe either the Laws of Cricket or the spirit of the game. We have no evidence that our confidence has been misplaced. Much as we regret accidents to Woodfull and Oldfield, we understand that in neither case was the bowler to blame. If the Australian Board of Control wish to propose a new Law or Rule, it shall receive our careful consideration in due course.

'We hope the situation is now not as serious as your cable would seem to indicate, but if it is such as to jeopardise the good relations between English and Australian cricket and you consider it desirable to cancel the remainder of the programme we would consent, but with great reluctance.'

SIR GEORGE ALLEN (1902-1989)

G.O.B. Allen, known to his many friends as 'Gubby', was not just one of English cricket's best-loved figures this century, but also one of its most influential. Born in Sydney to a half-French and half-Australian mother, Allen came to England with his family when he was six. He was educated at Eton and Cambridge before playing for Middlesex and England in the inter-war years as one of the fastest bowlers of his generation. Allen's greatest contributions to cricket would come after his retirement from the field, and his playing record is relatively modest. In his 25 Tests he took 81 wickets and once took ten wickets

Second Test England v. Australia, Lord's 1975. HM The Queen meets the team accompanied by G.O. Allen.

in an innings (eight of them bowled) for Middlesex against Lancashire at Lord's. On the 1936–37 tour Down Under, he took 5 for 36 to help dismiss the Australians for 58 in Brisbane. He made his highest score of 180 for the Free Foresters against Cambridge University at the age of 46.

He was a member of the team on the controversial Bodyline tour of 1932–33, famously refusing to bow to Douglas Jardine and employ intimidatory tactics against the Australians. Cynics said that he could afford to disobey his captain as he was a 'gentleman', but Allen took his stand as a matter of principle. It was Allen's cheerful diplomacy that did much to repair the severe damage in relations between the two countries when he returned as captain four years later, England losing a thrilling series 3–2. Allen was also in command, at the age of 45, when a weakened England squad toured the West Indies in 1946–47 and were overwhelmed by the brilliant batting of the three W's – Weekes, Walcott and Worrell – and lost the four-match rubber 2–0.

It was as an administrator that Allen made his greatest impression on the game. He dabbled in a number of careers outside cricket, working in the silk trade in France and briefly at the Royal Exchange, but most of his career was spent as a stockbroker, which made him enough money to provide him with the means to devote the rest of his life to cricket. He also distinguished himself in the Second World War, first in an anti-aircraft unit and then as an intelligence officer specialising in air defence.

Allen held most posts of consequence in English cricket at some point in his career. He was a member of the MCC Committee from 1935, President of the Club in 1963–64 and Treasurer between 1964 and 1976. He was chairman of selectors for seven years from 1955, represented England on the International Cricket Council for nearly twenty years and was involved in all manner of other sub-committees. Moreover, he still found time to play a central role in the administration of Middlesex CCC and a number of other cricket bodies. He never married and lived in a house leased by MCC next door to the ground.

Though part of the old guard, Allen was not lacking foresight and could not tolerate the less dynamic and more reactionary members of the MCC Committees on which he sat. He was the driving force behind a number of structural reforms to the MCC's administration, which helped the august old club keep pace with the changing world. His impact on the administration of cricket is too great to be done justice to in these pages, but perhaps his greatest achievement was his contribution to the development of youth cricket in England.

Disturbed by the lack of coaching in state schools, Allen set up the MCC Youth Cricket Association in 1952, which was later incorporated into the National Cricket Association. He had the foresight to understand that the standard of the national game would suffer irrevocably if facilities, grounds, coaches and equipment were not found or improved for the nation's youth. As a part of his crusade to help nourish young talent, he and H.S. Altham wrote the MCC Cricket Coaching Book for coaches as well as a pocket-sized *Cricket – Play the Game* for the young players themselves (royalties from the book ventures were re-invested in the project). The national sporting academy of Lilleshall was used to train coaches who, after gaining the Advanced Coaching Certificate, went to work around the country under the direction of Area Youth Councils. In the first ten years of the scheme, 15,000 schoolmasters and youth leaders attended the courses.

Though often openly hostile about some of his colleagues on the MCC Committee, Allen was given a lavish party in the Long Room for his 80th birthday in recognition of his contributions to the game. The guest list included every major figure in English cricket, and outside the floodlit scoreboard signalled 80 not out, just as it had for Pelham Warner. Allen, it is said, could be bullish and charming by turn, but English cricket should be grateful that, either way, he generally got what he wanted.

Allen bowling to McCabe in the 'Bodyline' match at Adelaide.

The great West Indian Learie Constantine battling against Middlesex at Lord's.

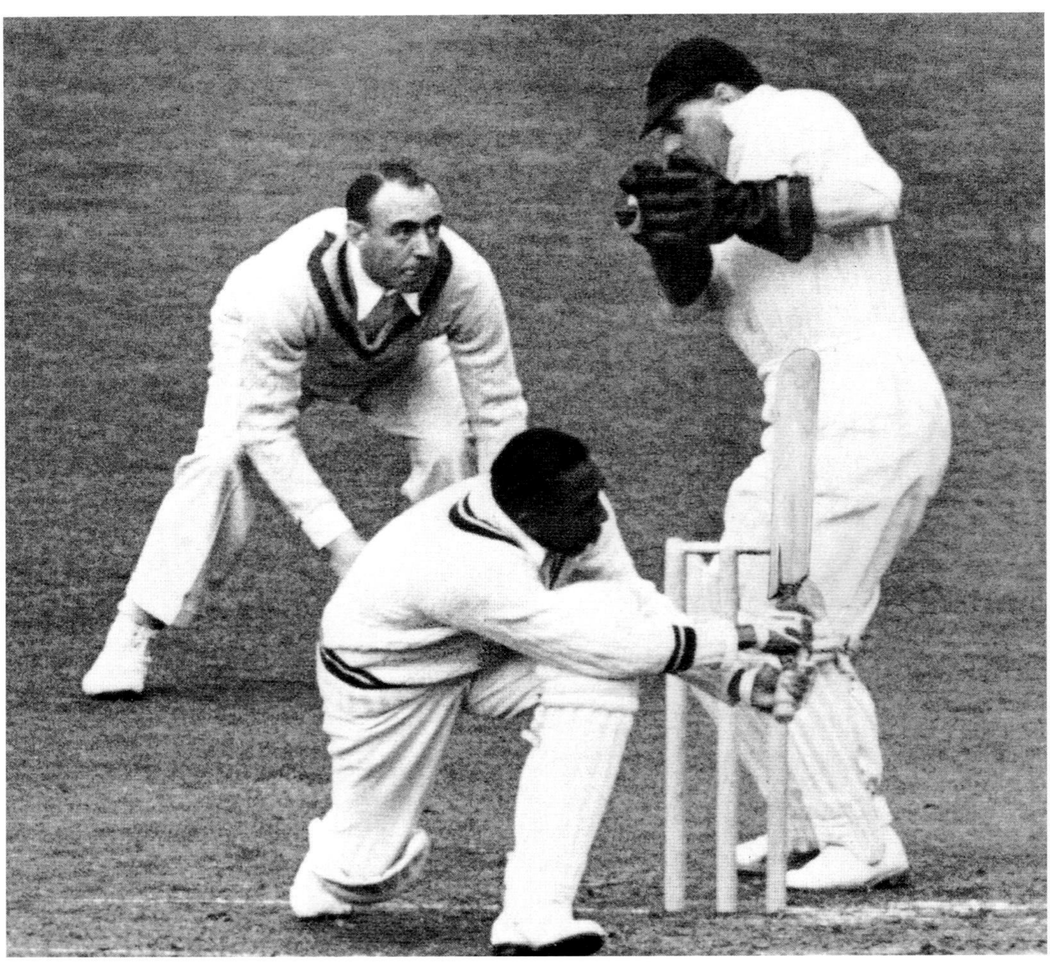

MCC and the cricketing public of both countries awaited Australia's response with anxiety. A few days later the following cable arrived at Lord's:

'We, the ABC, appreciate your difficulty in dealing with the matter raised in our cable without having seen the actual play. We unanimously regard bodyline bowling, as adopted in some of the games in the present tour, as being opposed to the spirit of cricket, and unnecessarily dangerous to the players.

'We are deeply concerned that the ideals of the game shall be protected and have, therefore, appointed a committee to report on the action necessary to eliminate such bowling from Australian cricket as from the beginning of the 1933–34 season.

'We will forward a copy of the Committee's recommendations for your consideration, and it is hoped co-operation as to its application to all cricket. We do not consider it necessary to cancel the remainder of the programme.'

England won the series (4–1), but the arguments continued to rage for years to come. As a footnote to the controversy, it is worth recording that Harold Larwood, the spearhead of Jardine's tactics, took 33 wickets in the series, while Gubby Allen, who refused point-blank to carry out his captain's instructions as a matter of principle, took 21.

After the tour the Australians implemented laws banning bodyline bowling without waiting for MCC to ratify their decision. MCC were later criticised by many for their attitude in the affair, but with the benefit of hindsight it seems that there was little else they could have done, being so far from the epicentre of the moral

earthquake that shook the sport to its foundations. Letters took up to a month to reach the other side of the world, and telegrams could only give a limited idea of what was really happening out in the middle.

Many felt that Warner and Jardine were the only ones with the power to act during the crisis, as they were the MCC representatives on tour and were on the spot. Warner has come in for much criticism for going 'missing' when strong leadership was most needed, but it should be borne in mind that tour managers then did not carry the same authority that they do today, particularly in matters on the field, which were left almost entirely to the captain. But MCC had few excuses for failing to deal with the issue once the team had returned to England and they had read the reports and heard first-hand accounts of what had happened. The Committee declined to pass the rule change as suggested and adopted by Australia, and for years the issue of intimidatory play remained a grey, cloudy area, and MCC's failure to clarify the situation invited considerable criticism from all quarters.

In 1933 the West Indies toured England for a second time, but they were no more successful than they had been five years earlier, losing all three Tests by an innings, just as they had done on their inaugural visit. The tourists' fast bowlers, Martindale and Constantine, were accused of employing intimidatory tactics when they hurled down a barrage of short balls during the Second Test at Old Trafford. Years later, Constantine claimed that MCC had actively encouraged the West Indies to bowl bodyline so that they could assess the policy for themselves.

The visiting West Indies side, 1933.

Denis Compton (left) walking back to the pavilion at the close of the 1938 Test v. Australia.

DENIS COMPTON (1918–1997)

Denis Compton was one of the most charismatic cricketers of all time and his name will be for ever associated with Lord's, where he is one of four Middlesex and England players to have a stand named after him (Allen, Warner and his 'terrible twin' Edrich being the others). He was an outstanding all-round sportsman who also starred as a centre-forward for Arsenal and represented England eleven times during the unofficial football internationals of the Second World War. He was a hero to schoolboys up and down the country and did much to help lighten the gloom during the austerity of the immediate post-war years with his astonishing feats on the cricket field. It was not until Ian Botham exploded on to the scene in the late 1970s that English cricket was again able to boast a figure of such heroic stature as the man they called the 'Brylcreem Boy' after the hair product he famously advertised. Like Botham, Compton began his career on the Lord's groundstaff and was not long in announcing his extravagant talents. In 1936 he scored 1,000 runs in his first season with Middlesex at the age 18, and the following season he made his Test debut against New Zealand. In 1938 he became the youngest Englishman to play against Australia, making 102 at Trent Bridge. During war service in India, he continued to dazzle the crowds with the bat, making 249 not out for Holkar against Bombay in the Ranji Trophy Final of 1944–45.

No mention of Compton is possible without reference to his Middlesex and England colleague Bill Edrich. In the baking hot summer of 1947 the pair were rarely out of the headlines as Compton scored 3,816 runs, setting a new record for the most runs in a season, while Edrich was not far behind with 3,539. Of Compton's remarkable eighteen centuries that year, thirteen were for Middlesex, four for England and one for the South of England against South Africa. Between them, Compton and Edrich scored an astonishing 2,000 runs against the hapless tourists.

Compton's highest first-class score was 300 for MCC v. NE Transvaal at Benoni in 1948–49, which he scored in a bewildering 181 minutes. His highest Test score was 278 v. Pakistan at Trent Bridge in 1954, with the runs flowing at just under a run a minute. He was troubled by knee injury towards the end of his career and played his final Test against South Africa in 1956–57. His removed knee-cap is kept in the archive at Lord's.

Compton's shot selection was the most remarkable aspect of his game, and he was a batsman with that rare gift of appearing to have all the time in the world to choose his stroke even against the fastest bowlers. His running between the wickets was famously and farcically poor, and he once even ran out his brother Leslie during his testimonial match. It was often said of him: 'If Compton calls for a run, remember it is only a basis for discussion.'

Jubilant South Africa celebrate defeating England for the first time on English soil, 2 July 1935.

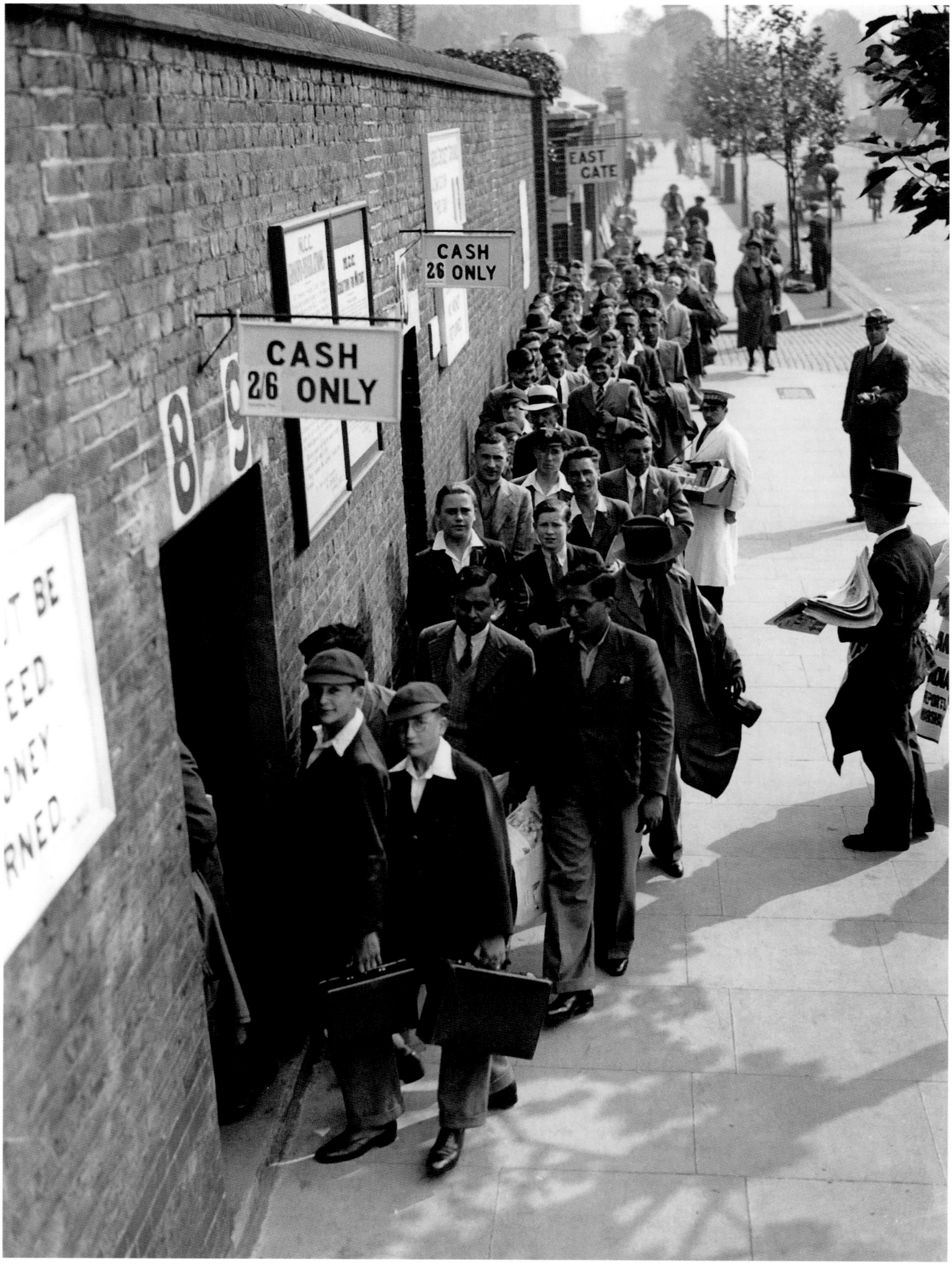
CASH
26 ONLY
CASH
26 ONLY
EAST
GATE
8
9

The tour also produced a new batting sensation in George Headley, 'the black Bradman', who scored 2,320 first-class runs at an average of 66, and hit seven centuries, including one in the Second Test. The rise of the West Indies as a power in Test cricket was underlined when an England party, albeit not the strongest they might have fielded, toured the Caribbean in 1935 and lost the four-match Test series 2–1. In the decisive fourth encounter at Kingston, Jamaica, England were crushed by an innings and 161 runs, thanks largely to a magnificent unbeaten 270 by Headley. The tourists' cause was not helped when captain Wyatt had his jaw broken by a short delivery in the first innings, but there were no excuses from the party, who accepted that in future only a truly representative England side could hope to compete with the islanders on their own wickets.

Meanwhile, as tempers began to cool, relations between England and Australia were slowly restored and the 1934 tour to England went ahead as scheduled. Jardine had made the best possible reply to those who questioned his tactics when he made a battling 127 against similar bowling by the West Indians. But in 1934, with Bradman free to wreak havoc once again and England unwilling to see a repeat of the Bodyline controversy, Australia gained some revenge by beating England 2–1 in their own backyard. Jardine and Larwood had made themselves unavailable for the series, and Bill Voce was surprisingly not picked. England's only success came at Lord's, by an innings and 38 runs on a rain-sodden wicket that made batting virtually impossible. The Yorkshire left-armer Hedley Verity took fifteen wickets – fourteen of them in a day – as England, watched by King George V, recorded their first win over the Australians at headquarters for 38 years. *The Times* reported: 'Helped as he was by a queer lack of confidence among the Australians, to whom the very sight of sawdust may suggest unknown horrors, Verity's achievement must be written down as one of the greatest in the whole story of Test cricket.'

England's series defeat was taken badly as the shock waves of the Bodyline tour continued to ripple through Australian and English cricket. Before the final Test the Australians were noisily jeered by the Trent Bridge crowd during the game against Nottinghamshire after Voce was ordered out of the attack for employing his leg-theory tactics. For many commentators, the incident was proof that the game was in crisis. 'Do we want to save Test match cricket?' asked Howard Marshall in his report of the match for the *Daily Telegraph*. 'A debatable question, perhaps, but one thing it seems to me is certain. Test match cricket is in a critical state, and it will be as dead as a doornail if we have a repetition of the scenes at Nottingham on Tuesday when the Australians were booed by the crowd.'

At the end of the tour two weeks later, an editorial in the same paper laid the blame squarely on the powers at Lord's, claiming that MCC's equivocation on Jardine's tactics eighteen months earlier meant that 'the whole series has been played in an atmosphere of doubt and mistrust'.

Early in 1935 the MCC Committee finally sought to put an end to the simmering row which had so badly damaged Anglo-Australian relations and tarnished their own reputation as an effective governing body. The Committee ruled that in future 'persistent and systematic bowling of short, fast-pitched balls at the batsman standing clear of his wicket' was no longer permissible.

The press's gloomy prognosis regarding English cricket worsened in the following summer of 1935 when England lost their first Test match at home to South Africa, the tourists going on to preserve their lead and

OPPOSITE: EARLY MORNING CROWDS AT LORD'S TO SEE ENGLAND V. INDIA IN THE FIRST TEST, 1936.

Opposite: Hutton and Fishlock walk out to open the batting in the first 'Victory' Test.

win the five-match series. A Greek chemist by the name of Xenophon Balaskas had destroyed England with some fine leg-break bowling. The *Telegraph*'s Howard Marshall reported from Lord's: 'By five o'clock this afternoon, South Africa had won their first Test match in England by 57 runs, and a generous Lord's crowd was cheering the players who thus made cricket history. A glorious victory, with blow after blow struck firmly home, and England must have felt as those in the lumbering Spanish galleons of the Armada did when they were harried and battered into amazed disaster.'

South Africa had provided stiff opposition to England touring teams on their matting wickets back home, but it was not until their first triumph in England that they firmly established themselves as a major force in Test cricket. The quality of their cricket and general sportsmanship won the tourists a great many admirers among the English public and press. '... without drawing invidious comparisons, it is safe to say no Dominion team has ever left more friends behind them after a visit home,' wrote H.S. Altham in *A History of Cricket*.

That summer of 1935 became known as 'the season of the leather-jackets' after a plague of the insects (the grubs of the cranefly) descended, destroying cricket pitches, golf courses and parks all over London and southern England. The outfield at Lord's turned a sickly yellow colour, and the authorities were at a loss as to how to eradicate the pestilence. Sir Pelham Warner described the outfield as looking 'like the sand on the sea shore'. *The Times* came up with an amusing proposal that schoolboys should not be allowed to ask for autographs at the ground unless they first went to Trafalgar Square and caught a starling, who fed on the leather-jacket, and deposited the bird at Lord's. Finally, the groundstaff, helped by a group of unemployed labourers, evicted the intruders by painstakingly picking up the grubs one by one and then burning them, sometimes as many as 1,500 in a day, until Lord's was restored to its lush green.

In 1936 England did not need to be at their best in the three-match series against All-India, which they won 2–0. England won a low-scoring contest at Lord's by nine wickets, and R.B. Vincent of *The Times* was less than impressed by the spectacle on the first day, reporting: ' ... a more riotous display of full pitches and long hops can never before have been seen in a Test match. Poor in quality the cricket may have been, but exciting also it was, for one never had an idea that swells such as these could get themselves out in such an amazing manner.'

In 1937 MCC celebrated its 150th anniversary and, from the columns of eulogies that appeared in the nation's newspapers to mark the occasion, it seems that the venerable old Club remained in good odour despite the fall-out from its role in the Bodyline controversy. Not for the first or last time, Neville Cardus provided the most eloquent words on the subject. His long tribute in the *Manchester Guardian* began:

'The antiquity of Lord's, which is being formally celebrated this week, has had its poets and prose poets these many years. But the proper greatness of Lord's, and all that it stands for in the estimation of cricketers, is its influence at the present time. It stands for that conservatism which at bottom is the game's secret; nearly everything changes nowadays, or is in a hurry, or is breaking up. Not Lord's. A few years ago I came home from a visit to the Continent, where the rattle of the tumbrils could be heard in the street, given some exercise of the imagination. In England at the same time we were going off the gold standard. I went to Lord's on the depressing morning of my arrival. The papers were full of the National Crisis. I sat in the pavilion seats, next to one of

Hammond hits out for England in the 'Victory' Test at Lord's in August 1945.

the hereditary occupants. After a while I said, "Things are looking bad sir." "Bad!" he snorted. "Much worse than bad. The country's going degenerate!" "But sir," I said, "'it's the same everywhere." "No!" he replied with emphasis. "We've no bowlers who can really spin the ball like O'Reilly and Grimmett." And at once I knew the heart of the Empire was sound and in the right place – Lord's on a sunny day.'

New Zealand were the touring side that summer, losing the three-match Test series 1–0, but making England battle for their success just as they had done six years earlier. The matches at Lord's and The Oval were drawn, and the result of the Second Test at Old Trafford hung in the balance for most of an evenly contested encounter.

In 1938 Australia toured England for what would be the last Ashes series for nine years. It finished level after one win each. The Second Test at Lord's, the first ever to be broadcast on television, ended in a draw after a brilliant century by Bradman on the final day saved the Australians from probable defeat. Live hour-long transmissions went out in the morning and afternoon sessions and proved so successful that an extra slot towards close of play was created so that workers in the City of London had the chance to see some cricket after work. Though Hammond had put them in a powerful position with a magnificent 240 in the first innings, England looked the more likely losers at the start of a thrilling final day when they collapsed to 142 for 6 before Denis Compton's unbeaten 76 lifted them to 242 for 8 and allowed them to declare. Chasing 314 to win in just over three hours, Australia lost wickets steadily, but England came across an immovable object in Bradman, who was unbeaten on 102 by the time he had steered the tourists to 204 for 6 at the close.

England were triumphant in their final two series before the outbreak of the Second World War, winning a five-match series in South Africa by a single Test and then triumphing over the West Indies by the same margin at home the following summer. That sole victory, by eight wickets, in the three-match rubber came at Lord's in the First Test and was achieved despite the fact that George Headley became the first player to score two hundreds (106 and 107) in a Lord's Test. For England, Len Hutton hit a masterful 196 and Compton an entertaining 120, while Copson, with nine wickets in the match, was the most impressive bowler.

When hostilities with Germany were renewed in September 1939, all international and English domestic cricket was suspended indefinitely. MCC were especially mindful of the public outcry which followed their original decision not to stop play at the start of the First World War. However, the government were keen for organised sport to remain in some form, both as a morale-booster for a war-weary public and as a palliative for servicemen on their visits home. Lord's was put to military purposes, principally as a recruitment centre for the RAF, but cricket was still played there during the six years of conflict, thanks in large part to the efforts of Sir Pelham Warner, an energetic right-hand man to President Stanley Christopherson.

In the absence of first-class cricket, Lord's went to great lengths to maintain a sense of 'business as usual' during the war. MCC made an important contribution to the war effort by staging a broad range of representative matches (many of them between branches of the services and most of them watched by good crowds paying reduced entrance fees), lifting the morale of players and public alike. MCC donated much of the gate receipts to charitable causes. In June 1941 the list of

HEDLEY VERITY IN ACTION AT LORD'S.

matches for the season at Lord's showed the changes brought about by circumstances. There were matches between teams of Home Guards, civil defence workers, and barrage balloon men: auxiliary firemen, anti-aircraft gunners, policemen, and the ATC; all had a chance to hit a boundary or take a wicket at Lord's.

There was cricket at Lord's on most Saturdays and many of the game's biggest names, including Compton, Edrich, Hammond and Hutton, all appeared at the ground at some point during the war. Among the most regular teams to appear at Lord's during the war were the British Empire XI, an entirely amateur team, and the London Counties XI, a side made up mainly of professionals. In 1942 tragedy attended one match, between Surrey Home Guard and Sussex Home Guard, when Andrew Ducat, the Surrey and England batsman who also played football for his country, dropped dead at the wicket.

On one day in August 1942 over 25,000 turned out at Lord's to see a combined Surrey and Kent side take on the joint forces of Middlesex and Essex. The day was made memorable by the remarkable achievement of an eighteen-year-old schoolboy who took three Surrey and Kent wickets in his first over. The boy was Trevor Bailey, who would go on to play 61 Tests for his country.

When the war was over it was clear that the people had lost little of their appetite for cricket. The unofficial 'Victory' Tests against Australia at the end of the summer of 1945 were attended by huge crowds, with over 85,000 pouring through the gates over three days of the contest held at Lord's. England won the five-match series 3–2, although they were unable to beat the Australians at Lord's, losing the second contest there by four wickets and drawing the fourth. After the second match, Wisden reported: 'About 17,000 people saw the finish, while altogether 67,660 paid the shilling admission during the three days, the proceeds of £1,935 3s. 6d. going to Red Cross and Australian charities. Entertainent tax absorbed £957 10s. 10d.'

One of the most memorable matches ever played at Lord's also took place at the end of August 1945 when, in front of another packed house, a Dominions XI beat England by 45 runs. Wally Hammond scored two centuries in the match, but it was a young Australian, Keith Miller, who stole the show with a magnificent hard-hitting 185. Miller, who had been serving with the Royal Australian Air Force, had a reputation for antipodean forthrightness and sardonic wit. Years later he recalled his first visit to the most famous cricket ground in the world: "'So this is the great Lord's,'" I thought. "What a crummy little ground.'" But in less provocative moments Miller admitted to his love for playing at Lord's, which had come to hold as much sentimental value for Australians as it did for Englishmen. The Australian Prime Minister Curtin, memorably said of the ground: 'Australians will always fight for those twenty-two yards. Lord's and its traditions belong to Australia just as much as to England.'

Lord's came through the Blitz almost entirely unscathed, although there were a number of near misses. Several bombs had exploded in the surrounding streets, but the only direct hit was by an oil-bomb, which burst on the pitch causing only superficial damage. Inside the bomb there was a picture of a German soldier bearing the message 'With Compliments'. In one match between the Army and the RAF the players were forced to throw themselves to the ground, while spectators cowered in their seats, in a reflex reaction to the sinister whine of a V-2 flying bomb overhead. The device exploded a few hundred yards away in Regent's Park, and the players got to their feet and continued as if nothing had happened. The only physical damage done to the ground was to Father Time, who was pulled from his perch by the trailing wire of a barrage balloon and fell into the seats nearby.

The war, though, did claim the lives of three of England's most prominent cricketers of the period. Fast bowler Kenneth Farnes was killed when his aeroplane went down on a training flight. Hedley Verity, the great Yorkshire slow left-armer, died of his wounds in a prisoner of war camp in Italy after being shot in action near Catania in Sicily. Maurice Turnbull, captain of Glamorgan, who played rugby for Wales and cricket for England, was killed in the Normandy offensive of 1944.

1945–1999

CHANGES AND CHALLENGES

The period between the end of the Second World War and today may seem a long time to those who have lived through it, and perhaps an even longer one to cricket-lovers, who have seen the game undergo momentous changes in that time. But for Lord's it has been just another era amounting to barely one-fifth of its entire history.

Visitors to the ground will walk through the famous Grace gates just as they might have done seventy years earlier. They will see the famous Old Pavilion, now comfortably into its second century, and the lush, beautifully kept playing area, the very *raison d'être* of the place, will of course be much as it always has been in the last hundred years. The slope, once described by Sir Pelham Warner as the height of 'a tall man in a top hat', continues to bemuse the visual senses. In the Pavilion, MCC Members put the world to rights in the Long Room, while the warren of offices on the upper floors continue to provide a home to the game's busy administrators. On match days, the stewards on the gate are as vigilant as ever, the printing shop pumps out its old-style scorecards and barmen dispense beer and other sustenance for the punters just as they did at the very first match on the current site in the year before the Battle of Waterloo.

OPPOSITE: CROWDS QUEUE TO SEE ENGLAND BATTLE BRADMAN'S INVINCIBLES IN THE 1948 SECOND TEST. SOME HAD SPENT THE NIGHT SLEEPING UNDER BLANKETS TO BE ASSURED OF A SEAT.

The construction of new stands will have given the ground a different appearance (and most would agree a far more impressive one), but the atmosphere of the place will be virtually the same. A day of Test match cricket will begin in virtual silence with only the rustle of newspapers, a dull whispering murmur from the full house, and a crisp crack of ball and bat to be heard. At 11.05 a passer-by, unaware of the entertainment taking place within, would barely know that 30,000 people are packed behind the brick walls just a few dozen feet away. As if to a preset programme, the decibel level slowly rises throughout the day as the ale starts to loosen tongues and events in the middle prompt a flurry of opinions from the onlookers before the crowds stream up the Wellington Road to St John's Wood tube station at close of play.

For while all around it there has blown a gale of change, Lord's has remained rock-like in its refusal to be buffeted or damaged by outside forces. None of this is to say that Lord's and the ancient private club that owns it have not adapted to the ever-changing face of cricket and the society in which they exist. For in the half-century or so years since the war, cricket has undergone a sweeping transformation, from the administration of the game at the top

LORD'S
M.C.C.
CAR PARK
ADMISSION BY PAYMENT
AT TURNSTILES Nos 11 TO 19 INCLUSIVE
WELLINGTON PLACE
PLAY NOT GUARANTEED
NO MONEY RETURNED

to the grass-roots at the bottom. It is only because we are living through the changes that they may not appear as remarkable as a longer historical perspective will make them seem to future generations.

The period has witnessed: the abolition of the distinction between amateurs and professionals, the transfer of power from MCC to other institutions, the Kerry Packer circus, the dramatic decline of county cricket, the isolation of apartheid South Africa and its subsequent return to the Test fold, the rapid growth of the one-day game, the rise of the West Indies as a major force, the gradual

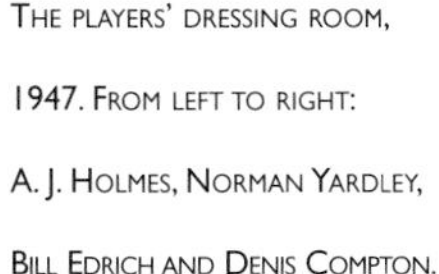

THE PLAYERS' DRESSING ROOM, 1947. FROM LEFT TO RIGHT: A. J. HOLMES, NORMAN YARDLEY, BILL EDRICH AND DENIS COMPTON.

decline of the mother country of cricket as a Test power, players dressed in pyjama-style kit, floodlit matches, the introduction of a four-yearly World Cup, the deterioration of cricket in English schools, the emergence of Sri Lanka and Zimbabwe as Test nations, the growing power of television in the game and, most recently, the MCC vote to allow women to join the club after 211 years – not to mention any number of changes in the Laws.

The Imperial Conference met at Lord's shortly after the war and a seven-year schedule for all the Test nations was drawn up. India, it was decided, would be the the first nation to tour England after the war, and fittingly it was Lord's that hosted the first Test match on English soil for seven years. England won the match by ten wickets to take what turned out to be a winning lead in the three-match series, with the Second Test at Old Trafford and the Third at The Oval both drawn. The Indian side, led by the Nawab of Pataudi, a former England player, won eleven of their fifteen matches that summer.

The summer of 1947 was dominated by the heroics of Compton and Edrich, whose avalanche of runs carried Middlesex to the Championship and England to a crushing 3–0 win over South Africa in a five-match rubber. Their 370 set a new record for a third-wicket partnership in Test cricket, only 12 short of England's highest for any wicket (Hutton/ Leyland's 382 at The Oval in 1938). Reporting in the *Daily Telegraph*, the newspaper he continues to write for over 50 years later, E.W. Swanton commented that 'the only flaw was the running between the wickets, which was an almost perfect example of how not to do it.' The match was attended by King George VI and Queen Elizabeth and their two daughters. The presence of Philip Mountbatten at the side of Princess Elizabeth prompted plenty of inches in the gossip columns of the nation's newspapers.

The following summer Compton hit the highest score of his career to date when he made 252 not out against Somerset at Lord's in an innings which included three sixes and 37 fours. It came in a partnership of 424 with Edrich which set a new record for the third wicket in English cricket, overhauling the 375 made by their Middlesex predecessors Hendren and Hearne in 1923. (Compton eclipsed his own highest score on the winter tour to South Africa when he hit 300 for MCC against North East Transvaal at Benoni.) Later that summer, Captain J. Deighton enjoyed a brief moment of fame when he took a hat-trick for MCC against Cambridge University at Lord's, having done the same the previous year playing for the Army against the Navy.

But the summer of 1948 was principally memorable for the tour of Bradman's 'Invincibles', who many, including 'the Don' himself, felt was the strongest Australian side of all time. There was barely a weak spot in the Australian team, who in Lindwall and Miller could boast one of the most formidable fast-bowling combinations cricket has ever known. They were backed up by the left-armer Bill Johnston and were greatly assisted by a change in the rules which allowed Bradman to take the new ball after 55 overs, so that England's batsmen were given little respite from the pace barrage. The top of the batting order made for awesome reading: Morris, Barnes, Bradman, Hassett, Miller and Harvey. The tourists visited Lord's four times that summer, sparking a rush through the turnstiles on each occasion. Middlesex, MCC and the Gentlemen of England were all comprehensively beaten, while England were crushed by 409 runs in the Test, which was watched by a record aggregate crowd of 133,000, generating record gate receipts of just over £43,000.

The Australians went on to take the series 4–0 and left for home undefeated. Bradman's final appearance at Lord's was in the game against the Gentlemen, during which he celebrated his 40th birthday. Bradman, who would be knighted in the New Year's Honours list, hit 150 and then gave his wicket away, as if to underline how easy he had always found the art of run-making. The Australians may have overwhelmed their English opposition throughout the summer, but their first visit for ten years had added considerable impetus to the resurgence of public interest in cricket after the war.

Bradman, one of the game's great ambassadors as well as batsmen, took the time to send a letter to the men at Lord's applauding the spirit in which the visitors had been received during their all-conquering visit. He wrote: 'I felt that our last tour was a great success from your point of view as well as ours. We may eliminate playing results because I am convinced we had a particularly strong side, but there is no doubt a splendid feeling existed, and I shall certainly continue to work for the spirit of goodwill between our countries.'

Valedictory tributes to Bradman filled Britain's newspapers when he set sail for home with the rest of the Australian party at the end of September. He had been the ruthless tormentor of English bowlers for over two decades, but it was with sadness that England bade him farewell. 'Some baby now toddling after a soft ball in New South Wales may grow up to be the scourge of English Test teams in the sixties,' wrote *The Times* in September 1948. 'Old stagers who then watch him piling up a century will be able, however finely he plays, to murmur: "Ah, but you should have seen Bradman."'

The Test cricket in the summer of 1949 was largely forgettable, as the four three-day matches against New Zealand failed to produce a single result. The Second Test at Lord's, in which the Kiwis scored 484 to England's 313 for 9 declared and 306 for 5, threw up an interesting legal question on the first day. England captain George Mann declared the first innings closed before the close of play so as to give his bowlers a brief stab at the tourists' top order. Mann, like so many others in the ground that day, was unaware that declaring on the first day of a three-day Test match was not allowed, but a difficult situation was averted as no wickets fell and New Zealand had no grounds for complaint.

If England's failure to beat New Zealand had been disappointing, morale was positively shattered the following summer when the West Indies won their first Test match and series on English soil. The home side could have had little idea of the setbacks

Jim Laker meets Her Majesty The Queen prior to the Second Test against India in 1952.

Above: The West Indies' 'spin twins', Valentine and Ramadhin.

Opposite: Len Hutton, the first professional to captain England in 75 years, in action against India, 1952.

that would follow after they sealed a comfortable win, by 202 runs, in the First Test at Old Trafford in early June. Nine weeks later, England left the field at The Oval to the deafening din of steel bands, having lost the fourth and last test – despite a masterful 202 from Hutton – as the tourists clinched a historic 3–1 success in the rubber.

In the Second Test at Lord's England slumped to 151 all out, to trail the West Indies by 175 runs, as Ramadhin took five wickets and Valentine four. Any hopes that England might fight their way back into the Test were dashed when Walcott was dropped early on. He went on to make an unbeaten 168, allowing the visitors to declare a massive 600 runs in front. Victory was out of the question, though England might still have managed a draw, but they were undone a second time by the magic of Ramadhin (6 for 86) and Valentine (3 for 79) as they slumped to a 326-run defeat.

England fared no better in Australia on their winter tour, losing the series 4–1, but the rot was stopped the following summer when they saw off South Africa 3–1 in the five-match rubber. In 1952 England beat India 3–1, having tied the series 1–1 on the tour to the subcontinent earlier in the year. A small piece

of social history was made at the start of the summer when MCC appointed Len Hutton as captain for the series. Hutton was the first professional in 75 years of Test cricket to lead England. 'Though there are many who will look back with anxious eyes and sorrow at the passing of an age, there are yet those who will welcome the ending of an anachronism,' wrote the distinguished sports reporter Geoffrey Green in *The Times*. The idea of the amateur, in the traditional use of the word, had been destroyed by the economic circumstances of the mid-twentieth century.

The summer of 1953 was a memorable one for England as they wrested the Ashes from Australia with their first series victory over the old enemy since the controversial Bodyline tour of 1932–33. The triumph came in the fifth and final encounter at The Oval in mid-August, the previous four Tests having been drawn. Appropriately, the winning runs were struck by Denis Compton, England's pre-eminent batsman of the period, sparking a mass invasion of the playing area as 15,000 jubilant fans assembled before the Pavilion to relish the moment. With hindsight, however, the crucial point of the series was seen to have come at Lord's on the final day of the Second Test six weeks earlier.

England faced near certain defeat after they had subsided to 12 for 3 on the previous evening. Compton and Watson withstood an Australian bowling attack which included Miller and Lindwall until twenty minutes before the lunch interval, when Compton was out. Trevor Bailey, arguably the greatest stonewaller of them all, then joined the left-handed Yorkshireman Watson at the wicket, where they remained until ten to six. Watson made 109 and Bailey 71 (in four hours and twenty minutes) in one of the great rearguard actions of Test cricket to deny Australia victory and boost England's confidence for the remainder of the series.

The English public were given plenty to cheer that year. In addition to England's regaining of the Ashes, 1953 also witnessed the Coronation of Queen Elizabeth, the conquest of Everest by Hillary and Tensing and 'the Matthews final', when the great Sir Stanley inspired a remarkable fightback by Blackpool to beat Lancashire rivals Bolton 4–3 and lift the FA Cup. After the misery of the war and the austerity and uncertainty that followed it, sport was playing a large part in restoring the morale of the nation. In a poignant ceremony that year, Lord's paid its own tribute to the cricketers throughout the Commonwealth who had fallen in the two world conflicts. The Imperial Cricket Memorial Gallery was officially opened by the Duke of Edinburgh in a ceremony attended by High Commissioners of Commonwealth countries and representatives of a number of cricketing institutions, among them some members of the touring Australian party. The Duke unveiled a simple engraving which read: 'To the Memory of Cricketers of all Lands who gave their lives in the Cause of Freedom: 1914–1918, 1939–1945, secure from change in their high-hearted ways.'

That summer Lord's experienced a 'revolution' in its scorebox, when for the first time light bulbs were used to indicate who was doing what in the field. When this innovation was announced before the start of the season, an amusing tongue-in-cheek piece in *The Times* claimed that 'Lord's, indeed, will be more like Piccadilly Circus than a respectable cricket ground'.

England retained the Ashes two years later, beating Australia 3–1 on their own turf as the home side crumbled against the pace of Frank Tyson and Brian Statham. England's hegemony continued back home in the summer when they triumphed over the green caps for a third successive time and the Surrey off-spinner Jim

OPPOSITE: THE SECOND TEST AGAINST AUSTRALIA IN 1953. LEN HUTTON AND TOM GRAVENEY GO OUT TO BAT.

Laker wrote himself into the history books at Old Trafford with match figures of 19 for 90 – a record in first-class cricket which still stands today. Laker's incredible effort propelled England to victory in the Fourth Test and put them 2–1 up in the series, thus ensuring that the Ashes were retained with just the Fifth Test at The Oval to be played.

England, though, lost heavily in the Second Test at Lord's and were never really in the match after they slumped to 171 all out on an unpredictable wicket to trail the Australians by 114 going into the second innings. Working on the assumption that he might get an unplayable delivery at any time, and with the luxury of a sizeable first-innings lead, Richie Benaud took a gamble and launched into the England attack in spectacular fashion before he fell three short of a richly deserved hundred. (Benaud had resumed on his overnight score of three, but he came close to forcing a delay in the start of play, and no doubt incurring some form of disciplinary action, when his taxi was caught in busy traffic and he only arrived at the ground with ten minutes to spare.) Miller then returned his second five-wicket haul of the match as Australia swept to a 185-run victory.

The Essex all-rounder Trevor Bailey was the hero at Lord's in the summer Test of 1957, taking eleven West Indian wickets as England won by an innings and 36 runs inside three days. Colin Cowrdey hit his second successive 150-plus in the series – which England won by three Tests to two – but it was Bailey who took the plaudits. Reporting for the *Daily Telegraph* on Bailey's 7 for 44 in the first innings, E .W. Swanton wrote: 'Among the cricketing arts that have developed, while others have been allowed to fall into decay, is that of using the seam of the ball to encourage it both to swing in the air and to change direction on hitting the ground. Of this type of bowling, Bailey is a master; while of all wickets, Lord's, in fine weather and especially at the start of a match, is ideal for his purposes.'

After tying the rubber 2–2 on their winter tour to South Africa, England continued their purple patch with a crushing 4–1 success over New Zealand in the summer of 1958. But the run of success which saw them not lose a series at home or abroad for eight years came to a shuddering halt on the tour to Australia in 1958–59. England were crushed 4–1 by a young side led for the first time by the leg-spinning all-rounder Richie Benaud, under whose inspirational leadership Australia would never lose a Test series.

England bounced back in the summer when they recorded their first ever 5–0 series win against a hapless Indian side. In a one-sided contest, the Lord's Test was enlivened by the appearance of an uninvited guest in the outfield. During the middle stages of India's first innings and in fine full view of the spectators and the television camera, a composed and confident cat fielded for a short period at square leg, changed to mid-off at the end of the over, then marched off the field. *The Times* reported that 'many a player must have envied him the easy grace and the absence of self-consciousness with which he made the long walk between the wicket and pavilion.'

But if the cool cat had won the respect of the Lord's crowd that day, the same could not be said of the thirty men who stripped to the waist on a baking hot August day that year during the championship match between Middlesex and Yorkshire. An official told the offenders to cover themselves, declaring, 'After all, Lord's is Lord's.' Later an MCC spokesman told the press: 'We do have regular complaints from ladies who object to seeing men with bare chests. We do our best to comply with their views and to persuade men to wear shirts.'

Essex all-rounder Trevor Bailey was England's saviour in 1957.

During the 1950s the committee men at Lord's were busy scrutinising all aspects of the game as they endeavoured to make the game more attractive in a social, commercial and cultural environment which had been substantially altered by the war. No area of the game escaped inquisition. Television coverage, changes in the lbw laws, re-structuring of the County Championship, the status of amateurs and professionals, time-wasting, sponsorship, 'throwing' and 'dragging' were all items on a full agenda at this time. Like all governing bodies, MCC has been criticised for prevaricating and failing to react quickly enough to changing events. But no such accusation could be rightfully levelled at the administrators of the

post-war years, who were alive to the necessity of adapting cricket in a changed and changing world. 'The problems faced by the various MCC Committees in the 1950s are fascinating because they belie the Club's reputation for being retrospective,' wrote Tony Lewis, ten years before his election as MCC President in 1998. 'There was an alertness and realism about their discussions which served cricket well: they might so easily have coasted serenely onwards in the wake of England's success at international level rather than taking note of the financial discomfort of certain counties and the falling attendances at county matches.'

If cricket, on the surface at least, continued in the 1950s much as it had done since the late nineteenth century, then the 1960s ushered in a period of upheaval, reflecting radical changes throughout society. The last outward sign of class division was removed from the game when MCC abolished the ancient distinction between amateurs and professionals, or 'Gentlemen' and 'Players'. Nor could cricket hide from the explosion of protest movements which swept through society as anti-apartheid campaigners used sport as a focus for demonstrations against the South African regime. The issue came to a head at the end of the decade when England's tour to the former Dominion was called off as a result of South Africa's attitude towards Basil D'Oliveira, a 'coloured' South African who had qualified to play for England. In cricketing terms the most significant development was the arrival of limited-overs cricket in the form of the Gillette Cup in 1963 and the John Player League in 1969.

England began the decade well enough with series wins over both West Indies and South Africa. In the Second Test at Lord's England beat the South Africans by an innings and 73 runs, and apart from the overwhelming superiority of England's cricket, particularly their batsmen, the match was memorable for the performance of the unfortunate South African bowler Geoff Griffin. Griffin, who was unable to straighten his arm when he bowled as a result of an accident in his childhood, was continually no-balled throughout England's innings, as he would be all summer. But after being removed from the attack earlier on the second day, he was recalled and became the first South African to take a hat-trick in a Test at Lord's. Sadly, young Griffin's second Test match was to prove his last, as his suspect action forced him into early retirement at the start of a decade which would witness plenty more 'throwing' controversies before it was out.

England's first Test defeat in nineteen matches came at Lord's in June 1961 when Australia withstood a late fightback by pacemen Fred Trueman and Brian Statham to squeeze home by five wickets. England had batted recklessly, scoring only 202 and 206, with Ken Barrington (66) the only player to reach his half-century. Australia needed just 69 to win, but they collapsed to 19 for 4 under the onslaught from Trueman and Statham before Peter Burge steered them to their target with a battling, unbeaten 37. England went on to lose the series 2–1, and would not regain the Ashes until the 1970s, even though they only lost one more rubber (in 1964) to the Australians, the other three series all finishing level.

In June 1962 Lord's played host to a well-attended match between the Lord's Taverners and an Old England XI, as some of the most famous names in cricket returned to action in a contest that descended at times into a highly amusing farce. The Middlesex and England heroes Compton, Edrich and Robertson, the great Australian all-rounder Miller and Cyril Washbrook all featured in the knockabout alongside entertainers Norman Wisdom and Roy Castle. "'Go on Keith, bowl him a bumper,'' came the cry as Compton took guard with the shadows beginning to inch their way across

OPPOSITE: FRED TRUEMAN BOWLING TO AUSTRALIA'S NEIL HARVEY, JUNE 1961.

The Lord's Taverners take on the Old England XI in June 1962. Denis Compton plays his famous leg sweep and scores four off a ball from Richie Benaud.

Lord's on Saturday evening,' reported Brian Moore in *The Times*. 'Miller, ever the man for such a moment, tossed that fiery mane of his, an action still capable of chilling English blood, and duly parted Compton's hair with what can only be called a fizzer. In that moment there was crystallized the whole purpose of this day's sparkling cricket between an Old England XI and the Lord's Taverners.'

On 26 November 1962 the first-class counties voted to abolish the distinction between the amateur and the professional, a decision later ratified by MCC. Henceforth all who played the game would be known simply as 'cricketers'.

Just as the First World War had shattered the old social order, the Second World War had also provided greater impetus towards a more egalitarian society. War had been a great equaliser, and MCC were quick to end the trappings of social apartheid in cricket. In the first game at Lord's after the war all Middlesex players, amateur and professional, shared a communal dressing-room and entered the pitch by the same gate. The old professional gate to the north side of the Pavilion was made redundant. Amateurs would no longer be referred to as 'Mr' on the Lord's scorecards, although, unlike the professionals, they would be given initials. It is difficult to explain to non-cricketers the amateur/professional divide without giving the impression that cricket had been a fearfully snobbish game while it existed. But the concept of amateurism in cricket was much more than the outward expression of a society divided along class lines.

Although there have been several professional 'rebels' over the years who resented the idea that they were in some way second-class citizens, they were exceptions. Most professionals understood the romance and the spirit of adventure which

characterised the amateur. The notion that someone was prepared to devote himself to a sport purely for the love of playing it without material reward – albeit because that person had the private means to liberate him from the job of earning money – was generally seen as something to be respected. The amateur spirit, as embodied by the Corinthians at the turn of the century, was seen as something noble, not mean and divisive. Only six years before the abolition of the distinction, the Monckton Committee, headed by the Duke of Norfolk, the incumbent MCC President, had reported that professionals were in favour of retaining amateur status. It was also felt by many that teams made up entirely of professionals would encourage dull cricket, as batsmen would err on the side of caution for fear of losing their job if a greater abandon were to lead to poor form and their demotion from the team.

When the distinction was finally abolished, it was not 'class' that prompted the change, but the issue of 'shamateurism'. The economic drain of war had impoverished people at all levels of society, and at the end of the conflict most amateurs could no longer afford to spend a whole summer playing cricket without receiving some kind of income from it. Indirect payments, in the form of massaged expenses or publishing and advertising deals, came to find their way into the flannel pockets of the 'gentlemen' cricketers, making a mockery of the whole concept of amateurism.

The *Daily Telegraph*, while ruing the end of an era in the game, welcomed the announcement: 'One does not have to be a revolutionary to feel that the right decision has been made. The time had come when the successful amateur, by writing and advertising, was making so much money out of cricket, that a form of legalised deceit was being practised.'

THE LAST EVER GENTLEMEN V. PLAYERS MATCH IN 1962. FRED TRUMAN LEADS THE PLAYERS OUT TO FIELD.

Colin Cowdrey walks out to bat against the West Indies with a broken arm, 25 June 1963.

ENGLAND V. WEST INDIES AT LORD'S, 1963. GARFIELD SOBERS ATTEMPTS TO PULL A BALL FROM SHACKLETON TO LEG.

In June 1963 Lord's was the scene of one of the most exciting finales to a match in Test history. All four results were possible as the Second Test between England and West Indies drew to its thrilling climax. England were six runs short of victory with just one wicket standing when Colin Cowdrey strode down the pavilion steps with his left arm, broken by a rising delivery the day before, plastered to the elbow. Shackleton had been run out at the bowler's end the ball before, allowing David Allen to negotiate the final two balls of the match as Cowdrey watched from the safety of the non-striker's end. The match thus finished in a draw, but England were well beaten in the series (3–1). *Wisden* commented: 'The game, which attracted 110,287 paying spectators and approximately £25,000 all told, gave cricket a fine boost which was reflected immediately in improved bookings for the Third Test at Edgbaston. The receipts were £56,300, not far short of a record for any match. Those who saw it, and the millions who followed the game's progress over television and radio, were kept in a constant state of excitement. It was a game to remember.'

The day after the Lord's match several West Indians were hauled before a magistrate, having been arrested the day before for being drunk and disorderly. The magistrate told them: 'I don't blame you. It was worth it.'

At the end of the summer, the final of the inaugural limited-overs competition in first-class cricket took place at Lord's. Knock-out competitions had been mooted several times in the past. After the Second World War the idea gained momentum and received a good deal of support in the press, but as the government began to consider a ban on midweek sport, in order to boost economic production, the idea

was dropped. Later, when cricket looked for ways of boosting county coffers to offset the decline in attendances at championship matches, the one-day plan was resurrected and in 1963 the Gillette Cup was born.

Many feared that the introduction of the one-day game would have a damaging effect on technique. Bowlers, it was predicted, would lose the art of bowling batsmen out, concentrating instead on run prevention, while batsmen would sacrifice orthodoxy and patience as they improvised for quick runs. On the other hand, it was widely accepted that the one-day game was neccessary to bring back the crowds, which had been dwindling for years, while boosting the coffers of the financially ailing counties. But as the arguments continued, the final provided an exciting spectacle for the 25,000 who squeezed into Lord's. Before a full house, who created a football-style cup final atmosphere, Sussex beat Worcestershire by fourteen runs with 1.4 overs to spare.

One observer who enjoyed the day and welcomed the advent of the new competition was the influential E.W. Swanton of the *Daily Telegraph*, who wrote in his report of the match: 'This instant cricket is very far from being a gimmick. There is a place in it for all the arts of cricket, most of which are subtle ones. That is why the day was so enjoyable, not only for the patriots with their banners and their rosettes "up for the cup", but for the practising cricketers, past and present, of all ages and types, who seemed to form the bulk of the 25,000 crowd.'

If the first final had been a close-run affair, then the third, between Yorkshire and Surrey in 1965, did little to promote the potential

The 1965 Gillette Cup Final, Surrey v. Yorkshire. Ken Barrington at gully looks on as Geoff Boycot hits out.

excitement of the limited-overs game. Yorkshire, the pre-eminent county of the 1960s, bursting with the talents of Boycott, Illingworth, Close and Trueman, crushed Surrey, the outstanding team of the previous decade, by a massive 175 runs. Another huge crowd was there to witness the rout as man-of-the-match Boycott struck a scintillating 146 and Close clubbed 79 to help the White Rose county reach a formidable 317 for 4 from their allotted 60 overs. Surrey were never at the races after Trueman picked up three wickets in four balls, and Illingworth mopped up with five of his own.

England enjoyed mixed fortunes in the Tests in the summer of 1965, winning all three Tests against New Zealand, but losing the three-match series to South Africa, whose one victory came at Trent Bridge.

Before the 1965 season began the issue of 'throwing' had come to a head. The Advisory County Cricket Committee met at Lord's and announced that they had set up a special board to monitor bowlers who had been repeatedly no-balled or reported as having a suspect action. It was decided that anyone with a suspect action would be filmed in action and that the special committee would have the power to suspend a bowler until the end of the season.

In 1965 and 1966 there was even greater controversy at Lord's. MCC faced a serious revolt from within, as many of its Members protested about proposals for the redevelopment of the south-west corner of the ground. The in-house rebellion became a cause *célèbre* in the national press as Members reacted furiously to expensive plans to do away

Sobers and Holford return to the Pavilion at the close of play on the fourth day of the 1966 Test.

with the famous Tavern and clock tower – as well as their dining-room – to make way for a new stand. 'Beer-drinking spectators of cricket outside the Tavern at Lord's this summer will need to order an extra pint to drown their nostalgia,' the news pages of *The Times* reported in May 1965 following the publication of MCC's plans. 'For at their backs, as they drink, time's winged chariot will be drawing near in the form of a redevelopment plan which will obliterate their century-old haven behind cover-point or mid-wicket, depending on which end is bowling.' Acrimony reigned as the Members argued among themselves at special meetings called to discuss the issue over the ensuing months, but in the end the Committee prevailed over its critics and the building got under way in 1967.

Two years later Lord's became the focus of one of the greatest controversies in twentieth-century sport. What began with the late call-up of Worcestershire all-rounder Basil D'Oliveira to the England party for the 1968–69 tour of South Africa ended in a full-blown international crisis that saw South Africa isolated from international sport for over two decades. D'Oliveira was a Cape Coloured who was debarred from playing representative cricket in his homeland on the grounds of his skin colour. His passage to England was arranged by the cricket broadcaster and writer John Arlott, whose commentary the player listened to on

the BBC World Service. D'Oliveira wrote to Arlott, who arranged for him to join Middleton in the Lancashire League. D'Oliveira, an attacking right-hand bat and useful off-spinner, topped the batting averages in his first season. In 1965 he made his debut for Worcestershire, scoring over 1,500 runs and hitting six centuries. The following year his remarkable rise from scrubland cricketer to the highest stage in cricket was completed when he was selected for England.

D'Oliveira, a hugely popular figure with the public, lost his form on the 1967–68 tour of West Indies and was dropped after the First Test against Australia in the summer despite making an unbeaten 87 in the second innings. On his recall to the side for the final Test following the withdrawal of Roger Prideaux, he hit a 158 which helped England to square the series. Though it was probably not going through his head at the time, D'Oliveira had compiled the most politically significant century in the history of the game.

Immediately, the country's cricket writers and followers understood its significance. In his match report for the *Daily Telegraph*, E.W. Swanton wrote: '... his fine innings here today may imperil MCC's tour to South Africa in the autumn. It is hardly conceivable now that he will not find a place on merit, when the party is named next Wednesday. And there is a persistent rumour from South Africa that D'Oliveira would not be persona grata.'

Swanton's would not have been the only eyebrows raised when D'Oliveira was not named in the party for the winter tour of South Africa announced that Wednesday. The many critics of his omission claimed it was a purely political act designed to avoid a face-off with the South African government. MCC insisted that the decision had been made on purely cricketing grounds and that D'Oliveira's bowling was unsuitable for South African pitches. Not everyone was so convinced, and the protests began to mount as the 'D'Oliveira affair' was splashed over front page and back page of broadsheet and tabloid alike. The row gave rise to heated protests by MPs in the House of Commons and a handful of MCC Members even resigned, while the former England captain David Sheppard, the future Bishop of Liverpool, headed a group of protesting MCC Members upset by the player's omission.

Then the withdrawal through injury of Warwickshire medium-pacer Tom Cartwright gave MCC the chance to silence their critics – at least at home – as they called in D'Oliveira as a replacement, even though he was originally left out on the grounds of his bowling. D'Oliveira's inclusion was widely welcomed in England, but that was not the case in South Africa, where the President, John Vorster, left no one in any doubt about his views on the matter. 'It is not the MCC team,' said Vorster, whose political career was ended ten years later when he was found guilty of the misappropriation of government funds. 'It is the team of the anti-apartheid movement. We are not prepared to have a team thrust upon us.'

Shortly afterwards, MCC cancelled the tour and thus begun South Africa's gradual expulsion from all forms of international sport until the release of Nelson Mandela from prison in 1990 and the repealing of apartheid laws the following year. Vorster's reaction was treated with near-universal scorn. *The Times* wrote: 'To the outside world Mr Vorster's speech about Mr D'Oliveira was one more indication of the mental weakness of apartheid, which is a fetish rather than a policy. To hear it said that Mr D'Oliveira had been chosen by the anti-apartheid league sounded like the murky justifications of *Pravda* or *Izvestia*.'

With no winter tour, England had to wait until the following summer before they resumed Test action. West Indies and New Zealand were the guests that year, and both returned home having lost a three-match series by two Tests to nil. Underwood, the Kent left-arm spinner, was England's hero against New Zealand at Lord's, when he bowled the team to victory on the fourth day, taking 7 for 32 on a pitch of unpredictable bounce as the visitors were skittled for 132.

In May 1970, just over a week before the South Africans were due to arrive in England, the authorities at Lord's called off their tour under pressure from the Labour government, and announced a series of matches against The Rest of the World in their place. The decision was greeted as a triumph by the Stop the '70 Tour Campaign, and with bitterness by South Africa, where the Minister of Sport, Frank Waring, launched a scathing attack on the decision "forced on" the Cricket Council.

Shortly before the announcement of the tour's cancellation, a student from London University, David Wilton-Godberford, had threatened to wreck the tour by covering the country's cricket pitches with half a million locusts that he had been breeding at his home in Wales. Wilton-Godberford told the press: 'I abhor apartheid and this is to be my personal protest. Anything up to 100,000 locusts will be let loose at a particular ground and I think the plan is foolproof. They will ravage every blade of grass and green foliage. The greatest care will

BASIL D'OLIVEIRA BOWLING FOR WORCESTERSHIRE AT LORD'S IN 1966.

D'Oliveira playing for England against Australia at the Oval in 1968.

be taken to ensure they are in the correct physiological stage. So that their insatiable appetites will not be impaired they will not be fed for 24 hours before the moment of truth ... the South Africans are going to dread this trip.'

Earlier in the year South Africa had unwittingly played their last Test match for 22 years when they completed a 4–0 series whitewash over the Australians. A powerful team including four truly world-class players in Richards, Pollock, Procter and Barlow beat Australia by 323 runs at Port Elizabeth. The following year South Africa's cricketers made a public protest about their government's apartheid policy in sport. At the start of the Transvaal v. Rest of South Africa match to celebrate ten years of the Republic, the players walked from the field and issued the following statement: 'We cricketers feel the time has arrived to make our feelings known. We accordingly support our Association in its approach to the Government with the stipulation that merit alone must be the main criterion for selection.'

In the mid-1960s MCC was beginning to feel the strain of running virtually every aspect of organised cricket. The financial costs were rising, and the administrative burden growing more onerous by the year. In theory, there were separate governing bodies managing the game at different levels. The Board of Control oversaw Test cricket and the Advisory County Cricket Committee attended to the first-class game – but these bodies were founded, funded and administered by MCC.

At this time the Government was starting to distribute grants to the country's sports associations via the Sports Council, but as a privately owned club MCC was not eligible to receive any of the hand-outs. As a way round this, the National Cricket Association was formed in 1965 to run all cricket outside the first-class game. (The NCA was an independent body in name, but it was administered by an MCC secretariat.)

MCC continued to run the first-class game, but when Gubby Allen, in his first year as Treasurer, announced a record deficit of £14,200 in the 1967 accounts, MCC was forced to accept that it could no longer afford to support Test and county cricket. Thus in 1968 the Test and County Cricket Board (TCCB) was formed and MCC, with a mixture of reluctance and relief, was obliged to hand over the power it had held over the game for 180 years. MCC was left only with custody of the laws of the game – a role it continues to fulfil today.

So, in theory, cricket now had an independent governing body, but in practice, MCC remained at the very heart of cricket's government and Lord's remained the physical seat of power. MCC provided the bulk of administrators for the new organisation while the Cricket Council, the new supreme, over-arching authority, was also administered by MCC. The Council would be made up of an equal proportion of representatives of MCC, the NCA and the TCCB, but its chairman and vice-chairman would be the MCC's President and Treasurer. Thus, for all the new cluster of abbreviations and positions, the transfer of power could be regarded as nothing more than a change in nomenclature.

It was logical, however, that MCC should continue to be involved at the very highest level of the game in the early years following the transfer of power. Who else had 180 years' experience of running the game, and who else could whistle down a corridor and call upon such a distinguished list of former cricketers and administrators? It would hardly have been sensible if the running of the game was handed over to those with only passing experience of cricket administration. But in 1974 MCC scaled down its involvement when it handed the NCA and TCCB the responsibility of setting up their own individual staffs.

As Britain's pre-eminent cricket club, whose members included virtually every major name in English cricket, MCC was unable to remove itself entirely from the running of the game, and this led to tensions within the new order at Lord's. Former England captain Tony Lewis, who succeeded Colin Ingleby-Mackenzie as President of MCC at the end of 1998, recalled in his book *Double Century* how, towards the end of the 1970s, the fact that all of the new bodies were housed at Lord's, that some members of the TCCB were the Members of the MCC Committees, and that a few men seemed to be trying to wear a number of hats at the same time, 'led not to a peaceful shift of power but to difficulty and deadlock … it became more a jockeying for position and fight for control.'

MCC also administered the International Cricket Council until 1993, when cricket's world governing body established its own secretariat. The ICC remains based at Lord's, as do the England and Wales Cricket Board (ECB), which replaced the TCCB in 1996 in another shake-up of the structure of the domestic game. MCC has never disentangled itself from the government of the game, even though that was its alleged intention at the end of the 1960s. So long as Lord's remains home to the various organisations now running the game, the Marylebone Club will remain at the centre of the cricketing world. There have been plenty of calls since MCC handed over its power for the headquarters of the TCCB, and now the ECB, to be moved to somewhere

more geographically and symbolically central, like Trent Bridge or Edgbaston. So far the urge has been resisted. Lewis singles out three major points in favour of MCC.

'First, any organisation which controls the organisation and running of cricket, albeit by the request of all, is bound to be criticised. The rule-makers in cricket cannot always be right or popular ... Second, throughout MCC's life as cricket's government, its many committees that run first-class cricket were all composed of nominees from the first-class counties and the universities ... The channels were always open for the widest possible discussion on any subject through the county system. MCC's governing process was far more democratic than many people believe ... Lastly, I must emphasise the immense responsibility which many men of Lord's have felt and feel towards cricket and cricketers. Imagine the number of times that long-serving committee men have boarded trains or cars in the dark on winter mornings and set out for Lord's – not half a dozen times, but hundreds. I have little sympathy with their detractors unless they themselves are prepared to devote the hours and match the conscience of such men, often former county players.'

In the First Test against the Rest of the World at Lord's in the summer of 1970, England slumped to defeat by an innings and 80 runs and went on to lose the series 4–1. The great West Indian all-rounder Garfield Sobers hit a magnificent 183 and took eight wickets in the match, while the South African all-rounders, the bespectacled Barlow (119) and Procter (55), also made significant contributions. In the summer of 1971, forty years after their first official tour, India won their first Test match in England when they triumphed by four wickets at The Oval to take the three-match series 1–0.

Twelve months later the Australians flew in, hoping to regain the Ashes, which they had surrendered after twelve years of 'ownership' six months earlier when Ray Illingworth became only the second captain after Jardine to regain the Ashes on Australian soil. But in a thrilling series, England, who had won by two Tests to nil in Australia, ensured the trophy remained in their hands as the rubber finished all square at 2–2.

The match at Lord's lasted just three and a half days, but over 100,000 people passed through the turnstiles to see it, generating £83,000 – the largest gate receipt ever recorded at a cricket match. That Second Test will be for ever known as 'Massie's match', after the medium-paced swing bowler Bob Massie, who took 8 for 84 and 8 for 53. His figures were comfortably the best to have been returned by a player on his Test match debut, and were the best ever by an Australian on English soil, surpassing fourteen wickets taken by 'The Demon Bowler', Fred Spofforth, at The Oval in 1882.

Massie had arrived from nowhere and would return there as soon as the series was over. 'But who is Bob Massie?' asked John Woodcock in *The Times* after the Australian had bowled his team to the brink of a series-levelling victory by close of play on Saturday. A 25-year-old bank clerk from Perth in Western Australia, Massie took 8 for 84 in England's first innings and was suddenly a name to be reckoned with. England began their second innings half an hour after lunch on the Saturday, 36 runs behind Australia, with Massie bowling from the Nursery End and Lillee working up a pace at the Pavilion End. By 6.30 Massie had taken 7 for 38 in 24 overs.

Lord's was again an unhappy place for England followers in the summer of 1973, when they subsided to their second heaviest defeat in nearly 100 years of Test matches. England lost by an innings and 226 runs to the

OPPOSITE: ENGLAND V. AUSTRALIA AT LORD'S, 1972. CHAPPELL (131) RETURNS TO A STANDING OVATION.

West Indies, the emerging superpower in world cricket. E.W. Swanton applauded the all-round strength of the tourists, who won two of the rubber's three Tests. In his match report of the fourth and final day, he wrote in the *Daily Telegraph*: 'Kanhai and his team deserve the warmest congratulations on their first success in a rubber for seven years. On giving reasons for the victory, Kanhai laid stress on the great improvement in the West Indian catching. This is true but, fielding apart, I would ascribe the rejuvenation of the West Indies to three factors, the emergence of Julien, the sudden and unexpected elevation of Boyce to new heights of achievement, and not least to the glorious Indian summer of Sobers.'

England emerged with credit from their tour of the Caribbean that winter, after they levelled the five-match series on the final day of the final Test at Port of Spain, Trinidad, thanks largely to superlative bowling by the towering all-rounder Tony Greig. The South African-born future England captain, his six feet seven and a half inches an intimidating sight at the crease, capped a highly successful series by taking 5 for 70 in the West Indies' second innings to add to his 8 for 86 in their first. Greig also finished second in the batting averages, ahead of the prolific Geoff Boycott but well behind Dennis Amiss.

In 1975 Lord's staged the inaugural World Cup final amid a carnival atmosphere only possible when the West Indies are on the billing. At the end of a beautiful June day, the West Indies clinched victory after having set Australia the highest ever target in a 60-over match on English soil. John Woodcock in *The Times* wrote: 'As much as a cricket match, the final of the World Cup for the Prudential Trophy, won by West Indies, had been a piece of theatre; of drama, tragedy, carnival and farce all rolled into one.'

Boycott is bowled by Massie in 'Massie's Match.'

ENGLAND V. WEST INDIES, 1973. BERNARD JULIEN IS CONGRATULATED ON HIS CENTURY AS THE CROWD INVADES THE PITCH.

Amid the lengthening shadows and a cresendo of clattering tin cans and car horns, Jeff Thomson became the fifth Australian to be run out in the match as Ian Chappell's battling side finally yielded under the pressure of the exacting run rate. Captain Clive Lloyd, dropped on 26 with the score on 83 for 3, was the hero of the West Indies' innings. His 102 included two huge sixes, one a hook off Dennis Lillee, and earned him the Man of the Match award. Replying to a daunting 291 for 8, the Australians fought to the end and Thomson and Lillee even threatened a remarkable victory when they thrashed 41 off six overs for the last wicket. However, their realistic hopes of success had evaporated in the early evening sunshine when the Chappell brothers, Greg and Ian, were run out as they strove to keep on top of the run rate.

Australia fared better in that summer's Test series against England, which they won by a single Test to retain the Ashes. The series will be for ever remembered for the vandalism which forced the abandonment of the Third Test at Headingley. On the final day of an evenly balanced match the groundsmen arrived to discover that the wicket had been dug up and oil poured into the holes. The damage had been caused by one Peter Chappell, who had been leading a vigorous campaign to overturn the prison sentence handed to George Davis, a London taxi driver who had been convicted for armed robbery. Earlier in the year, Chappell achieved the publicity he sought for his campaign when he rammed the gates of Buckingham Palace as well as the doors of the *Telegraph* building in Fleet Street and then draped a 'Free George Davis' banner across the dome of St Paul's Cathedral. In January 1976 he

ABOVE: STREAKER MICHAEL ANGELOW PROVIDES A SPECTACLE DURING THE SECOND ASHES TEST IN 1975.

OPPOSITE: WEST INDIAN FANS CELEBRATE DURING THE FIRST WORLD CUP FINAL.

was jailed for eighteen months for damaging the Headingley wicket.

Cricket seemed to be attracting trouble-makers in the heatwave of that summer. In August Michael Angelow, a merchant seaman, was fined by Marylebone Magistrates for streaking across the hallowed turf at Lord's. When Angelow told the court he had been bet £20 to do it, the magistrate, Lieutenant-Colonel William Haswell, told him: 'The court will have that £20. Please moderate your behaviour in future.'

In the summer of 1976 England captain Tony Greig was made to pay for his injudicious declaration that England would 'rub West Indies noses in the dirt'. The tourists won by three Tests to nil, with the victories coming at Old Trafford, Headingley and The Oval as England folded under the ferocious onslaught of West Indies' formidable fast bowlers, Andy Roberts and Michael Holding, whose elegant run-up to the wicket earned him the soubriquet 'whispering death'. Only Greig himself and David Steele, who cut an incongruous figure in the middle with his bank clerk glasses and silvery hair, truly distinguished themselves with the bat.

England, who had shown their vulnerability against the Australians Lillee and Thomson in preceding seasons, once again showed that they had little answer to the quick stuff. 'Obviously England's Test batting is not yet geared to cope with the fastest bowling,' wrote Michael Melford in the *Daily Telegraph*. 'The frequency with which batsmen were beaten outside the off-stump showed the difficulty of getting into position in time to play bowling a yard or two faster than is normally encountered in domestic cricket.'

AUSTRALIAN GOLD AUSTRALIAN CANNED FRUIT
PIA Great people to fly with
ED FOR ENGLAND

Above: Michael Holding bowls to Brian Close in the Second Test at Lord's, 1976.

Opposite: Kerry Packer and Tony Greig leave the High Court in London on the first day of Packer's legal action against the ICC and TCCB.

If the 1960s had ended on a stormy note with the D'Oliveira affair, the 1970s drew to a close in positively tempestuous circumstances as the Australian media magnate Kerry Packer sparked the biggest upheaval that international cricket had known since Test matches were first played 90 years earlier. The root causes of the crisis were the attractions of the one-day game for spectators and television audiences as well as good old-fashioned greed.

The leading national sides were severely weakened when many of their top players joined the exodus to Packer's circus. At Lord's the news that the defectors had signed contracts with Packer's Channel Nine network was greeted with dismay. 'There are wide international ramifications which will require discussions between all countries concerned,' said TCCB Secretary Donald Carr. 'As far as English cricket is concerned it will be, of course, most disappointing to everyone if three or four of our leading players decide to join up with a commercial "circus" rather than be available to tour with England.'

In all 35 players from England, Pakistan, West Indies, South Africa and Australia, signed three-year contracts for the World Series, which would involve 'Test matches', three-day games and one-day contests between an Australian XI and the Rest of the World. Many of the players were either approaching their retirement or had passed it, but the very fact that international cricketers were prepared to jeopardise Test cricket caused a major shock in the cricket world.

Greig, Knott, Snow and Underwood were the ageing Englishmen to put pen to paper, but

World Series cricket poster featuring vilified former England captain Tony Greig.

Australia's Test ranks were far more severely depleted by the desertion to the Packer cause of eighteen of their leading players, who included Lillee, Thomson, Ian and Greg Chappell, Redpath and Marsh. The South Africans, Pollock, Barry Richards, Procter, Barlow and Hobson, had little to lose as their country remained in isolation from international sport. But the West Indies were perhaps the hardest hit as they lost four of their greatest players – Lloyd, Viv Richards, Holding and Roberts – to the lure of the Australian dollar. Pakistan, too, would be seriously enfeebled by the departure of Asif Iqbal, Imran Khan, Mushtaq Mohammed and Majid Khan.

The announcement of Packer's project, which had been kept a well-guarded secret in the months of behind-the-scenes negotiations, came as a sudden shock in May 1977. Overnight, the world of cricket was thrown into turmoil as the established authorities at Lord's and elsewhere considered how to react. Thirteen of the Australian players who had only just arrived in England for the summer Ashes series had signed up for Packer. The Australian Cricket Board, who had twice rebuffed Packer's approaches to show Test cricket in Australia, were seething, and not least because they had recently approved a package of measures that substantially improved the financial position of their leading players.

The authorities at Lord's, meanwhile, said England's four Packer-bound players would still be available for Test selection that summer, although they took the step of stripping Tony Greig of the captaincy after it was revealed that he had been actively involved in persuading players to join the venture. In arriving at their decision to remove Greig as skipper, the Cricket Council said that they had taken into consideration 'his clearly admitted involvement, unknown to the authorities, in recruitment of the players for an organisation which has been set up in conflict with a scheduled series of Test matches. His action has inevitably impaired the trust which existed between the cricket authorities and the captain of the England side.'

Greig became the focus of vilification in the English press, whose 'traitor' and 'greed' headlines would come in handy again two months later when the England football manager Don Revie deserted his post for a far more lucrative one with the United Arab Emirates. John Woodcock, one of the most highly respected commentators of the day, certainly took a dim view of Greig's behaviour. He wrote in *The Times*: 'However plausibly Greig may claim that what he is doing is for the good of English cricket, however unselfish an act he may say it is, however truculently he may express the hope that the authorities at Lord's will be "sensible" in how they react to the Packer circus, no one is likely to be convinced that he has acted less than miserably as the reigning captain.'

The International Cricket Conference called an emergency meeting and arranged showdown talks at Lord's with Packer and his colleagues, but the talks broke down over Packer's insistence on exclusive television rights in Australia. The last chance of peace had gone, and Packer's band of rebels were effectively abandoned by the international cricket community. The ICC authorities at Lord's ruled: 'No player who after October 1 has played or made himself available to play in a match previously disapproved by the Conference shall thereafter be eligible to play in any Test match.'

Packer took immediate legal action against the ICC and the TCCB, and in September the case was heard in London's High Court, where Greig, Snow and Procter claimed illegal restraint of trade. The seven-week hearing ended in a shattering defeat for the authorities, as the court found in the players' favour and ordered the defendants to pay the costs of the case, amounting to £250,000. Nevertheless, the judge, Mr Justice Slade, said he had sympathy for cricket's established authorities, but said that as the law stood, their integrity stood for nothing. In delivering his judgement Justice Slade said: 'If they can be regarded as fairly representative of it, I am not surprised that cricket has traditionally been regarded by many as embodying some of the highest professional standards in sport. These witnesses all clearly regarded the official Test match structure as something which should represent the pinnacle of any cricketer's ambition. They thus find it difficult to understand how any cricketer could, even for good commercial reasons, bring himself to do anything which could be thought likely, directly or indirectly, to damage the structure of international cricket, of which Test matches at present form the all-important part.'

The World Series finally got under way, but with only limited success, and television figures showed that more Australians watched their official Test team in the series against India than tuned into the Packer circus. The High Court ruling may have obliged national boards to allow their cricketers freedom to work for any master, but it did not prevent them from ignoring their claims for a Test place. The Lord's

TONY GREIG IN HIS 'PYJAMAS'.

authorities did not consider the English rebels for the tour of Pakistan, where the Third Test was almost called off after protests from England about the possible inclusion of Imran Khan, Mushtaq Mohammed and Zaheer Abbas in the Pakistan side. Then, on the eve of the match, the President of the Pakistan Board announced that the players would not be considered for selection and the match went ahead.

The second season of the World Series was more successful, but in 1978–79 the circus was finally driven out of town after the Australian Board agreed a deal with Packer, granting his Channel Nine exclusive TV rights to Test matches. Packer had won, but he cannot have imagined at the outset of his project the spoils of victory that would come his way. In an extraordinary deal, the Australian Board, previously so obdurate in its refusal to mollify Packer, granted him not just an exclusive television contract but also the right to promote the game in Australia. It was a decision that would change the face of cricket, as Packer was given a free rein to effect whatever changes he felt would make cricket more attractive to television audiences. Thus Packer was given power to introduce day/night matches, pyjama clothing and any other American-style gimmicks he felt desirable.

A month after the Packer crisis erupted in 1977, England and Australia tried to ignore the distractions of the arguments raging off the pitch when they got down to the traditional business of fighting for the Ashes. By the end of the summer England were celebrating a 3–0 victory over their oldest enemy, who a few months earlier had beaten them by 45 runs in the Centenary Test at Melbourne. The hero of that contest had been England's Derek Randall, whose 174 had taken England to the brink of what would have been comfortably the highest winning score in a Test. By the end of the summer, however, England had a new hero in the form of a precocious young all-rounder, Ian Botham, who did enough in the two Tests he played to establish his reputation as a great player in the making. The highlight of the summer came at

OPPOSITE: DEREK RANDALL HOOKS A BALL FROM JEFF THOMPSON IN THE TEST AGAINST AUSTRALIA AT LORD'S, 1977.

VIV RICHARDS BATTING FOR THE WEST INDIES IN THE 1979 WORLD CUP FINAL.

Headingley, where Geoffrey Boycott, back in the side after a self-imposed 30-match Test exile, scored his 100th hundred on his home ground as England took an unassailable 3–0 lead in the series.

The following summer Botham wrote himself into the record books with a remarkable all-round performance against Pakistan at Lord's. Having clubbed 108 in England's first and only innings, the young Somerset player wrapped up victory with a devastating spell of bowling on the final morning. On a cloudless day, he made the ball swing extravagantly and took seven wickets for fourteen runs in 13.5 overs to finish with figures of 8 for 34 as England wrapped up victory by an innings and 120 runs. Botham's figures were the best by an

IAN BOTHAM FLATTENS THE STUMPS OF IQBAL QASIM ON HIS WAY TO A RECORD-BREAKING 8 FOR 34 AGAINST PAKISTAN.

England player since Laker took nineteen wickets against Australia at Old Trafford. The Lord's match was only his seventh Test, but by the end of it the bullish 22-year-old could boast three hundreds, one fifty and five hauls of five wickets.

Even Botham's emerging all-round genius, however, could not prevent England's defeat in the final of the second World Cup in the summer of 1979. The trophy was retained by the West Indies, who won the match by a crushing 92 runs after England had subsided from 183 for 2 to 194 all out. The giant West Indian fast bowler Joel Garner was the cause of the dramatic collapse as he ran through England's middle order with five wickets in eleven balls.

Earlier, Viv Richards (138 not out) struck one of the great one-day innings as he and Collis King (86) made the most of England's lack of a fifth bowler. Bob Willis had been ruled out by injury, and part-time bowlers Boycott, Gooch and Larkins were used to fill the void in the 60-over quota. Their twelve overs cost 85 runs, but more importantly their harmlessness relieved much of the pressure on the West Indies batsmen. A glance at the close-of-play scorecard might suggest to those who were not there to see it that England had got off to a flying start. Boycott and Brearley both passed 50 as they put together an opening partnership of 129, but unfortunately for England they had scored at such a slow rate that England's more progressive batsmen were left with the near impossible task of scoring 152 off the final twenty overs. Once Garner returned to the fray, they did not even get close.

Richards and Garner made a triumphant return to Lord's in September, when Somerset took on Northamptonshire in the Gillette Cup final. A full house, swelled by thousands of raucous, cider-guzzling fans from the West Country, saw man-of-the-match Richards blaze a brilliant 117 as Somerset clinched their first ever trophy in the 104 years of their first-class existence. Botham, never one to be pushed out of the limelight, made a sparkling cameo appearance alongside the West Indian when he scored 27 out of their 41-run partnership. In reply Northamptonshire folded against the mean, lifting pace of Garner, who finished with remarkable limited-overs figures of 6 for 29.

West Indian captain Clive Lloyd congratulates England's Graham Gooch on reaching his first Test century at Lord's in 1980.

In the Second Test against India at Lord's that summer Botham took his 100th Test wicket when he had Gavaskar caught at slip, and in the Fourth Test at The Oval he scored his 1,000th run. The 21 Tests he needed to achieve the all-rounder's double was comfortably fewer than the 33 needed by fellow Englishman Maurice Tate in the 1920s to reach the landmark, and considerably fewer than the 48 taken by the great Sir Garfield Sobers.

The 1980 Centenary Test at Lord's, commemorating the first ever Test between England and Australia on English soil, was a profound disappointment. The weather, naturally oblivious to the emotion of the occasion, blew in from the Atlantic to ensure that the match petered out into a tame draw. The biggest talking point of the match came off the field of play, when umpire David Constant was jostled and had his tie pulled by angry MCC Members as he made his way up the Pavilion steps after making one of his numerous inspections of the pitch during the rain-wrecked match. The two captains, Greg Chappell and Ian Botham, were caught up in the unseemly melee, intervening to protect Constant when a young member lunged at the umpire and grabbed him by the tie. 'It was the kind of behaviour one expects from football hooligans,' said Botham, who was hit on the head. Short of a four-letter word appearing in the Queen's Christmas address, it is difficult to imagine an event more likely to shock the English public, who long ago had come to regard Lord's as one of the last bastions of dignified behaviour. 'Has civilisation as we know it ended with the disgraceful scenes in the Members' Enclosure at Lord's before the start of the third day of play in the Cornhill Centenary Test?' asked *The Times*.

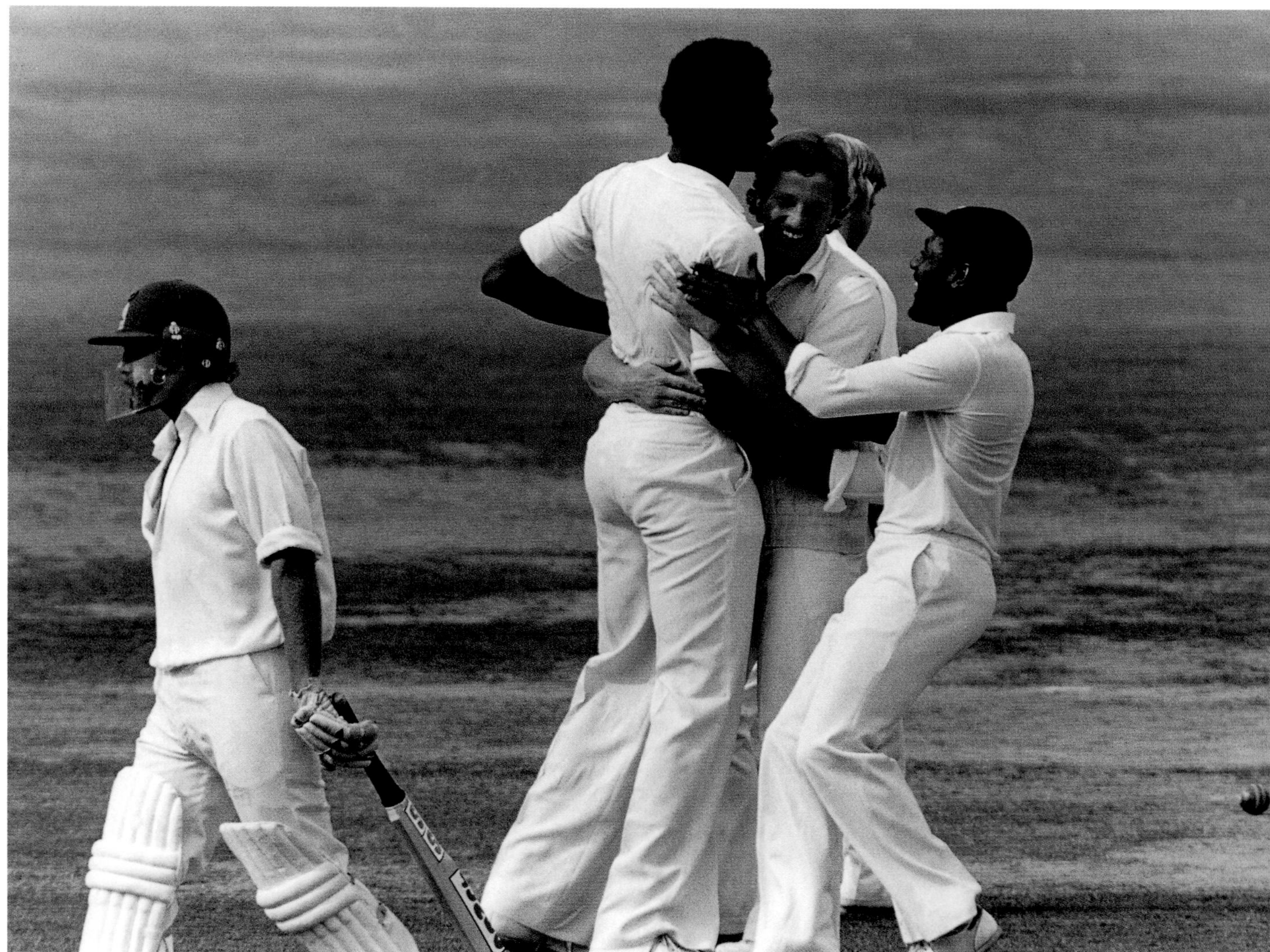

THE 1979 GILLETTE CUP FINAL AT LORD'S. IAN BOTHAM AND VIV RICHARDS CONGRATULATE JOEL GARNER.

While Botham had taken just 21 Tests to reach 1,000 runs and 100 wickets in Test cricket, another future England captain, Graham Gooch, needed 22 before he reached the first of his twenty Test centuries earlier that summer. It came at Lord's on the first day of the Second Test against the West Indies and provided a classic illustration of batsmanship against fast bowling of the highest quality. Gooch, who had bagged a pair of ducks on his Test debut against Australia in 1975, struck 123 out of England's first-innings total of 269, mixing aggression with vigilance in equal measure. Against the West Indies' unrelenting battery of pace the moustachioed Essex opener seized on any ball that varied even slightly in line or length as he punched seventeen boundaries (including one six) on either side of the wicket and mainly in front of square.

Throughout the summer, England's batting had a tendency to fold once either or both Gooch and Boycott had been removed. On this occasion, England lost five wickets in the final 130 minutes after Gooch had departed. At the other end of the wicket for the greater part of his innings was the phlegmatic figure of Chris Tavare, who contributed just 26 runs to their partnership of 145. In reply, the West Indies experienced no such difficulties in finding runs as they amassed a mighty 518. Young opener Desmond Haynes, who would become a familiar face at Lord's when he

GEOFF BOYCOTT CELEBRATES HIS CENTURY IN THE CENTENARY TEST, 1980.

joined Middlesex, hit 184 – the highest innings by a West Indian at Lord's – while Richards struck a typically majestic 145. England, having lost the thrilling First Test at Trent Bridge, were spared a further reverse when rain washed out more than half of play on the last two days. The West Indies preserved their lead in the series and the remaining three matches all ended in draws.

The 1980 Gillette Cup final at Lord's was a disappointing affair in that it failed to provide an exciting climax to the game, as Middlesex cantered to a seven-wicket victory over Surrey with six overs to spare. But there were no complaints about the entertainment six weeks earlier when another full house at Lord's passed through the turnstiles for the Benson and Hedges Cup final. Set a modest 210 runs for victory by Northamptonshire, Essex seemed well on course to reach their target when Gooch and McEwan had steered the county to 112 for 1 by the 33rd over. Six overs later, however, Essex were in disarray at 121 for 4, and despite a late slog by Norbert Phillip, Northants crept home by six runs, having pulled off one of the great fightbacks in domestic one-day cricket.

The summer of 1981 provided one of the most astonishing series in the history of Test match cricket, and it was at Lord's that the drama began. Botham's explosive arrival in Test match cricket in the late 1970s had made him an irresistible candidate for the England captaincy, and he was duly appointed to succeed the scholarly figure of Mike Brearley. It was perhaps unfortunate that England's opponents over successive series would be the mighty West Indies, who were fast establishing themselves as one of the most formidable teams the game had ever seen. Having narrowly lost the home series by a single Test, England were outplayed in the Caribbean, losing two out of the four Tests. Botham's form suffered horribly, and whereas England's most charismatic cricketer since Compton had previously looked inexhaustible, it now seemed that the triple responsibilities of batting, bowling and captaining were too much even for him.

Matters worsened at the start of the summer, as England went 1–0 down to Australia in the First Test at Trent Bridge. Shortly after the Second Test at Lord's, where he had bagged a duck in each innings, Botham beat the TCCB axe and hastily resigned the captaincy. It was a depressing moment for English cricket. It was not just that England had gone twelve matches without a Test win, or that Australia were apparently heading for a comfortable series triumph over an England side that had lost direction and determination. It was the decline and fall of Botham himself that seemed more deflating than anything else: the schoolboys' hero, who had seemed set to inspire England to a new era of glory, was mortal after all. What hope was there now if even I.T. Botham could not compete at the highest level?

The England selectors, headed by Alec Bedser, did not have an obvious alternative captain to turn to. Gower was considered too young, as was Gatting, who had yet to transform his youthful promise into concrete and consistent success at the highest level. Boycott, Fletcher and future MCC Secretary Roger Knight were all considered, but in the end the invitation went out to Brearley, who only the year before had passed on the responsibility of leadership to Botham. It proved to be a master-stroke. Brearley brought with him a shrewd tactical mind, a wealth of experience and an avuncular bearing that inspired the younger players to perform for him. Brearley, a keen student of psychology, knew how to bring out the best in players, and in Botham, his First Test captain, he found a willing, if unwitting, student.

What happened over the next three Tests is well known to those with even just a passing interest in cricket. England squared the series in the Third Test at Headingley after Botham produced one of the greatest all-round performances in the history of the game. England were heading for an innings defeat, having scored just 174 in reply to Australia's 401. The only heartening feature of the opening three and a half days had been the apparent return of Botham's confidence. He took 6 for 95 in Australia's first innings and followed it with a half-century in England's feeble reply. But when England batted again, months of pent-up frustration seemed to be unleashed as Botham launched himself into the Australian bowlers, Lillee, Alderman, Lawson and Bright.

England captains: Brearley and Botham leave the field during the 1981 Ashes series.

England were 135 for 7 – still 92 runs adrift of Australia – when the lumbering figure of Graham Dilley joined Botham at the wicket late in the afternoon session. Thirty-five overs

Above: Ian Botham and Bob Taylor are mobbed as Australia are all out for 111 at Headingley in 1981.

Right: Botham on his way to a sensational 149 at Headingley.

later England were 351 for 9, Dilley had made 56 and Botham had struck one of Test cricket's greatest ever innings. The wider context of the innings (his poor form and resignation at Lord's) made his unbeaten 145 all the more dramatic, but as an innings in its own right it will be remembered for ever as one of the great sporting moments of its generation. Botham added four more runs the following morning before Willis was out and Australia were set 130 runs to win.

On that final morning the common prediction was that Australia would reach their target after a small struggle, but that England and Botham would emerge from the match with credit for putting up a fight. What followed surpassed even the wildest dreams of England's most fervent followers. After switching from the football stand end to the Kirkstall Lane end, Willis was a bowler transformed and he tore through the Australians, who slumped from 56 for 1 to 111 all out as England claimed one of

Botham, who resigned as captain after the Lord's Test, returned to form in spectacular fashion.

their most famous victories of all time, winning by eighteen runs. Ladbrokes the bookmakers had offered odds of 500-1 against them.

In the Fourth Test at Edgbaston, England again came back from the dead to record another famous victory. Needing just 151 runs to win, the Australians were bowled out for 121 as this time Botham chose the ball as the medium for another heroic performance.

The remarkable recovery of both England and Botham from the nadir of Lord's was completed in the Fifth Test at Old Trafford, where England clinched the Ashes with another victory inspired by Botham. His second-innings 118, which rescued England from a parlous 104 for 5, has been described by many as the greatest Test innings of all time. It came from just 85 balls, and though the great Jessop – the man to whom Botham has been constantly compared – took ten fewer for his century against Australia at The Oval, the context of Botham's innings, with the Ashes hanging in the balance, made his effort all the more remarkable.

The events described above may not have taken place at Lord's, but what happened at Headingley, Edgbaston and Old Trafford over those dramatic few weeks carried a significance that extended well beyond the boundary ropes of those grounds. When Botham resigned the England captaincy after the Second Test at Lord's, the morale of English cricket was at its lowest ebb for years. What he achieved in the three Tests that followed had an immeasurable impact on a young English generation that was crying out for a national hero. Talk to any number of first-class cricketers who grew up at the time and, to a man, they will single out Botham's heroics that summer as the most memorable episode of the period.

The remarkable summer of 1981 ended, appropriately, with a thrilling climax to the final of the NatWest Trophy (formerly the Gillette Cup) at Lord's. Michael Melford in the *Daily Telegraph* began his report of the contest between Derbyshire and Somerset as follows: 'What more could anyone ask after the cricket of the last two months than a last cloudless day at Lord's and victory off the last ball in the most exciting limited-overs final ever played?' It was the tightest possible finish, as Derbyshire scrambled a last-ball run to level the scores – and win on fewer wickets lost.

Political controversy returned to international cricket in 1982 when twelve English players, including Geoff Boycott, Geoff Cook and Graham Gooch, set off, wallets bulging, for a rebel tour of South Africa, which was still isolated from international sport. The TCCB had warned the players that they were jeopardising their chances of representing their country in future. India and Pakistan, who were due to tour England that summer, had intimated that they would pull out unless the English authorities took a strong stance against the rebels. The TCCB reacted decisively by banning the rebels from Test cricket for three years.

England's revival continued when they beat both Pakistan and India in three-match series. England, though, lost their first ever match to Pakistan at Lord's, as the tourists recorded only their second win over them in 35 meetings. Mohsin Khan was the Pakistan hero, hitting the first double century in a Test match at Lord's in 33 years as England lost by ten wickets.

The following year the West Indies failed in their attempt to win a third consecutive World Cup when they were beaten by India in a low-scoring final at Lord's. The West Indies were set what looked like a straightforward task of scoring 184 in 55 overs on a benign wicket. There seemed little reason to doubt that they would get there as Richards swept them to 57 for 2 from just fourteen overs. Richards was playing as though he were in a charity match, stroking Madan Lal for three fours in an over, but his insouciance got the better of him when he had reached 33 and skied a catch to Kapil Dev at mid-wicket. Madan Lal then picked up the wickets of Gomes and Lloyd, who had called for a runner, and the match had swung decisively in India's favour. Dujon and Marshall kept alive West Indian hopes with a seventh-wicket partnership, but once it was broken, India ran through the tail to win by 43 runs.

1984 was a dreadful year for England's cricketers, who slumped to one of their most humiliating defeats in Christchurch, New Zealand. Bob Willis's side were beaten by an innings and 132 runs, having been bowled out for 82 and 93. The other two matches of the series were drawn, and confidence was not high when, later that year, the all-conquering West Indies flew into Heathrow for the start of a five-Test tour. When they flew out at the end of the summer, the newspaper headlines were proclaiming simply: 'Blackwash!' In what made almost painful viewing, England were hopelessly outplayed by the visitors, whose quartet of

Andy Roberts walks in the 1983 World Cup final between West Indies and India.

Captained by David Gower, England regained the Ashes in 1985.

pace bowlers remorselessly battered England's batsmen. England's low scoring created a vicious circle in that the bowlers rarely had the platform of a sizeable total of runs, which would have allowed them to take a few risks against the West Indian batsmen.

The Second Test at Lord's was especially dispiriting for England followers. England went into the final day with faint hopes of victory and a near-certain belief that the match could not be lost. But five hours later the West Indians were celebrating a remarkable victory after Gordon Greenidge had played one of the greatest innings ever seen on the ground. The Reading-born Hampshire opener hit an unbeaten 214 as, to the mounting astonishment of those who saw it, the West Indians raced to their supposedly daunting target of 344 from 66 overs without serious alarm and with the loss of only Haynes' wicket – a run-out. Only Bradman's 1948 Australians had made a higher final innings total to win a Test match in England, and it was only the tenth time in Test history that a side had scored more than 300 to win a match.

Greenidge's blistering innings was the third highest in a Test match at Lord's, but curiously, and a little embarrassingly, he was obliged to share the Man of the Match award with Botham. The England all-rounder, generally so unsuccessful against the West Indies, played a major part in keeping England in a competitive position by taking eight wickets in the first innings and scoring 111 runs in the match. In the West Indies' second innings, however, he was made to look very ordinary by Greenidge, whose Herculean effort will be remembered for ever by those privileged to witness it. The victory put the West Indies 2–0 up in the series and dealt a major blow to England's confidence. Even when they appeared to have battled themselves into a strong position, it seemed that the West Indians could simply raise their game one level higher. England lost the final three Tests to lose a home series 5–0 for the first time. Echoing the famous obituary notice which appeared 102 years earlier in *The Sporting Times* after England had lost to Australia, the Announcements columns in *The Times* featured the following entry after the Fifth Test at The Oval:

IN MEMORIAM
ENGLISH CRICKET
which finally passed away at The
Oval, 14th August 1984, will be sadly missed.
R.S.V.P.
T.I.S.

England had to wait until 1991, when they drew the Test series with the West Indies 2–2, for their first win over them since 1969. The arrival of Sri Lanka at the end of the summer for their first Test match in England raised hopes that England might end the summer on a winning note. But it was not to be, as the Sri Lankan batsmen treated the Lord's crowd to an exhibition of stroke-play of the highest quality. Three of their batsmen hit hundreds, and Mendip fell just six runs short of a second century in the match.

England's Test fortunes picked up the following year. After a successful tour to India, where they won the five-match Test series 2–1, they returned to England to face an Australian side who had regained the Ashes two years earlier. England grew in confidence as the series progressed, and helped by 723 runs from captain David Gower they swept to a 3–1 triumph in the rubber. It was to be England's last success for some time. In the winter they suffered a second 5–0 'blackwash' at the hands of the West Indies in the Caribbean, and in the two home series that followed they were beaten 2–0 by India and 1–0 by New Zealand.

The first half of 1986 was a busy period for the authorities at Lord's. Prompted by the relentless bombardments of the West Indies' pace attack, the TCCB met in March to discuss the issue of intimidatory bowling and drew up a proposed amendment to the laws which they would put before the ICC at their annual general meeting later in the year. The proposal suggested the following amendment: 'The bowling of fast, short-pitched balls is unfair if, in the opinion of the umpire at the bowler's end, they are either frequent or by their length, line and height, are likely to inflict physical injury on the striker standing upright at the crease. The relative skills of the striker should be taken into consideration.'

Two months later, the TCCB Executive Committee met to discuss what action should be taken over Ian Botham's newspaper revelation that he had smoked marijuana. Botham, England's greatest sporting hero of the decade, had been convicted and fined earlier that year for the possession of a small quantity of cannabis. Shortly after the TCCB meeting

THE QUEEN MEETS THE AUSTRALIAN TEAM BEFORE THE SECOND TEST, 1985.

the disciplinary committee banned him from first-class cricket for two months.

In the 1987 NatWest Trophy final at Lord's the great New Zealand all-rounder Richard Hadlee bade farewell to English cricket with a match-winning unbeaten 70, thrashed from just 61 balls, to see his beloved Nottinghamshire home with three balls to spare. 'On a day when the script might have been written in advance for the occasion of his last appearance at Lord's, Richard Hadlee carried Nottinghamshire to a remarkable three-wicket victory over Northamptonshire in the delayed final of the NatWest Trophy,' wrote Peter Deeley in the *Daily Telegraph*. The task looked beyond even Hadlee when Nottinghamshire, whom he had served with great distinction for nine years, needed to score more than ten runs an over in the final five. Off the final ball of the last but one over, with eight still needed, Hadlee ran out wicketkeeper Bruce French, but then smashed a six and a four off the next two deliveries to secure Notts their first win in a knock-out competition.

The summer of 1987 also saw Lord's host a match between the MCC and the Rest of the World to celebrate the club's bicentenary. A powerful Rest line-up included the talents of Gavaskar, Haynes, Border, Imran Khan, Kapil Dev, Courtney Walsh and Abdul Qadir. The MCC scorecard was equally impressive, featuring Greenidge, Gower, Gatting, Gooch, Rice, Hadlee, Marshall and Shastri. A highly entertaining match was watched by over 80,000 spectators, who were treated to sparkling centuries from Greenidge, Gooch, Gatting and Gavaskar, but ended in disappointment when rain washed out play on the fourth and final day.

Nottinghamshire won the NatWest Trophy for a second time two years later when the plump figure of off-spinner Eddie Hemmings smashed a four off the last ball to overhaul Essex's 243 for 7. But the summer of 1989 was a disappointing one for England, as they were comprehensively outplayed by Australia, who won the series 4–0 to begin what would be a long period of domination over the English. The Ashes defeat represented the worst possible start for Ted Dexter, who was appointed earlier in the year as chairman of a new selection board calling itself the 'England committee'. The team manager Mickie Stewart, the father of England batsman and future captain Alec, would also serve on the committee, as would Alan Smith, the TCCB's chief executive, and Ossie Wheatley, the TCCB chairman.

A fresh controversy involving South Africa erupted in 1989 when a rebel England tour, led by former captain Mike Gatting, was organised in defiance of the worldwide sporting boycott of

PAKISTAN'S IMRAN KHAN (OPPOSITE) AND INDIA'S SUNIL GAVASKAR (BELOW) IN THE MCC BICENTENARY MATCH AT LORD'S, 1987.

GRAHAM GOOCH GLANCES TO LEG ON HIS WAY TO A MASSIVE 333 AGAINST INDIA AT LORD'S, 1990.

the country. Gatting and his fellow rebels came in for a barrage of criticism, and the TCCB later banned them from representing England. Gatting and his colleagues justified their decision on the grounds that they were simply cricketers and not politicians. The 1990 trip, though, was cut short amid anti-apartheid protests, and the second leg of the tour, due to be played the following year, was cancelled.

England's Test fortunes improved in 1990 when, after a 2–1 defeat in the Caribbean, they beat India and New Zealand – each by a single Test in a three-match series – to avenge their defeats by the same opposition four years earlier. England's victory over India came in an extraordinary Second Test match at Lord's in which Gooch, Azharuddin, Shastri and Kapil Dev produced some of the finest batting seen on the ground in modern times.

In his innings on the first two days Gooch threatened to break the record for the highest innings in Test cricket (Len Hutton's 364, since surpassed by Brian Lara's 375 against England at St John's). The 37-year-old England captain, watched by Sir Leonard shortly before his death, bludgeoned his way past the 300 mark with a devastating display of attacking batsmanship. In front of a capacity crowd Gooch homed in on the record, but after ten hours at the crease fatigue appeared to get the better of him when he was bowled by Prabhakar attempting to drive. His mammoth innings of 333 included 43 fours and three sixes, and he was given a prolonged and fulsome standing ovation as he sloped back towards the Pavilion. But that was not to be the end of the batting exhibition – nor of Gooch's insatiable appetite for runs.

Undaunted by England's first-innings 653 – the fifth highest total in their history – India counter-attacked in style. Shastri hit a century before his captain Azharuddin picked up the baton with a hundred of his own, which arrived off just 87 balls. When he was out for 117, India were still in danger of being forced to follow on, but with just one wicket remaining and 24 needed, Kapil Dev smashed off-spinner Eddie Hemmings for four consecutive sixes. Even Dev's heroics, reminiscent of Botham and Jessop at their most belligerent, were not enough to save India from defeat, however, as England recorded a rare win at headquarters by 247 runs. In England's second innings Gooch hit 123 to become the first player to score in excess of 300 and 100 in the same first-class match.

Lord's was treated to another pulsating NatWest final at the close of the 1991 season, when Hampshire recorded their first ever win in the competition, defeating Surrey in the deepening gloom with two balls to spare. The broadcaster and writer Christopher Martin-Jenkins, the latest in a long line of distinguished cricket reporters for the *Daily Telegraph*, wrote: 'Robin Smith provided the match-winning surge, revelling once more in the inspirational vibes of Lord's on the big occasion. His 78 took his aggregate from five innings in the competition this year to 331, at an average of 165.'

In 1992 a full house of 25,000 was inside Lord's to see one of the most exciting finishes to a Test match in the history of the ground. On an extraordinary final day seventeen wickets tumbled on a blameless wicket as the balance of the match swung first one way, then the other, and then back again. Pakistan were the favourites when they ran through England's second innings in the first part of the day. Only Alec Stewart (69) distinguished himself as he became the first Englishman to carry his bat in a Test at Lord's. By tea, though, England had captured four Pakistani wickets, and when the visitors subsided to 95 for 8, Gooch's side seemed virtually certain to secure their first win over Pakistan in ten years. Then, showing admirable composure under pressure, fast bowlers Wasim Akram and Waqar Younis disappointed their hosts by carrying Pakistan to victory with a ninth-wicket partnership of 46. England levelled the series in the Fourth Test at Headingley, before Pakistan won the decider at The Oval.

England's disastrous form against Australia continued in 1993, when they were comprehensively beaten 4–1 on their own pitches, leg-spinner Shane Warne wreaking havoc with his extraordinary box of tricks. From the moment in the First Test at Old Trafford when Gatting was turned inside out by what has been described, if only a little extravagantly, as the greatest ball ever bowled, England struggled to compete. Warne spun a mesmerising web over England's batsmen, whose only previous experience of high-quality leg spin had come against Pakistan's Abdul Qadir, with equally unhappy consequences. The Second Test at Lord's was England's seventh successive defeat to four different countries.

The two domestic finals at Lord's that summer provided compulsive viewing for lovers of the one-day game. In the Benson and Hedges Cup, Derbyshire beat Lancashire by six runs, thanks largely to Dominic Cork, whose unbeaten 92 rescued them from a parlous 66 for 4. Lancashire's left-handed captain Neil Fairbrother, one of the finest one-day batsmen in the world, kept the contest alive until the last over, when the eleven runs needed for victory proved to be beyond even him.

Even the excitement of the Benson and Hedges was as nothing compared with what unfolded at Lord's two months later, when Warwickshire met Sussex in the final of the NatWest Trophy. A full house saw just under

645 runs scored in what most commentators agreed afterwards was the best domestic one-day game they had ever seen. A century by David Smith helped Sussex register 321 – the highest score in a final in the history of both one-day competitions. Amazingly, Warwickshire surpassed it. The foundations of victory were laid by Asif Din's 104, but it was the one-day expert Dermot Reeve, all guile and guts, who led them to victory with a brilliant unbeaten 81. The Edgbaston club needed 46 off the final five overs and then 15 off the last. Reeve hit 4-2-2-4-1 off the first five balls, to leave Twose with the responsibility of hitting the winning runs from the first ball he faced – which he did with a slash over the covers.

After 1994 England showed a steady improvement, and in the summer of 1998 they won their first five-match series in eleven years when they beat South Africa 2–1 after mounting a spirited fightback to win the final two Tests. Victory was a highly unlikely prospect in mid-June, when Alec Stewart's side capitulated by ten wickets at Lord's. Jonty Rhodes hit 117 in the tourists' first-innings 360 before Allan Donald, widely regarded as the best fast bowler in the world at the time, took five wickets as England collapsed to 110 all out. In the follow-on a century by Hussain and a fifty from Stewart saw England reach a healthy 222 for 3 before they lost six wickets for eleven runs and South Africa cantered to victory inside four days.

It was South Africa's second resounding triumph at Lord's since their return to the international fold in 1992. In 1994 they had crushed England by 356 runs in a match which began charged with emotion and ended in high controversy. South African openers Andrew Hudson and Gary Kirsten were given a standing ovation by the Lord's crowd when they trotted down the Pavilion steps on the morning of the first day. It was an historic moment for the South Africans, as they were welcomed back to the spiritual home of cricket, and it was unfortunate that their return would be overshadowed by the Mike Atherton dirt-in-the-pocket affair and the England captain's confrontation with match referee Peter Burge. Television pictures showed Atherton reaching into his pocket and then rubbing something into the ball.

Sadly for the South Africans, the joy of their victory was buried under an avalanche of

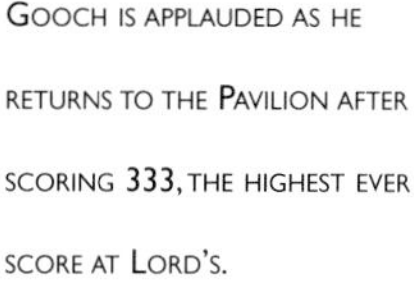

Gooch is applauded as he returns to the Pavilion after scoring 333, the highest ever score at Lord's.

speculation and recrimination, as the affair dominated the headlines throughout the match. Atherton was fined £2,000 by England's chairman of selectors, and the young England skipper later admitted that he had dealt poorly with the incident and had given the press plenty of rope with which to hang him by not 'coming clean' when the story first erupted. The summer, though, would end happily for Atherton and his team as they levelled the series at The Oval, where Devon Malcolm took 9 for 57, the sixth best figures in Test match history.

In the four-year gap between the two defeats at Lord's by the South Africans, England drew 2–2 with the West Indies in 1995, beat India 1–0 and lost 2–0 to Pakistan in 1996, and lost 3–2 to Australia in 1997.

The Second Test against the West Indies in 1995 ended in a rare victory for England at Lord's. The Derbyshire seamer Dominic Cork was England's hero as he took 7 for

43, including a hat-trick, in West Indies' second innings. The following summer England drew with India, but all the media attention was focused on umpire Dickie Bird, who was invigilating in his last Test match. The colourful Yorkshireman, who shed tears as he left the field, had officiated in a record 66 Tests.

Bird might also have been moved to tears by what he saw at Lord's a few weeks later, when England collapsed in dramatic fashion against Pakistan, whom they had beaten just

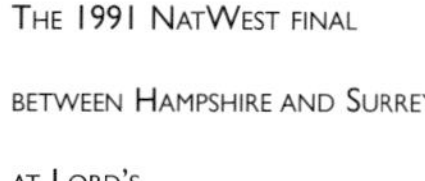

The 1991 NatWest final between Hampshire and Surrey at Lord's.

once in sixteen Tests since 1987. It was the first meeting between the two sides in four years and was given extra edge by the controversies over ball-tampering and Gatting's notorious confrontation with Pakistan's provocative umpire Shakoor Rana a few years earlier. On the final morning, England, with nine wickets still standing, needed 334 for victory. Stewart and Atherton steered them to within sight of their target, but from 164 for 1 England's hopes suddenly imploded as they crashed to 208 for 9.

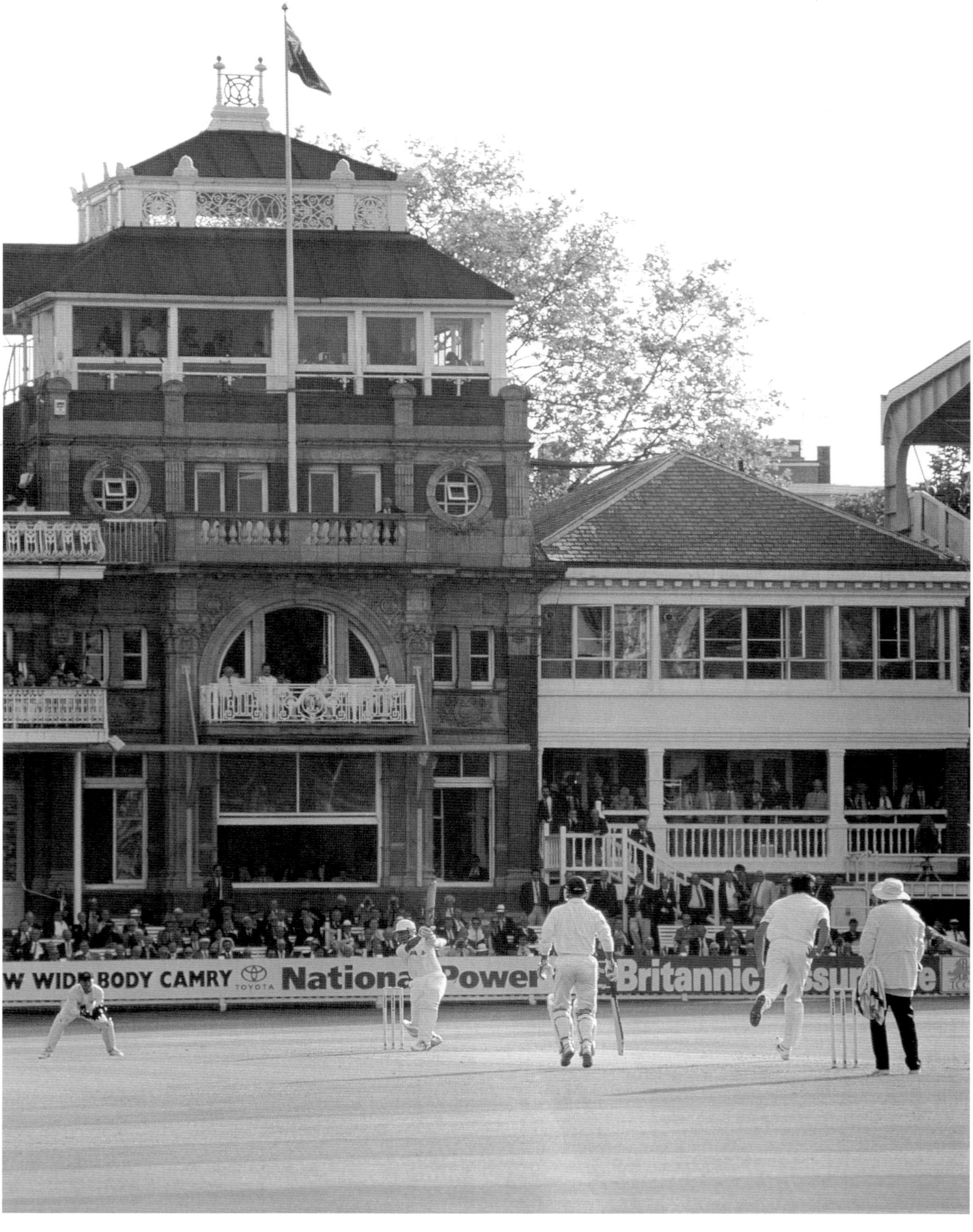
W WIDE BODY CAMRY
TOYOTA
National Power
Britannic

In 1998 the long-running and contentious issue of whether women should be allowed to become Members of the MCC was finally resolved. Against a cultural backdrop of increased political correctness, the 17,250 Members of one of the oldest private clubs in the world voted, by the necessary two-thirds majority, to admit women into their inner sanctum. The news was greeted with relief by the 'Yes' campaigners at Lord's, who, regardless of their own personal feelings on the matter, had been worried about the negative publicity attracted by previous refusals to admit women. The 'No' campaigners argued that a private club is a private club and its members should be free to decide whom they wanted to be part of it. In the press the debate was always presented as a straightforward battle between feminism and old-fashioned male chauvinism. In the end, Sir Pelham Warner's famous description of MCC as 'a private club with a public function' rang as true as it ever has done, as a tide of social change finally swept away 211 years of tradition at Lord's.

The last time an attempt had been made to introduce female members was in 1991, when Rachael Heyhoe Flint, the former England women's captain, backed by influential MCC Members, failed to gain the necessary

Above: June 1994: South Africa celebrate their first Test win at Lord's since 1935.

Opposite: Lord's on a beautiful summer's day during the 1993 Australian tour.

Dickie Bird gives his last decision, ruling Jack Russell out lbw – England v. India, June 1996.

two-thirds majority. It was decided then to raise the matter again in five years. A working party was set up in 1996, which reported the following year that there were still mixed feelings among the membership. MCC President Colin Ingleby-Mackenzie made no secret of his desire to see women admitted. Other influential Members, including former England captains Ted Dexter and Tony Lewis – soon to be Ingleby-Mackenzie's successor as President – were also strongly in favour. MCC was also under pressure to change the constitution for financial reasons. Discrimination was cited as one of the five reasons for the rejection by the Sports Council of MCC's application for £4.5 million of National Lottery money to rebuild the Grand Stand at Lord's.

In December 1997 the MCC Committee sent out a report to its Members announcing that a vote on the issue would take place in February. The report left the Members in no doubt as to the Committee's own views on the matter.

In its December statement it said: 'The report stressed that MCC has always played a dual role as a prominent custodian and promoter of cricket on the one hand and, on the other, as a private association of members devoted to the game. It is fully understood that the election to membership of ladies would have an impact on both of these functions. The Committee also recognises that the question is of fundamental importance to the future role and character of MCC and, by a large majority, it has now reached the view that the time has come to adopt the rule changes necessary to

Jonty Rhodes takes another run for South Africa in the 1998 Second Test at Lord's.

NASSER HUSSAIN ON HIS WAY TO 105 AGAINST SOUTH AFRICA IN JUNE 1998.

allow for the election of ladies to the membership of the Club. While the Committee hopes that the membership will share these conclusions, it acknowledges that this is a matter for each individual Member to decide for himself. A two-thirds majority of votes cast will be required.'

The ballot was welcomed by Rachel Heyhoe Flint, but she was not optimistic that change would be forthcoming. 'Seven years on I'm still not confident that there's going to be a majority. Last time round 10,000 members didn't bother to vote and there needs to be a two-thirds majority,' she said. Heyhoe Flint pointed out that women had been playing cricket since 1745 and had long been accepted as making a valuable contribution to the game. 'It seems hypocritical of the MCC if they chose not to admit women, as they are happy to promote cricket at every level. Even if they did vote to admit women there's an eighteen-year waiting list, so I would be 76 by the time I was able to join.'

Heyhoe Flint's pessimism proved justified, for on 24 February 1998 it was announced that MCC Members had voted against the proposed change. In fact the vote was won decisively by those in favour of admitting women – by 6,969 to 5,538 – but the figure fell 1,369 short of the two-thirds required to change the Club's constitution. Reacting to the vote, Heyhoe Flint said: 'I just feel very sorry for the Committee, because they've spent nearly eighteen months researching, discussing and on working parties. I think they are very keen to change the image of the MCC. The public perception is of a rather stuffy and elitist

organisation.' She said that other male-only preserves, such as the RAC Club at Epsom and the Stock Exchange, had changed, and that MCC should follow suit. 'I just think that they would have far more support from the corporate world in general,' she said.

The Equal Opportunities Commission admitted it was disappointed but acknowledged that, as a private club, MCC was entitled to operate exclusively for men. 'Cricket is not an exclusively male preserve,' said EOC chairwoman Kamlesh Bahl. 'The sport is played by girls and boys at school, and Lord's welcomes fee-paying female spectators. It would seem to be a natural extension to allow women to become Members of the MCC, given its public role.' In a submission to the Government on equality a few weeks earlier, the EOC said it did not wish to require genuinely single-sex clubs and organisations to open up membership to both sexes.

Ingleby-Mackenzie, who had said before the vote that he wanted to rid the Club of its 'fuddy-duddy image of old men puffing on

Former England women's captain Rachel Heyhoe Flint batting against Australia in 1976 (above) and (left).

THE ASHES
The Ashes Trophy
Presented by Marylebone Cricket Club
January 1999

pipes', declared himself heartened by the result. He pointed out that the 12,507 voters represented 69.6 per cent of those eligible to vote and also represented a 68.8 per cent swing in favour of electing women since the last vote in 1991. MCC Secretary Roger Knight said he did not expect a legal challenge following the announcement of the results. 'People will be disappointed perhaps that the membership wasn't able to support sufficiently the recommendation of the Committee,' he added.

The ECB, which had thrown its weight behind the 'Yes' campaign, said it was 'disappointed' at the result. Prime Minister Tony Blair criticised the decision, and Sports Minister Tony Banks, never one to steer clear of a controversial view, added his voice to the chorus of disapproval. By early May the issue had refused to die down, and after the Club's Annual General Meeting at Lord's it was decided that a questionnaire would be sent out to ascertain the exact views of the membership on the admission of female members. In late August the Club announced that for the second time that year it would ask its Members to vote on the matter. But the Committee stressed that women would join the end of the Club's long waiting list like any other applicants; men already on the list would not have to wait any longer because of a flood of female applicants. Announcing the fresh vote, Ingleby-Mackenzie said: 'Although some Members are absolutely opposed to the concept of women membership, irrespective of the detail, it seems that a substantial number who voted against in February may well have done so because of unfounded concerns about the impact of women membership on the existing waiting list and on Members' facilities.'

On 28 September the MCC Committee got their way and, after 211 years, the exclusion of women was brought to an end. The ballot resulted in a 9,394 (69.8 per cent) vote for change, with 4,072 (30.2 per cent) against. Although women would have to join the back of the eighteen-year waiting list, some women would be allowed to jump the queue under a system of elected Honorary Memberships as a nominal gesture. Membership would give women Members permission to enter the Long Room and to wear MCC colours. The vote was hailed by Ingleby-Mackenzie who said: 'The Committee is absolutely delighted with this important decision, which clears the way for the Club to play its rightful part in the regeneration of cricket, both in this country and around the world. MCC emerges from this vote stronger, more united, and better equipped to play a major public role.' But the decision was condemned by many of MCC's Members, some of whom voiced their anger in a packed and acrimonious Special General Meeting at Lord's. One Member, who refused to give his name, said: 'I'm very upset about it. We've all been steamrollered and blackmailed into this.' Another accused the Committee of 'looking like propagandists in a communist state'.

The following day incoming MCC President Tony Lewis announced that he would be overseeing the establishment of an MCC women's team. 'I take over this week with the chance to take the game forward after the historic vote that we all wanted, that formally allows women to become an integral part of the Lord's set-up,' he said. 'As a solid indicator of our intention to put the Members' vote into tangible cricket terms I want to set up an MCC Ladies XI.' After years of campaigning, Rachel Heyhoe Flint said: 'I almost can't believe it. After seven years. I'm absolutely thrilled to bits, not for my own personal gain but for the sake of cricket, because the MCC needs funding. It is great that people will now respect the MCC fully. I reckon that over the last two or three years the club has been looked on in a very poor light, but now its image is brilliant.'

OPPOSITE: FOLLOWING THE 1997 AUSTRALIA TOUR THERE WAS MUCH DISCUSSION ABOUT WHETHER AUSTRALIA SHOULD BE ALLOWED TO TAKE THE ASHES HOME WITH THEM. TO PREVENT ANY FURTHER SPECULATION MCC DECIDED TO COMMISSION A PERMANENT TROPHY IN WATERFORD CRYSTAL TO BE PLAYED FOR IN FUTURE ASHES SERIES. IN KEEPING WITH THE TRADITION OF THE ASHES, THE TROPHY IS A HAND-CRAFTED REPLICA OF THE ORIGINAL URN.

BEHIND THE SIGHTSCREENS

It might be imagined that shortly after the umpires draw stumps at the close of play of the final match of the season at Lord's in mid-September, a steward waves goodbye to the last of the Middlesex players in their sponsored cars before turning out the Pavilion lights, padlocking the Grace Gates and hanging up a sign saying, 'Popped out for six months, back in April.' In fact, far from finding the place boarded up and the dustsheets thrown over the heirlooms, those who visit Lord's during the winter months walk into a hive of activity. Lord's is far more than a cricket pitch. Coaches, groundsmen, builders, cooks, cleaners,

administrators, curators, shopkeepers, bar staff, tour guides, security men, MCC Committee Members, employees of the ECB, Middlesex CCC and the ICC are all busily going about their jobs, despite the fact that a cricket ball has not been bowled in anger at the ground for several months.

The winter months are as busy as any in the calendar. The eight MCC Sub-Committees (Finance, Cricket, Tennis and Squash, Estates, Arts and Library, General Purposes, Marketing, Players and Fixtures) all meet regularly; dinners are laid on for Members; the Real Tennis courts (to the rear of the Pavilion) echo to the sound of that ancient and arcane game; the sound of bat on ball can be heard at the indoor coaching school; the Lord's shop does a brisk trade in books, souvenirs and equipment; the ever-improving museum, housing the famous Ashes urn, throws its doors open for guided tours, and the curators

LORD'S DURING THE SECOND TEST, ENGLAND V. SOUTH AFRICA, IN 1998.

The dramatic new media centre under construction in June 1998.

The Compton and Edrich stands by night.

patiently show visitors around the library and field telephone enquiries about any cricket curiosity imaginable.

In the warren of offices in and around the Pavilion, MCC employees attend to sackfuls of paperwork, the marketing department strikes new sponsorship deals, the estate managers paint fences and drain pipes, and the groundstaff get to work on the wickets and the outfield before the first frost. At the time of writing, an army of builders and decorators have set up camp as they race to finish the state-of-the-art Nat West Media Centre as well as a new electronic scoreboard above the Allen Stand in time for the 1999 World Cup.

Lord's provides an awesome spectacle even when empty, and it is unlikely that any cricket ground in the world can boast such a wide variety and high quality of architecture. Thomas Verity's imposing red-brick Pavilion, opened in 1890, is the oldest building on the ground. Directly opposite it stands the new press centre, designed by acclaimed architects Future Systems and opened in May 1999. The centre, which will be capable of housing over 200 journalists, provides a striking addition to Lord's, and its bold design is a testament to MCC's vision of the future.

Directly to the left of the Pavilion is the Warner Stand, which has housed the press on its upper level since it opened in 1958. The Allen Stand is directly to the left of the Pavilion and seats guests of the players. It is connected to the Pavilion by a corridor, which allows the players to see their families and friends without having to leave the building first. The Warner Stand, designed by Kenneth Peacock, is the second smallest of the stands after the Allen Stand, and backs on to the Coronation Gardens, which were laid out to commemorate the coronation of HM Queen Elizabeth II. The stand was opened by the man who gave it its name, Sir Pelham Warner, one of the most influential and active characters in the history of Lord's and of English cricket. The lavatories beneath the stand have windows looking out over the outfield, allowing spectators to keep in touch with the action while they answer a call of nature.

Walking around the ground clockwise from the Pavilion and the Warner Stand, one next comes to the largest and most recent stand, the Grand Stand, which sits at three o'clock to the Pavilion's midday. Designed by Nicholas Grimshaw, its lower terrace was ready for use in 1997, but it was not until the Second Test against South Africa in 1998 that the whole of the Grand Stand was officially opened by the Duke of Edinburgh. All seventeen surviving donors who had contributed to the cost of building the previous stand by accepting Life Memberships at £200, were invited to the opening. The earlier Grand Stand, the second to occupy the site, was erected in 1926 and was designed by Sir Herbert Baker, who presented MCC with the famous Father Time weather-vane.

Next to it in the north-west corner is the Compton Stand and then, separated from it by the NatWest Media Centre, the Edrich Stand, both of which were opened in 1991. Standing between the two stands provides the best perspective of the famous Lord's slope – a six-

Father Time in his new position on top of the Mound Stand lift shaft.

Crowds watch England play the West Indies in 1991 from the highly acclaimed Mound Stand (right).

foot six-inch drop running from the Grand Stand down to the Tavern Stand. While the slope is there for all to see, the 'ridge', the other famous feature of the Lord's outfield, remains something of a Loch Ness monster issue in cricketing circles. Romantics say it exists (or at least did), while sceptics say it is nothing more than a figment of the imagination, used to explain any abnormal lift in the wicket. MCC were sufficiently convinced that there was a 'ridge', and that it was caused by the line of an old sewer, to have had it dug up and relaid in 1962.

Directly behind the Compton Stand is one of the scoreboards, and behind that the offices of the ICC in the North Clock Tower. Visitors who come in via the North Gate entrances pass by the Nursery ground and the row of brown brick sheds and offices which are home to the groundstaff and the estate managers. Mick Hunt, the Head Groundsman, lives in a small block of flats about twenty yards from his sheds. He shares the block with the Estate Manager, Gareth Williams, as does Jonathan Hawke, the man responsible for ensuring that

Construction of the Compton and Edrich stands in 1990. They were opened the following season.

the whole of the ground other than the playing area is in pristine condition on match days.

Hunt is a key figure at Lord's as well as a colourful one. Glenys Williams, the Assistant Curator, puts his role into persepective: 'If the museum doesn't open on time or the caterers don't turn up or the Committee overslept, then Lord's would still operate, but if anything happens to that pitch or it's not ready, then we are in real trouble. Cricket is the whole point of the place, so in a way the most important person of MCC's 111 employees is Mick Hunt.'

Hunt's 'office' is a delightfully cluttered and ramshackle affair furnished, or rather 'filled', exactly how you might expect. A kettle, TV (complete with Sky Sports), crates of beer and a revealing poster of a big-chested model jostle for space with boots, anoraks, tools of indeterminate function and boxes and bags of indeterminate contents.

For years Hunt worked as assistant to the long-serving Jim Fairbrother before taking over from him in 1989, when his mentor fell ill with cancer. Hunt, who was born and brought up close to Lord's, cannot remember exactly when he first came to the ground, but 'I was definitely wearing flared trousers and probably sporting sideburns', he says. His brief is simple: 'If it's green, it's my responsibility.'

So how does Mick feel about having the onus of the very existence of Lord's resting on his shoulders? 'To be honest, on the night before and the morning of a big match, like a Test or a Cup final, I feel physically sick with nerves. Occasionally, when I see the postman walking around with his sack over his shoulder, I think, "I'll have his job", and get away from all this, but the truth is I love cricket and I love working here. The people are good to me here and the people who genuinely know what they're talking about don't criticise me. I have a love-love relationship with the place. It's my little kingdom.'

Although he is too modest to admit it, Hunt has not produced a 'shocker' of a wicket since he took over in 1989, but that has not stopped him from coming in for criticism. The 1996 NatWest Trophy final was won by Lancashire after Essex, batting second, were shot out for 57. 'People gave me stick, saying that the bounce was uneven and there was exaggerated movement off the seam, but if that

Mick Hunt and his groundstaff at work.

was the case then Lancashire would have been bowled out for nothing in the morning, when there is always more moisture in the wicket and in the air. They made 180-odd, which is not a great one-day score, but they did it batting first when traditionally runs are harder to come by.

'I don't mind being knocked if the wicket was poor, but I have no control over what happens in the air. If the ball swings like a banana, what do they want me to do about it? Or if they get themselves out playing poorly, it's not my problem. It's too easy for batsmen and

OPPOSITE: AN AERIAL VIEW TAKEN DURING THE LORD'S BICENTENARY MATCH IN 1987.

BELOW: IN PREPARATION FOR MIDDLESEX V. NEW ZEALAND IN 1990.

the media to point the finger at the groundsman. If all people want is a bucket-load of runs which a batsman can score in his sleep, then they might as well just sack me and play on an artificial wicket. But if you do that then you will kill off most of the magic and the mystery as well as the art of good batting. A long time ago when batsmen had to bat on uncovered wickets, it was occasionally a bit of a joke if a downpour reduced the wicket to a marsh, but it also improved a batsman's technique because they had to improvise.'

Hunt, a useful wicketkeeper/batsman for London Schools and Middlesex Colts, was particularly upset and surprised when he came in for criticism after the famous 1990 Test against India, when Gooch hit 333 and 123, Azharuddin and Shastri hit centuries and Kapil Dev hit four consecutive sixes to save India from the follow-on. One of the most memorable Test matches of modern times ended in a 247-run victory for England. 'There was a result and some brilliant entertainment, but some people still said the wicket was too flat. Sometimes you don't know what people want, but I try not to let it get to me any more. But even if you know it's not your fault, you always worry that the pitch will be blamed or used as an excuse for someone else's failure.'

Lord's has never been a quick pitch, although some of Hunt's relaid pitches are starting to produce some lift. Hunt believes that the ball now swings more than it has ever done, following the construction of the new stands, which have enclosed the outfield and 'thickened' the atmosphere. 'The ball can be doing nothing, but if it suddenly clouds over then it starts moving about all over the place whatever the time of day.'

There are eighteen wickets at Lord's, with the central ones reserved for the most important games of a packed fixture programme. 'Ideally, you only want to use each wicket for one match a season, but it's just not

possible. Some grounds have that luxury, but this is Lord's and a lot of matches are played here.' Hunt, who has six full-time staff working for him, has been relaying some of the wickets since 1991. 'It's a very old square out there and we get a lot of cracking because of the many layers of top dressing that have been put on it down the years. When we relay a wicket it's only about six inches deep, but it still needs about four to five years to mature and consolidate. If we relaid one in 1998, then we would not use it in 1999. In 2000 we would use it for a couple of one-dayers, but if at all possible we would not want to put it to full use until about 2002.'

Jonathan Hawke is the preparations (or 'prep') manager who works alongside Gareth Williams in the Estates Management department. He has the responsibility of making sure that Lord's is in immaculate condition before a match. At the close of play in a Test match or after a Cup final Hawke oversees the removal of 24 tons of rubbish – an operation which often continues well past

A Cross Arrows match on the Nursery ground.

midnight, aided by the hordes of helpers who have been turning up at Lord's for years to earn a few extra pounds. 'It is always a lot messier after it has rained for much of the day, because without anything to watch people tend to eat and drink more.'

Hawke admits that one area of his job has become easier since the old wooden benches were replaced by plastic seating. Instead of endless painting ('It was a bit like painting the Forth Road Bridge,' he says), the new seats are simply blasted with a powerful jet wash.

At the end of the season the Nursery ground stages the games of Cross Arrows Cricket Club, which has become something of an institution within an institution. The fixtures provide some light-hearted fun for the Lord's staff at the close of an inevitably and invariably busy summer. Anyone employed at Lord's is entitled to play for the team, and a number of illustrious guests such as Garfield Sobers, Fred Titmus and any number of Middlesex 'ringers' have appeared in the club's scorebook in its 120-year history. The club was originally known

as the St John's Wood Ramblers but allegedly changed its name when one team member, giving directions to somewhere in north-west London, declared, 'It's 'cross 'arrow way.' The Cross Arrows will play virtually any team who are prepared to take their beer as seriously as they take their cricket. A club called The Stage, made up of actors and with its origins in the Actors v. Writers fixture, which began at the turn of the century, provide regular opponents. The Metropolitan Police and the Royal household from Windsor Castle also put up teams each year, as do a number of wandering clubs with exotic names such as Incogniti, The Frogs, The Stragglers of Asia and The Adastrians. Traditionally, the Cross Arrows President is the MCC Secretary, and at the time of writing the captain is the former Warwickshire and England player John Jameson, the MCC's Assistant Secretary of Cricket.

The outdoor nets at Lord's are to be found at the northernmost end of the Nursery Ground, a short distance from the new Indoor Cricket School, where Clive Radley, the former Middlesex and England batsman, is Head Coach. The original school, opened by Sir George 'Gubby' Allen in 1977, was replaced by more modern facilities in 1995. The nets are

THE MOUND STAND DURING THE BICENTENARY MATCH.

used by Middlesex players, MCC Members and their sons, as well as members of the public. Radley took over in 1990 from the former left-arm spinner Don Wilson, who has returned to his native Yorkshire to coach the schoolboys of Ampleforth College. Radley's main brief is to school MCC's young professionals, who come from all over the country for six- or twelve-month periods, having impressed during trials in the winter. The boys come on the recommendation of counties or local clubs or following a letter from ambitious parents. Only a handful get past the trial stage and even fewer make it into first-class cricket, although some famous names such as Denis Compton, Fred Titmus, John Murray, Ian Botham and Phil Tufnell are all graduates of the coaching programme. There are eight nets in total, as well as video cameras, which Radley employs to record deficiencies in technique and show the culprits where they are at fault.

Next to the Indoor School are the offices of the England and Wales Cricket Board, the Lord's shop and an area set aside on match days for bookmakers. Continuing our clockwise journey from the Pavilion, the next building is the magnificent Mound Stand with its marquee-style roof. The Mound, which was opened in 1987 to commemorate MCC's bicentenary, houses the majority of the Lord's hospitality boxes and units on the upper levels. Much of the money for its construction was provided by the multimillionaire MCC Member Sir John Paul Getty, and its designer Michael Hopkins earned great acclaim from the world of architecture for his highly original design.

Separating the Mound Stand from the Tavern Stand is the old scoreboard, above which the hunched figure of Father Time perches proudly, having been moved there from the Grand Stand during building work. Plans for the Tavern Stand's reconstruction in the late 1960s sparked a revolt among MCC Members, who did not want to see the disappearance of their dining-room and the famous pub from which the stand took its name. The MCC Committee rode the storm, but they decided to preserve something of the old boisterous atmosphere of the Tavern by building a long bar that ran under the upper tier and looked out on to the playing area. The bar, as rowdy as you like at the end of a Cup final, was removed in the early 1980s at the same

THE HARRIS MEMORIAL GARDEN IN BLOOM.

time that it was decided that spectators were no longer allowed to sit on the grass behind the boundary ropes. The only bar to be found there nowadays is a fairly functional affair at the foot of the Stand, facing the high brick wall running alongside the St John's Wood Road. But the Tavern continues its existence in the form of a pub situated ten yards to the right as you leave by the Grace Gates, and it remains a favourite watering and eating hole for the staff at Lord's.

The extension behind the Pavilion, which is connected to the main building by corridors on the first floor, is home to the museum, the library, the tennis and squash courts, the Club Office and a film theatre funded by Sir John Paul Getty and dedicated to the memory of the broadcaster Brian Johnston. The small theatre was officially opened in 1998, and the original plan was to use it for showing archive films to MCC Members, with a view to allowing in members of the public at a later date. Next to the pavilion extension are the modest offices of Middlesex CCC which look out over the Harris Garden. The gardens were laid out in memory of Lord Harris, one of the great figures of Lord's, captain of Kent and England and President of MCC. A plaque on the wall at the back of the gardens bears the following inscription:

ERECTED TO THE MEMORY OF
GEORGE ROBERT CANNING
1851 LORD HARRIS 1932
IN RECOGNITION OF INVALUABLE SERVICES
RENDERED TO CRICKET AND TO THE CLUB OVER
A PERIOD OF MORE THAN FIFTY YEARS HE WAS
A GREAT CRICKETER A GREAT GENTLEMAN
AND A WISE COUNSELLOR WHOSE
ENTHUSIASM FOR THE GAME NEVER WANED

The eleven benches in the garden are dedicated to leading figures in the history of Middlesex CCC, including Patsy Hendren, Bill Edrich, F.T. Mann, J.W. Hearne and N.E. Haig.

When the great Australian all-rounder Keith Miller walked into Lord's for the first time during the Second World War, he was famously unimpressed. He had grown up hearing Australia's returning heroes talk about the place with unalloyed reverence. He had imagined a ground of unparalleled grandeur which dominated the London skyline and intimidated all those who stepped through its hallowed Grace Gates.

Miller was not the first or the last person to experience a feeling of bathos on first walking into Lord's. Most sports stadiums dominate their immediate surroundings and they generate a sense of growing awe as they are approached by visiting teams or spectators, who as they get nearer have time to reflect on the legends that have been created and the feats of heroism that have been performed there. Wembley, just a few miles up the road from Lord's, is a prime example. Visitors head towards it along Wembley Way, with the 'twin towers' looming ever larger, so that on entering the stadium ten minutes later they have experienced a sense of mounting excitement.

Visitors to Lord's, on the other hand, barely know that they are there until they get inside. Whichever way one approaches the ground, Lord's resolutely refuses to reveal its full majesty, preferring instead to nestle modestly into the anonymity of residential St John's Wood. Entering the ground by the Grace Gates maintains this impression, as one can still only see the side of the Pavilion and the back end of the Allen and Tavern stands. It is only when the outfield is glimpsed through a gap in the stands that a vague sense of disappointment begins to turn into something like spine-tingling awe. Miller, who was quickly to change his mind about Lord's once he had had the experience of playing there before a full house, would find today that almost all the stands he saw then have since been replaced by bigger and better constructions. Only the Allen Stand (formerly the Q), which has been comprehensively refurbished, and the lower tier of the Mound Stand were there in the 1940s.

The only building overlooking the pitch which remains is the Pavilion, and not even Miller at his most iconoclastic could have failed to be moved once he had seen it in its full imposing grandeur from the outfield or walked down its sombre wooden staircase, through the Long Room and out to bat.

THE HARRIS GARDEN PROVIDES A QUIET SPOT FOR MEMBERS OF MCC BEHIND THE PAVILION.

THE FAMOUS LONG ROOM.

The Long Room dominates the Pavilion. It is ninety feet long and runs along the ground floor looking out on to the concourse below. The concourse is the only part of the ground that still uses wooden benches, and to reserve seats in that area one has to have been an MCC Member for over 25 years and be over 70. Once this area is full, Members take seats on a first-come, first-served basis. Even MCC Members have to queue. On the morning of an important match it is not uncommon to see a horde of distinguished Members, complete with straw hats, egg and bacon ties and full picnic hampers, jostling amiably inside the Grace Gates from seven o'clock onwards before racing to get the best seats. There are 18,000 Members in total, and although they never all turn up at once, there is nothing like enough room to accommodate them all in the Pavilion area, and so the Tavern and Warner stands are used as an overflow. The rules of the Long Room are strict: no drinking, smoking or eating, and non-members are not allowed in on match days.

MCC Members and the curators of the Lord's museum often find themselves involved in a good-natured tug-of-war over the paintings and exhibits on display in the Long Room. Understandably both sides covet the Club's prized possessions. The numerous paintings that hang in the Long Room include portraits of the great England bowler Sydney Barnes, Lord Frederick Beauclerk, Keith Miller, the long-serving MCC Secretary F.E. Lacey, John Nyren of Hambledon, the Earl of Winchilsea (one of the founding fathers of MCC), Thomas Lord himself, the ghostly figure of William Beldham, Don Bradman,

Douglas Jardine, Denis Compton and Len Hutton. Glass cases on the back wall of the Long Room are full of memorabilia that includes bats and balls presented to cricketers for outstanding achievements in a match. There is the ball used in the first ever Test match between England and Australia at Sydney, and another presented to Yorkshire's Wilfred Rhodes after he took 15 for 124 against the Australians at Melbourne. One of the more curious items on display is a bat dedicated to 'Little Joey in 1792–93 died of cricket, lbw'. It is thought that this may refer to John Ring (1758–1800), who died as a result of a blow in the face from a ball bowled by his brother George. William Beldham credited the first introduction of the lbw law in 1774 to the shabby tactics of John Ring, but as Ring was then only sixteen and, moreover, the inscription anticipated his death by seven to eight years, both its inference and Beldham's statement are in doubt. Also on display are bats belonging to Weekes, Bradman, Rhodes, Sutcliffe and Hobbs, as well as one, heavily taped around the middle, used by Sir Pelham Warner in his last triumphant match as captain of Middlesex in 1920.

The ground floor also accommodates the Writing Room, the Old Library and the Committee Room, where between 1890 and the late 1960s all the major decisions affecting the future of cricket were made by the elder statesmen of MCC sitting around the great wooden table. At the front of the room there are several leather-bound armchairs, and it is here that Her Majesty the Queen, until recently the only woman allowed into the Long Room on match days, looks out over her subjects to the play in the middle.

Next to the Committee Room are the offices of the marketing department, which is run by Chris Rea, the former Scottish rugby international, and his assistant Karen Marshall. To them falls the delicate task of ensuring that Lord's and MCC operate as an effective commercial enterprise while maintaining the traditions of a venerable private club. Both are

THE LONG ROOM PORTRAYED BY DENIS FLANDERS IN 1953.

Members in the Long Room during a match.

cricket fanatics and both are keenly aware of the difficulties of balancing tradition on one side with progress on the other.

Rea, who admits to having been a poor wicketkeeper and only a reasonable bat at school and university level, joined MCC at the end of the 1995 Rugby World Cup. There was no Marketing Department or Committee until then, but since their establishment they have proved to be highly successful in raising money for the Club as well as in helping to promote the Club's public image and drive through the 'Yes' vote in the debate on the admission of women.

Rea says that one of his main aims is to turn the negatives of the Club's image into a positive. 'Part of the strength of the Club is the tradition and history, the quality and integrity that exists

within this club. It is a huge strength that must not be tampered with, but it is also a weakness in that inevitably we are perceived as "establishment" and reactionary.

'There is the idea that the MCC is wholly resistant to change, but nothing could be further from the truth. It is a problem we have to deal with, but it is more a problem of public perception than actual truth. I have seen various sports administrations at close quarters, but the quality of Committee Members here is exceptional. The Main Committee is one of the most high-powered bodies you could ever wish to come across. To hear the quality of debate is a privilege.'

The new MCC President Tony Lewis, an eminent journalist, broadcaster and writer as well as cricketer, believes that irresponsible

THE MUSEUM AT LORD'S.

reporting has much to do with the negative public perception of MCC. Writing in the Club newsletter shortly after taking his new office, Lewis said: 'There are lesser journalists who enjoy scything away in print at an MCC which does not exist, of elitism and of brain-dead anti-feminism. Their art is that of holding an ancient ghost up against the ropes with one hand to sock him with the other. They would have nothing to hit unless they fabricated it. It means that their inkwell is nearly empty.'

Much of the Pavilion has the feel of a Victorian boarding school about it, with its dark wood panelling, broad staircases, honours boards, imposing canvases of great cricketing figures, and its pleasant smells from a kitchen catering for as many as a hundred at a time. But the hoppy odours emanating from the Members' bar, which runs along the back of the Long Room, remind visitors that they are somewhere else entirely. At the foot of the stairs leading up to the first floor is a wooden honours board commemorating MCC Members who gave their lives in the First World War (curiously, there is no Second World War equivalent). Nearly 350 names fill the board in an impressive if grim reminder of the epic sacrifice in the Great War. Only four of the names on the board are not preceded by an Officer's rank in a list which includes such distinguished names as Major The Earl of Suffolk, Admiral Sir G.J.S. Warrender, Rev. R.M. Kirwan, Rear-Admiral Sir R.K. Arbuthnott and Major The Hon. A.A. Tennyson.

The offices of the MCC Secretariat are located on the first floor, and it is there that

one can find the Secretary, Roger Knight. A former captain of Surrey and headmaster of Worksop, Knight became only the thirteenth Secretary of the Club when he succeeded Lt.-Col. J.R. Stephenson at the beginning of 1994.

The MCC Secretary has three roles: he is the head of a private club with 18,000 Members, he is a kind of chief executive of Lord's as a property and a commercial asset and, thirdly, he is an ambassador who travels the country and the world promoting the interests of cricket in conjunction with the ICC. Diplomacy is perhaps the most important quality needed for the job, given the highly public nature of the position, and in Knight MCC seem to have found the perfect man for the post.

Like the new President, Tony Lewis, Knight is an open-minded traditionalist who was delighted by the recent vote to admit women. 'We had to decide if we were a cricket club or a private club,' says Knight, who sat on the Players and Fixtures Sub-Committee before joining the Main Committee. 'If you decide that you are a cricket club, why should people who play the game, umpire the game, administer the game, support the game and love the game not be allowed to take as full a part as anyone else? If MCC decide they are a purely private club then they are perfectly entitled to do so. But if you accept that the club has a public function which transcends the private club, then that is different. I would say that the public function of MCC is to look after the laws of the game, to be responsible for the running of the headquarters of cricket and to have a development role within ICC. All those three facts mean we cannot just sit back and say we are a private club. I think the recent vote to admit women was a crucial one for the Club, not least because the issues forced the Club to define its identity.'

Knight is hoping that, now that the women's issue has been dealt with once and for all, the Club may start to receive some praise for its contribution to the development of cricket.

The offices of the MCC secretariat back on to the visitors' dressing-room. There is nothing pretentious or glamorous about the players' changing-rooms, which are virtually identical in their utilitarian decor. In the centre of each airy room are wooden cupboards, or 'coffins' where the players can lock up their kit-bags at the close of play. Green plastic benches run along the walls, and there are French windows opening out on to the balconies with their white, wrought-iron balustrades. In each dressing-room there is a basin in the corner, a television set, a physiotherapist's bed and honours boards on the walls with the names of all those who have scored a century or taken five wickets in an innings or ten in a match during a Lord's Test.

THE SPARROW KILLED BY A BALL IN 1936, BOTH OF WHICH NOW RESIDE IN THE MUSEUM.

The boards in the visitors' dressing-room show that Australia's H. Graham in 1893 was the first visitor to score a century, and that South Africa's J. Rhodes in 1998 the most recent. The first to take ten wickets was Australia's G.E. Palmer in 1884 during the first ever Test at Lord's, and the last was New Zealand's Dion Nash in 1994. In the home dressing-room A.G. Steel's 148 in 1884 is the first recorded Lord's Test century, while the latest entry is Nasser Hussain's 105 against the 1998 South Africans. J. Briggs was the first Englishman to take more than ten wickets in a Test match while, in a mildly depressing reminder of England's recent fortunes, the name of I.T. Botham is the last name on the ten-wicket list for his 11 for 140 against New Zealand in 1978.

To the back of each dressing-room are the wash areas, each with four huge baths (showers have only recently been installed). In the home team's area one of the baths has been made the personal property of the Middlesex and England seamer Angus Fraser, who has put up a warning sign on the door announcing menacingly 'Fraser's Bath'. The angry stud marks on the door to the England area, meanwhile, stand as a physical testimony to the frustrations of the national team in recent years. During the 1996 Test match against Pakistan, which the visitors won after one of the most exciting climaxes to a Test in living memory, the drama on the pitch spread into the wash area and ended in a minor domestic crisis. The tension was clearly too much for one of the Pakistanis, who turned on the taps to run his bath, only to return to the balcony to watch Waqar Younis and Wasim Akram steer Pakistan to a two-wicket victory. Celebrations in the dressing-room followed, and when the player finally returned to attend to his personal hygiene he found that gallons of piping hot water had overflowed on to the floor and brought down the ceiling below.

The second floor of the Pavilion is largely given over to wining and dining. One kitchen caters for the Committee dining-room, the Pavilion restaurant and the players' dining-room. The current cook is Linda Leker, who works all year round, laying on several dinners and lunches a week for MCC Members as well as for benefit evenings. She took over in 1995 from the redoubtable Nancy Doyle, who had achieved legendary status by the time she hung up her pots and pans and retired with an MBE.

At the other end of the second floor, there is the Members' lounge, the Members' bar and the increasingly popular Bridge Society (where P. Donovan is said to be the foremost exponent of the ancient game).

The Curator's Office, the Library and the Museum can all be found in the extension at the back of the Pavilion. The long-serving and highly knowledgeable Stephen Green is the Chief Curator and presides over the running of the museum, the library and the archives. In the same warren of stairwells and corridors are the MCC Club Offices where, *inter alia*, staff attend to the arduous tasks of allocating tickets and membership applications.

At the last count there were approximately 18,000 MCC Members, and each year the office receives hundreds of applications from hopefuls wishing to join the eighteen-year waiting list. Until the end of 1998 the 72 hospitality boxes around the ground could be hired out over a five-year period for £50,000, but from 1 January 1999 all of the available boxes were put out to tender. The length of tenure has been reduced to two years and the boxes are allocated to those making the best offers. Those who cannot afford a box but want to guarantee that they will have a seat can buy a debenture for £2,500, which gives them first call on tickets for the ensuing ten years. Tickets for debenture holders are £38 for Test matches and £50 for one-day finals. For the rest, the prices of Test match tickets start at £15 for seats with restricted viewing and rise to £34; County Championship match tickets cost £7, and Sunday League games £8.

The Pavilion extension has also become home to the print shop, which was forced to relocate from under the Grand Stand. Lord's is the only ground in the country still printing the old-style scorecards – long and thin so as to fit into a gentleman's coat pocket. The original print shop was set up by James Dark in 1848, and today it is run by Andrew Anderton, who took over from the long-serving Vince Miller.

The museum houses some of the most important artefacts in the history of cricket. In addition to the Ashes urn, which takes pride of place in a glass case at the centre of the room, other exhibits include Bradman's surprisingly small boots, the balls with which Jim Laker took nineteen wickets against Australia in 1956, and the sparrow (after a trip to the taxidermist) which was killed by a ball bowled by Jehangir Khan in Cambridge University's match against MCC in 1936. The exhibits come from three sources: sales, donations and commissions. The Curator's office are finding it increasingly difficult to get cricketers to part with the tools of their success, and several of the items on display, such as the bat with which Graham Gooch hit 333 and 123 against India in 1990, are only on loan. At the same time there has been a boom in the cricket memorabilia market in recent years, and the curators have occasionally relied on MCC Members tipping them off about items up for auction.

MIDDLESEX AND LORD'S:
An Enduring Partnership

Lord's lost something of its lustre in the middle years of the nineteenth century. There were fewer fixtures and smaller crowds, and the state of the ground deteriorated to the point where, at the end of the 1850s, Surrey and Sussex both refused to play there. The MCC Secretary R.A. Fitzgerald, aware that the future of cricket lay with the counties,

THE NAT WEST FINAL, 1988, MIDDLESEX V. WORCESTERSHIRE.

set out to woo Middlesex to the ground in a bid to boost MCC's dwindling coffers and restore its reputation as the pre-eminent venue in English cricket. His overtures were unsuccessful, as the county had already settled on playing their matches at Prince's Ground, but contact had been established and in 1877, the year after Fitzgerald was replaced by Henry Perkins, Middlesex took up tenancy at Lord's.

'Lillywhite' (or *James Lillywhite's Cricketers' Annual*, to give it its full name) praised the good business sense behind 'the Club's' decision to co-habit with the county, commenting: 'The addition of the Middlesex fixtures fitted a decided blank in the Marylebone programme, and there was certainly more life in the appearance of matters at headquarters than in the previous year.'

In its earliest years, in contrast to the mainly professional northern counties, the Middlesex club was almost entirely amateur in composition. Founded in 1864, they originally played their matches at the Cattle Market Ground in Islington, but property developers forced them to relocate after just four seasons. For a brief period they moved to the Athletic Ground at Lillie Bridge and then, in 1872, to Prince's in the heart of Chelsea, before finally settling in St John's Wood. Although the club was dominated by 'gentlemen' cricketers, Middlesex's leading player of the day was the professional Tom Hearne, a star of the United XI, who achieved fame with a masterful unbeaten 122 for the Players against the Gentlemen in 1866.

In the Walkers, Middlesex are able to boast one of cricket's most famous families. Only the Graces of Gloucestershire and the Fosters of Worcestershire can match them for one family's contribution to cricket. The best of the bunch was V.E. Walker, who produced one of the great all-round performances of the nineteenth century when playing for England against the mighty Surrey at The Oval in 1859. Walker took all ten Surrey wickets in the first innings and then struck an unbeaten 108 in England's second. (Walker would take all ten wickets on two other occasions before his career was out.)

His achievement with the ball is all the more startling because Walker was a 'lob' bowler and, according to H.S. Altham, 'probably the best exponent of the art that ever lived'. His brother I.D. Walker was captain of Middlesex for many years and was said to be one of the best players on the off-side in his day as well as a useful underarm bowler. I.D. Walker was also the founder of the Harrow Wanderers and was the game's leading exponent of the 'Harrow drive', a sort of front-foot cut that has been largely consigned to history in the first-class game, although it remains popular with the more agricultural of village cricket hitters. In 1883 he figured in an astonishing partnership with Alfred Lyttelton, when the pair put on 341 against Gloucestershire, 226 of which came in just 100 minutes.

R.D. Walker, meanwhile, was a first-rate batsman who played in the Varsity match a record-equalling five times. R.D. Walker's association with Middlesex was the longest of all the Walker brothers', beginning as a player when the club was founded and ending with his appointment as the county's President. What made the batting achievements of I.D and R.D. Walker all the more remarkable was the fact that both declined to use pads even on the famously unpredictable Lord's wickets of the period or against the country's fastest bowlers.

From the very beginnings of cricket until the period between the two world wars, batting was generally a gentleman's pursuit while bowling belonged to the professionals. There is a simple socio-economic explanation to the trend. It was largely on the intitiative of the nobility and the gentry that organised cricket came into existence, and batting was seen as the game's principal purpose. Though bowling was an essential feature, it was seen as the inferior of the two disciplines. Gentlemen would employ 'professionals' to bowl at them, and so it came to be that, with a number of notable exceptions, the best batsmen were gentlemen and the best bowlers were professionals. No county highlighted this truth better than Middlesex in the early years. As a team made up largely of amateurs, they were a formidable batting side, but their bowling was weak. In addition to the Walker brothers, Middlesex could also boast the talents of A.J. Webbe (whom Altham considered to be the best batsman of the day after the great W.G. Grace and the Nottinghamshire professional Arthur Shrewsbury), the Studds, the Lytteltons, the Fords and, towards the end of the century, A.E. Stoddart, T. O'Brien, P.F. Warner, C.M. Wells, R.S. Lucas and T.J. and R.N. Douglas.

C.T. Studd was the most effective bowler for Middlesex in the 1880s, and his departure on missionary work overseas enfeebled the attack further. It would not be until the arrival of the great Albert Trott from Australia in the last years of the century that the county's bowling recaptured any sort of venom. In the 1890s their only effective bowler was J.T. Hearne, one of the greatest of Middlesex players, who took 3,061 wickets in his extraordinarily long career. Hearne managed to stay at the top of the first-class game for just over twenty years. He made his debut for Middlesex in 1889 and played his last first-class match in 1923 at the age of 56 for MCC against Scotland in Edinburgh. In 1910, some twenty years after making his debut in the county game, the 43-year-old Hearne topped the bowling averages, but 1896 was his most successful season, when he took 257 wickets (including 100 before 12 June) at an average of 14.28. When Australia were skittled for just 18 by MCC, Hearne had figures of 4 for 4, and in the second innings he claimed nine of the tourists for 73. He returned to torment the Australians later that summer when he took 6 for 41 and 4 for 19.

The most dominant player in the early part of the new century was Albert Trott, the Australian. Trott had been outstanding against the England side that toured Down Under in 1894–95 but, curiously, was omitted from the Australia side to tour England in the summer of 1896. Put out by this rejection, Trott travelled to England under his own steam later that year and turned up at Lord's, where he was employed on the groundstaff. By 1898 he had forced his way into the Middlesex side and for the next six or seven years he was one of the best performers on the county circuit with

A.E. Trott, the Australian who became one of Middlesex's greatest all-rounders.

B.J.T. Bosanquet, the originator of the googly.

both ball and bat. In his second and third seasons with Middlesex he achieved the remarkable feat of taking 200 wickets and scoring 1,000 runs. Trott, who was also one of the best slip fielders in the country, remains the only man to have hit the ball over the present Pavilion. By a delicious irony, the great hit was made off the bowling of Monty Noble when Trott was playing for MCC against his native Australia on 31 July 1899. Three weeks earlier Trott made what many claimed was an even bigger hit for MCC against Sussex, but his towering shot struck the MCC insignia high above the roof and bounced back down into the Pavilion seats.

Trott was not the only Middlesex star of this period, for in Pelham Warner and B.J.T. Bosanquet, one of the great all-rounders of the day, the county could boast two of the most famous names in the game. Bernard Bosanquet will always be remembered as the inventor of the googly, and in Australia the delivery is often still referred to as the 'bosie'. Frequently flat wickets combined with the batsman-friendly lbw laws made bowling a more back-breaking and unrewarding enterprise at this time. The necessity of taking wickets was the mother of Bosanquet's invention, and his great idea was conceived not out in the middle but in the Pavilion. During breaks in play, the players would often amuse themselves playing 'twisti-tosti' or 'twisty-grab', in which a player sitting at one end of the table would try to bounce the ball off the other end so that his opponent would be unable to catch it. Thus was the art of Bosanquet's deception born, as he sent his team-mates spilling out of their chairs while his 'googly' spun off in the other direction.

Bosanquet worked on his brainchild in the nets and he claimed to have first used the delivery for real when playing for Middlesex against Leicestershire at Lord's. The art was still to be perfected, but when Bosanquet was chosen to tour New Zealand and Australia with Lord Hawke's team in 1902–03, he used it to devastating effect. When the tourists played New South Wales, Bosanquet bamboozled the great Victor Trumper and clean bowled him with his first delivery. No Tests were played on that tour, but on his return the following year with Plum Warner's triumphant party Bosanquet made a major impression at the highest level and his six wickets in the second innings helped clinch the Fourth Test at Sydney. From about 1906 Bosanquet, an amateur, drifted out of the first-class game, although he continued to play cricket on and off until shortly after the First World War.

Another great Middlesex player of the time was, like Albert Trott, an Australian who started his Lord's career on the groundstaff. H.S. Altham thought that in the ten years before the outbreak of the war Frank Tarrant was the best all-rounder in the world alongside the Yorkshireman George

Frank Tarrant, who like Trott started on the groundstaff at Lord's before joining Middlesex.

Hirst. Tarrant, a slow left-arm bowler and a cautious bat, is one of the small band of players to have taken ten wickets and scored a century in the same match – a feat he achieved playing for the Maharaja of Cooch Behar's XI v. Lord Willingdon's XI in Poona in 1918.

In 1909 Middlesex gave a debut to another J. Hearne, who quickly became known as 'Young Jack' to distinguish him from his illustrious older namesake. The younger Hearne, who was one of the county's great all-rounders and whose name would always be associated with his contemporary Patsy Hendren, shot from the anonymity of the Lord's groundstaff and into the England Test side in less than three years. In 1909 Middlesex gave him his debut at the age of eighteen, and two years later he found himself on the boat to Australia with the 1911–12

J.T. Hearne, responsible for much of the success of Middlesex before the First World War.

The incomparable 'Patsy' Hendren examines the roughly cut willow planks which are to become cricket bats at Warsop's factory, near to Lord's, in the spring of 1938.

E.H. HENDREN (1889–1962)

Elias 'Patsy' Hendren was the dominant Middlesex figure of the inter-war years. An ebullient cockney, famous for his quick wit and practical jokes, Hendren served the county for an astonishing 27 seasons before he finally retired from the game at the end of 1937 season with a first-class average of 50.80. During that time he compiled 170 centuries and played for England in 51 Tests. Like a number of his cricketing contemporaries, he was also a prodigiously talented footballer and represented Manchester City, Coventry City and Queen's Park Rangers, as well as England in the 'Victory' international against Scotland in 1919.

Only Sir Jack Hobbs has scored more first-class centuries than Hendren, and only Hobbs and the great left-hander Frank Woolley have exceeded his aggregate of runs. Elias Hendren, known as Patsy as a result of his Irish roots, began his career on the groundstaff at Lord's in 1905, aged fifteen, and made his debut for Middlesex two years later. His short, powerful frame leant itself to cutting and hooking, and yet he was as happy on the front foot as he was on the back. His footwork was exceptional, and the speed with which he could get to the pitch of the ball proved a great asset on the more difficult wickets. He was also an outstanding fielder in the deep and took over 700 catches in his career. He made his highest score, 301 not out against Worcestershire, in 1933 at the age of 43, but his most prolific season was 1928, when he hit 3,311 runs with thirteen centuries at an average of just over 70. In four matches he hit a hundred in each innings and he topped 2,000 runs in a season on twelve occasions. Many of his biggest partnerships were made with his lifelong friend Hearne, whose more circumspect approach to batting established an intriguing contrast of styles. In 1933 Hendren's comic persona was given outward expression when he took to the field to face West Indies' battery of fast bowlers wearing a makeshift helmet fashioned by his wife. Two flaps made from rubber sponge had been sewn on to his cap and hung over his ears, giving him the bizarre appearance of a fighter pilot.

Hendren remained active in cricket long after his retirement as a player. He coached the boys at Harrow, served on the Middlesex Committee and was made a Life Member of MCC.

His outrageous talent as a cricketer was matched by an irrepressibly cheerful nature.

Following his death in 1962 at the age of 73, Wisden paid tribute to his engaging personality, saying: 'Apart from his achievements, "Patsy" was a "character" of a type sadly lacking in modern cricket. No game in which he was engaged could be altogether dull. If it looked like becoming so, Hendren could be relied upon at one time or another to produce some antic which would bring an appreciative chuckle from the onlookers. Furthermore, he was a first-rate mimic and wit.'

W. J. EDRICH (1916–1986)

To draw an analogy from the world of comedy, Bill Edrich was Ernie Wise to Denis Compton's Eric Morecambe. Compton was the more celebrated and glamorous of the famous double act for both Middlesex and England which brought so much joy to cricket-lovers in the immediate post-war years, but if Compton was flamboyant and cavalier, Edrich was gritty and tough. He was at his best against fast bowling and, far from ducking the challenge of short-pitched bowling, he seemed at his happiest when cutting, hooking and pulling the quicks. One of his most memorable innings came when he dug in on a terror track at Brisbane in the first innings of the First Test of the 1946–47 Test series and made 16 in 105 minutes as he repelled the menace of Lindwall and Miller. Batting on a surface that had been drenched by a violent thunderstorm, Edrich was hit at least ten times on the body as he stood his ground against one of the most feared pace attacks in the history of Test cricket. Australia enjoyed the better of the weather conditions and overwhelmed England by an innings and 332 runs, but Edrich emerged from the contest with his reputation enhanced rather than diminished.

Edrich made his name in his native Norfolk in the early 1930s before making his debut for Middlesex in 1937, when he impressed by scoring 2,154 runs at an average of 44.87. The following year he hit 1,000 runs in May and was called into the Test side, but he failed to reproduce his county form against the Australians and scored just 67 runs in six innings. However, his talent was obvious for all to see and the selectors kept faith with him for the winter tour to South Africa. Failure continued to dog him in the early part of the rubber and he scored just 21 runs in five innings, making it eight consecutive matches of failure for the unfulfilled talent. But in the famous unfinished Fifth Test in Durban, when England rushed to catch their boat home after the tenth day, Edrich finally came good with an innings of 219. Curiously, despite finally proving himself at the highest level, Edrich was dropped for the summer series against the West Indies, and when Test cricket resumed in 1946 after the war he played in just the one Test – though he did not bat – against India. During the war, Edrich served as a bomber pilot in the RAF and earned a DFC for his brave and distinguished service.

Edrich, who switched from professional to amateur after the war, confirmed his talent at the highest level in the 1946–47 tour to Australia, when he followed his heroics in the First Test with scores of 71, 119, 89 and 60 in subsequent matches. The following year, together with his 'terrible twin' Compton, his run-scoring reached remarkable heights. He scored a total of 3,539 runs (Compton scored a couple of hundred more) for his county and country. In all, Edrich scored 36,965 runs in first-class cricket, including 86 centuries, at an average of 42.39. In Tests he scored 2,440 runs at 40, and for Middlesex 25,738 at 43.40, and his achievements would have been immeasurably greater had the war not robbed him of his prime years. The ever cheerful Edrich, a fine outfielder as well as 'slipper', was also a useful medium-fast change bowler who took 479 first-class wickets at 33.31.

DENIS COMPTON AND BILL EDRICH TAKING PART IN A CHARITY WALK TO RAISE FUNDS FOR MIDDLESEX CCC IN 1971.

tour party which several months later would return home having regained the Ashes in emphatic fashion with a 4–1 series victory. Hearne made his own significant contribution to the glorious cause with 114 in the Melbourne Test. However, 'Young Jack' never established himself as a truly great player at Test level and it was for Middlesex that his greatest achievements were made. In five seasons for the county he completed the all-rounder's double of 100 wickets and 1,000 runs, and in three of those seasons he topped 2,000 runs. The last of his 'double' seasons came in 1923, after which his career was dogged by poor health, and though he continued to figure in the game for another thirteen years, he was never able to recapture the sparkling form of his early playing days. His greatest individual performance came against Sussex at Lord's in 1923, when he scored 140 and 57 not out and took twelve wickets. He batted with a ramrod straight bat and was rarely seen taking the attack to the bowler. His was a studied, defensive approach to the art of run-gathering, and his unflappable temperament provided the perfect foil to the explosive genius of Hendren, whose most glorious years would not come until after the war.

Thanks in large measure to the efforts of their all-rounders Tarrant and Hearne, Middlesex had been well placed to win the County Championship in 1914, before the outbreak of war eventually forced the suspension of all first-class cricket. When competition resumed in 1919 the county performed poorly, but the following year they were crowned champions amid jubilant scenes at Lord's after a remarkable climax to the season. With nine matches to be played, Middlesex were languishing in mid-table, but under the inspired captaincy of Warner, playing his final season in the first-class game, they won

Frank Mann, captain of Middlesex and England.

all their remaining matches and clinched the title late in the evening of the last day of the season against Surrey, their long-standing rivals from across the Thames.

Surrey, who held the advantage for much of the match and took a lead of 73 into their second innings, were set 244 to win in three hours. Andrew Sandham, one of the most prolific batsmen of the day and best known for his 325 for England against the West Indies in Kingston, was the greatest threat to Middlesex hopes, and once he was caught and bowled by Hearne victory came quickly. Warner was chaired from the field as the crowd poured on to the field and chanted his name beneath the Pavilion balcony. Warner later described that day as the happiest in his long and remarkable career, but it was not only his inspirational captaincy that made Middlesex's triumph possible. The leg breaks of the Oxford 'Blue' G.T. Stevens, a future England captain, as well as the runs of Hendren and the all-round contribution of Hearne, were also critical factors in the county's finest hour.

Under the captaincy of Frank Mann Middlesex retained their title the following season. Like his son George, Mann had the distinction of captaining both his county and his country. He was also one of the biggest hitters of the ball that the game has ever seen. In 1924 he struck consecutive deliveries from the great Yorkshire all-rounder Wilfred Rhodes on to the Pavilion roof and was just inches from matching the achievement of his Middlesex predecessor Albert Trott. In a replay of events twelve months earlier, Middlesex needed to beat Surrey at Lord's to take the title, and they achieved their target thanks to centuries from Twining and Hearne. The championship triumph of 1921 was to be Middlesex's last for 26 years, as the great northern powers of Yorkshire and Lancashire then dominated the county scene until the Second World War. Yorkshire won the next four titles, Lancashire the three after that, and between them the 'Rose' counties won sixteen of the eighteen championships between 1922 and 1939. Part of the problem for Middlesex during this time was the frequent unavailability of their amateur players, who, like many 'gentlemen' cricketers after the First World War, no longer had the private means to fund a life playing unpaid cricket and were forced to make a living outside the game. In G.O. Allen, R.W. Robins and I.A.R. Peebles, however, the county could boast three players of the highest quality who all distinguished themselves at Test level.

Though success in the championship eluded them, the Middlesex sides of the 1920s and 30s were invariably good entertainment, and under the vibrant and bullish captaincy of Robins they came close to pipping Yorkshire for the title in 1937, when a young batsman called Denis Compton, then in his second season, established himself as one of the most extravagant talents the county had ever produced.

In the cavalier figure of Compton, Middlesex supporters found a more than adequate replacement for Hendren. It is difficult to utter his name without the word Edrich emerging in the same breath, as the two were virtually inseparable at the wicket as well as in the minds of cricket-lovers in the immediate post-war years. Without question Compton and W.J. 'Bill' Edrich were English cricket's great stars of the period, plundering thousands of runs for both Middlesex and England. 'They go together in English cricket as Gilbert and Sullivan go together in English opera,' wrote R.C. Robertson-Glasgow in Wisden. 'It should be doubted that in the art of giving pleasure to an English audience, both pairs lack rivals.' In the glorious, baking hot summer of 1947 the pair scored a remarkable 7,355 runs between them and were especially severe on the touring South Africans. Compton played in all five Tests and hit 753 runs for an average of 94.12, while Edrich played in four, scoring 552 runs at 110.4. In all, the beleaguered South African bowlers surrendered 2,000 runs to the dashing duo.

Compton was undoubtedly the more naturally talented of the two, and his swaggering charisma made him the darling of the cricketing public and a hero to schoolboys of his generation. The sheer weight of runs scored by Compton and Edrich was a major factor in Middlesex's success after the war, when they were runners-up to Yorkshire in 1946 and champions the following season. They were, however, not the only outstanding figures on the books at Middlesex. Many counties took years to replenish their playing resources after the six years stolen by the war, but Middlesex were blessed with a glut of talent when first-class cricket resumed. Jack Robertson and Sid Brown were also prodigious scorers, and in the celebrated 1947 season the four made more than 12,000 runs between them. The inspirational and tactically shrewd Walter Robins returned as captain in 1946 at the age of 40 and, like Warner before him, won the title in his final season before handing the responsibility to George Mann. Middlesex's domination in 1947 is borne out by the statistics. They exceeded the 400-mark in eleven innings and declared twenty times, while on only three occasions did their opponents top 400.

Denis Compton batting for Middlesex against Worcestershire.

Given the fact that so many of the Middlesex players, most of them amateurs until the 1930s, were also members of MCC it was perhaps inevitable that the running of the county's affairs should have become submerged within the administrative machinery of Lord's. The influence of Sir Pelham Warner and Sir George Allen, monumental figures within both institutions, as well as a combination of common sense and common decency on both sides ensured that a potentially fractious relationship never developed into anything more confrontational. But in 1949 Middlesex wrested some independence from their landlords and today they operate much as any other county, though, of course, they remain tenants with only limited proprietorial rights. Middlesex, like all counties, have been forced to consider ways of making a profit in a climate of dwindling public interest for the county game. Commercial initiatives, such as sponsorship and advertising, have often run into difficulties with the MCC authorities, who enter into their own separate deals with business partners. Moreover, many of the club's members feel strongly that they do not want their famous ground to be exploited for commercial profit. One example of this conflict of interest came in 1981 when the clothing retailers Austin Reed entered into a deal with Middlesex which would involve the promotion of their goods on match days. A display stand was planned and girls were to be hired to wander around the ground button-holing spectators about Austin Reed's products. But the deal collapsed when MCC took exception to the prospect of their ground being turned into a mini-trade fair and Middlesex were forced to look elsewhere for additional revenue.

Middlesex, who have one of the largest memberships of all the counties, are not currently in financial difficulties, but their opportunities for generating revenue are limited by the fact that they do not own their ground. And as a result of the congested fixture list at Lord's they have to play some of their home matches away from Lord's at Uxbridge or Southgate, which is a drain on their resources. Many of the players say they love playing on the smaller club grounds, particularly in championship games, because there is more of an atmosphere. Lord's, they say, can be a dispiriting place to play when there are just a handful of die-hards and some passers-by to cheer them on.

Financially, however, it is far more profitable for Middlesex to play their matches at Lord's. Vinnie Codrington, the current Secretary of Middlesex, explains the difficulties:

'The demand on the pitches at Lord's is probably the most emotive issue. We would like to play nine 4-day championship games and nine one-day games at Lord's per season because every time we have to play a home match away from Lord's the set-up costs are up to £50,000. Each time we play at Uxbridge or Southgate, we are effectively building a temporary home with all the facilities and that's an expensive business. We don't recoup that money because most of the people who come to see 4-day cricket are members.

'We would rather play at Lord's for the whole season. That goes for most of our members too. A lot of them simply do not contemplate coming to watch if we are not playing at Lord's. I hate to admit it but some of our members are more interested in being at Lord's than watching Middlesex. The fact that they can come to the home of cricket is the attraction for those members.'

Codrington, who spent six and a half years at Richmond Rugby Club before joining Middlesex, believes the advantages of playing at the home of cricket outweigh the disadvantages.

'The arrangement is a simple one: MCC are the landlords, Middlesex the tenants. We pay the MCC a flat fee for the season which is good from our point of view in that we do not have to deal with money every time we have a match. The down side is that we don't have any control. If the beer is poor or the stewards are surly and so on we have to complain to the MCC, we can't deal with complaints ourselves. But it is generally a good arrangement for both parties: we get to play at the headquarters of cricket and the MCC get a whole season of first-class cricket to watch. One of the most difficult aspects for us is that the opportunities to generate income here at Lord's are very limited because it is not our ground to use as we want. The MCC are very wealthy and they do not actually need county cricket to make ends meet.'

The success of Middlesex after the Second World War mirrored their triumphs after the First, when they twice won the championship in the early years after the conflict. The only differences this time round were that Middlesex did not win the title in consecutive years and on the second occasion they were obliged to share it. In 1948 Glamorgan won the championship for the first time in their history, four points ahead of Surrey and eight ahead of Middlesex, whose hopes of retaining the title were seriously diminished by the unavailability of Compton and Edrich for much of the campaign. The pair played in five Tests against the Australians, which meant that they missed nine championship games. The left-arm spinner Jack Young missed seven county games when he was called on by the selectors for three of the matches. The problem of accommodating Middlesex in the Lord's fixture list was highlighted that year, when the county were asked to play their first ten championship matches at home and their remaining eleven away. This was not a state of affairs that delighted the Middlesex members, who felt attendances were often affected by the generally wetter weather at the beginning of the season.

The following season Middlesex, at full strength for most of the summer despite Test match calls for Compton, Edrich, Robertson, Mann and Brown, seemed on course for their second outright title in three years when they reached August without defeat. However, after being beaten twice by Surrey and then losing to Sussex at Hove, they were forced to share the championship spoils with Yorkshire. One of the highlights of the campaign was Robertson's 331 not out at Worcester, which remains the highest ever score for the county. There was also a memorable day at Lord's for Compton, whose benefit match against Sussex attracted a total of just under 60,000 spectators through the turnstiles and netted the idolised beneficiary a cool £12,000. Compton started nervously and did not get off the mark for fifteen minutes, but he finally rose to the occasion with a magnificent 182, the last 79 runs coming in a swashbuckling three-quarters of an hour. 'He began soberly,' reported E.W. Swanton for the *Daily Telegraph*, 'launched gradually into his full range of strokes, and, when both his hundred and the Sussex score were left behind, blossomed forth into one of those dazzling exhibitions which are so difficult for the bowler to compete with and so impossible to describe.'

Middlesex would not taste championship success for another 27 years, as they drifted into mid-table obscurity and even into the lower reaches of the table. Only twice over the next twenty years were they to be found above fifth place in the end-of-season standings. Part of the problem was the semi-retirement of captain Mann, whose appearances grew more and more infrequent as he attended to

Peter Parfitt, Middlesex and England.

John Murray pictured celebrating breaking the world record number of dismissals by a wicketkeeper in 1975.

business outside cricket. In 1950 as many as seven different players were called upon to captain the side. Compton's troublesome knee was another factor behind Middlesex's decline after their mini-Golden Age. He underwent an operation in 1950, forcing him to miss two months of the season, and although he continued to play for another nine years he was no longer the irresistible force that he had been. The measure of his decline is reflected in the averages. In the first four seasons after the war, Compton averaged just over 68 per innings, but in his final four seasons in the 1950s the figure had slumped to 29. Edrich, who had made his debut for Middlesex in 1937, also lost some of his lustre as the ageing process inevitably took its toll. Middlesex had been fortunate that Compton and Edrich were on the groundstaff when Hendren and Hearne put away their boots and bats. In the 1950s they were not so lucky, and it would be years before players approaching their calibre would grace the team.

By the end of the decade the left-hander Peter Parfitt and the elegant Eric Russell had bolstered the county's batting, while Fred Titmus emerged as an all-rounder of the highest quality. A hard-hitting bat who could

MIDDLESEX AND ENGLAND CAPTAIN MIKE BREARLEY HITS OUT FOR HIS COUNTY.

J.M. BREARLEY (1942–)

It is a sign of the respect in which Mike Brearley was held that not since Douglas Jardine in the early 1930s had England boasted a captain who so riled the Australians. Captain of Cambridge University, his county and his country, Brearley was without question one of the most thoughtful, scholarly and successful captains ever to grace a cricket field. His modesty would have him admit that he was not a Test batsman of the highest rank, although he would often pull out a big innings when his reputation as a batsman had put his place in the team on the line. That same humility would prevent him from blowing his trumpet about his achievements in charge of the national side, which he led to eleven victories over the Australians and just five defeats. Against other Test nations he presided over seven English victories and no defeats. Brearley, who took a First in Classics and a Second in Moral Sciences, was a shrewd tactician and strategist, but perhaps his greatest quality as a captain was his ability to bring out the best in his players. Though the fiercely competitive Ian Botham needed little outside help to ignite his motivation, Brearley is widely credited with restoring the great all-rounder's confidence, having returned to replace him as captain in the 1981 Ashes series, which England went on to win 3–1 against all the odds.

It should be said that Brearley enjoyed a dose of good fortune as England captain in that he inherited an improving side with a number of highly talented youngsters including Botham and David Gower. The Packer affair also worked in his favour, as England suffered the least of the leading nations from the mass defection of Test players to the World Series. In the final series before Packer's circus began, England regained the Ashes under Brearley with a 3–0 series win at home in 1977. Two years later Brearley oversaw their defence as England overwhelmed a young and inexperienced Australian side by five Tests to one on their own soil.

Brearley was handed the Middlesex captaincy in 1971 after returning from his studies at Cambridge, and he retired from the game in 1982 having steered the county to their fourth County Championship title in seven years over the most successful period in their history. After leaving the game, he became a lecturer, writer and psychotherapist.

bowl medium pace or off-breaks, Titmus had attracted the attention of the selectors as early as 1955, when he played in two Tests against South Africa. It was another seven years, however, before he established himself as a regular in the national side. His Test career came to an end in 1968 after he lost four toes in a horrific boating accident in the West Indies, but remarkably he recovered well enough to re-establish himself as a fine slow bowler on the county circuit. Though not a prodigious turner of the ball, Titmus was a master of flight and variation. John Murray, who took over the wicketkeeping role from Leslie Compton, was the fourth player of international class in the Middlesex ranks in the late 1950s and early 1960s. An excellent attacking batsman, if frustratingly inconsistent, Murray was considered the best keeper in the country for a while and represented England 21 times.

The late 1960s saw the emergence of two future England batsmen on the Middlesex books, Mike Brearley and Clive Radley. Brearley began his county career while studying at Cambridge, and for several seasons he divided his time between scholarship and cricket. Both were called into the Test side in the late 1970s following the mass defections of established stars to the Kerry Packer circus in Australia. Brearley, ever thoughtful and intelligent in his leadership, distinguished himself as captain of both his county and his country. Though neither Brearley nor Radley established himself as a Test batsman of the first order, they were prolific run-scorers on the county circuit.

It was under Brearley's shrewd leadership that the glory days returned to Middlesex in the mid-1970s and, rivalled only by Essex, they remained the most powerful county side until the early 1990s. In 1975 Middlesex reached the final of both knock-out competitions and the following year they won the County Championship title for the first time since they shared top place with Yorkshire in 1949. In 1977 Middlesex were joint champions with Kent, as well as Gillette Cup winners, and in 1980 Brearley guided the county to their seventh outright win in the championship. Their success was sealed not at Lord's but at Sophia Gardens, Cardiff, where Brearley's masterful 124 not out helped the London county to victory over Glamorgan. Afterwards Brearley singled out his giant South African fast bowler, Vincent van der Bijl, as the major factor in their success. His 85 wickets that season took him to the top of the national bowling averages. Lord's, though, did provide Middlesex fans with an occasion to cheer their heroes four days later when Brearley's men again lifted the Gillette Cup (in the last year of Gillette's sponsorship) after beating Surrey in one of the less thrilling climaxes in the history of the final. Needing just 202 for victory at an easy rate of about three an over, Brearley, fittingly, with an unbeaten 96, saw his charges home with 36 balls to spare, helped by the colourful stroke-play of Roland Butcher, who thrashed a half-century in just 45 minutes.

In 1982 Middlesex, enjoying their most successful period since the immediate post-war years, won their second championship in three years in the game against Worcestershire at Worcester. It was a triumphant end to the career of Mike Brearley, who had captained the side for twelve years, during which they won four championships and two Gillette Cups. Brearley was fortunate to have a strong bowling line-up in spinners John Emburey and Phil Edmonds and pacemen Wayne Daniel, Norman Cowans and Neil Williams, as well as Vincent van der Bijl, but his imaginative and positive leadership was a significant factor in the county's success during his tenure.

One of the advantages of being Middlesex is that if you get to the final of one of the two domestic knock-out competitions you are

MIDDLESEX V. NORTHAMPTONSHIRE, 1986 – MIKE GATTING REACHES HIS 150.

guaranteed home advantage. In 1984 Middlesex, under the bullish leadership of Mike Gatting, went 'home' to contest the NatWest Trophy final, and in one of the most exciting finishes in the 21-year history of the competition they beat Kent by four wickets off the last ball in near darkness. The veteran England left-armer Derek Underwood appeared to have bowled Kent into a winning position when he bowled nine overs for just twelve runs. Inexplicably he was taken off by Kent captain Chris Tavare, and Middlesex regained the initiative through Radley and Downton, who made 87 together at nearly six runs an over before the England spin twins Edmonds and Emburey kept their nerve to see Middlesex home.

The following year Middlesex recaptured the County Championship on the last day of the season against Warwickshire at Edgbaston,

M.W. GATTING (1957–)

A bulldog both in appearance and attitude, Mike Gatting was a pugnacious and highly successful batsman and captain for both Middlesex and England. His career was a catalogue of remarkable highs and equally spectacular lows. He was only the third England captain after Jardine and Illingworth to regain the Ashes on Australian soil, and he captained Middlesex to triumph in all four domestic competitions. In later years, however, his career was dogged by controversy. The beginning of the end came in December 1987, when he was involved in a furious on-pitch row with the provocative Pakistan umpire Shakoor Rana at Faisalabad. The following summer he was forced to resign the England captaincy after an encounter with a barmaid in his hotel room, and he then provoked a barrage of criticism when he led a rebel tour to South Africa.

Born in Kingsbury, Middlesex, Gatting established his reputation as a cricketer of outstanding promise in the early 1970s when he represented England Schools. He made his debut for Middlesex in 1975 and was awarded his county cap two years later. Gatting, stocky, powerful and aggressive, quickly showed that on his day he was capable of destroying any bowling attack, and in 1978 he was chosen for the England squad to tour Pakistan. However, it was not until his 54th innings that he made his first Test hundred. The selectors, though, had little choice but to persevere with him in the early 1980s when his sheer weight of runs for Middlesex confirmed that he was a batsman of the highest pedigree. In 1981 he finished eighth in the national averages, in 1982 he was sixth, in 1983 third, and in 1984 he finished at the top, having scored 2,257 runs at 68.39. It was in the 1984–85 tour of India that he finally came good at international level when he hit 136 at Bombay and followed it with 207 at Madras to finish the series with an average of 95.83. Against Australia in England's successful Ashes campaign the following summer he scored two more centuries and had considerably improved his miserable Test average, having scored a remarkable 1,102 runs in eleven matches.

In the 1986 tour to the West Indies, Gatting and England suffered a painful blow when he was struck by a short-pitched delivery from Malcolm Marshall that broke his nose. Such was the force of the impact that part of his nose was found embedded in the ball, and when he recovered from the injury he soon broke his thumb and was ruled out for the rest of the series. Following England's 5–0 whitewash in the Caribbean Gatting succeeded Gower as captain and, despite losing home series to New Zealand and India, he was confirmed as captain for the Australia tour. The 1986–87 Ashes success was perhaps Gatting's finest hour, as England, defying the form book and the bookmakers' odds, triumphed over their old adversaries under Gatting's aggressive and intelligent leadership.

Following his dismissal as England captain, Gatting's career went into decline and he was banned from Test cricket for three years after leading the controversial rebel tour to South Africa. He returned to the Test scene in 1992–93 with moderate success before retiring from the game in 1997, since when he has become a key figure in the England management team.

where Edmonds and Emburey once again led the charge towards victory. They took eight of Warwickshire's second-innings wickets as Middlesex sealed an overwhelming win by an innings and 74 runs. It was their fifth championship title in ten years and the ninth in their history. Gatting, who had succeeded Brearley as captain at the start of the 1983 season, played a major part in their triumph. His bold leadership would soon land him the England captaincy, and that summer he enjoyed some of the best form of his career, finishing at the top of the England batting averages.

Lord's was the scene of another thrilling NatWest final that summer as Essex, who rivalled Middlesex as the pre-eminent county side of the mid-1980s, beat Nottinghamshire by just one run on the last ball of a high-scoring contest. Essex had amassed an intimidating total of 280 for 2 in their 60 overs, thanks largely to an opening partnership of 202 between Gooch (90) and Hardie (110). But Nottinghamshire's openers, Robinson (80) and Broad (64), laid the foundations of an extraordinary run chase with a first-wicket stand of 145. With the field set back, Derek Randall (66) was at his inventive best as he kept Notts in the chase. In the final over Notts needed eighteen runs, and Randall took them to the brink of what would have been an

RAIN-SOAKED FANS GATHER IN FRONT OF THE PAVILION AFTER MIDDLESEX'S VICTORY OVER KENT IN THE B&H FINAL, 1986.

MIKE GATTING ACCEPTS THE WINNER'S CHEQUE FOR MIDDLESEX IN THE 1990 COUNTY CHAMPIONSHIP.

astonishing win with a string of drives off Pringle, but was caught at mid-wicket with just two runs needed.

In 1986 Middlesex added more silverware to their burgeoning trophy cabinet when they beat Kent in the final of the Benson and Hedges Cup at Lord's. The 1980s had produced a number of riveting cup finals, but none more so than this contest, which went down to the very last ball. Again, Lord's was in near darkness as the match reached its climax; but after Kent had turned down the offer to complete their innings the following day they failed to get the six runs needed off the final three balls and Middlesex had won by two runs.

Middlesex were triumphant again in the final of the 1988 NatWest Trophy, but there was no such excitement on this occasion as they overhauled Worcestershire's 161 with three wickets and 27 balls left. Teenager Mark Ramprakash was named Man of the Match after showing composure beyond his years to steer Middlesex out of choppy waters with a fine 56. Mike Gatting's side had the chance to retain the trophy the following season but were beaten by Worcestershire in the final over. Middlesex's success continued, however, when, buoyed by the runs of Gatting and Ramprakash and the wickets of Fraser, Tufnell and Emburey, they won the championship in 1990 and 1993 to cement their status as the foremost county (alongside Essex) in the modern era.

Middlesex's fortunes have dipped in recent years, partly because the production line of young talent is no longer what it was. 'Apart from Ramps (Mark Ramprakash), Tuffers (Phil Tufnell) and Owais Shah, the well is a bit dry at the moment, although we have a very promising batsman, Andy Strauss, who I think could go on to great things,' admits Codrington. 'But we have just appointed Mike Gatting as Director of Coaching and in Ian Gould we have a very good Club Coach. They are aware of the pressing need to discover and bring through some young players. With them in charge of playing affairs I do not think it will be long before we are back where we were a few seasons ago.'

MCC PRESIDENTS, SECRETARIES AND TREASURERS

PRESIDENTS

Year	President
1825	C. J. Barnett
1826	Lord Frederick Beauclerk
1827	H. Kingscote
1828	A. F. Greville
1829	J. Barnard
1830	Hon. G. Ponsonby
1831	W. Deedes
1832	H. Howard
1833	H. Jenner
1834	Hon. A. H. Ashley
1835	Lord Charles Russell
1836	Fourth Baron Suffield
1837	Fourth Viscount Grimston
1838	Second Marquess of Exeter
1839	Sixth Earl of Chesterfield
1840	First Earl of Verulam
1841	Second Earl of Craven
1842	Earl of March
1843	Second Earl of Ducie
1844	Sir John Bayley
1845	T. Chamberlayne
1846	Fourth Earl of Winterton
1847	Twelfth Earl of Strathmore
1848	Second Earl of Leicester
1849	Sixth Earl of Darnley
1850	Lord Guernsey
1851	Seventh Earl of Stamford
1852	Viscount Dupplin
1853	Marquess of Worcester
1854	Earl Vane
1855	Earl of Uxbridge
1856	Viscount Milton
1857	Sir F. H. Hervey-Bathurst
1858	Lord Garlies
1859	Ninth Earl of Coventry
1860	Second Baron Skelmersdale
1861	Fifth Earl Spencer
1862	Fourth Earl of Sefton
1863	Fifth Baron Suffield
1864	First Earl of Dudley
1865	First Baron Ebury
1866	Seventh Earl of Sandwich
1867	Second Earl of Verulam
1868	Second Baron Methuen
1869	Fifth Marquess of Lansdowne
1870	J. H. Scourfield
1871	Fifth Earl of Clarendon
1872	Eighth Viscount Downe
1873	Viscount Chelsea
1874	Marquess of Hamlilton
1875	Sir Charles Legard
1876	Second Lord Londesborough
1877	Eighth Duke of Beaufort
1878	Second Lord Fitzhardinge
1879	W. Nicholson
1880	Sir William Hart-Dyke
1881	Lord George Hamlilton
1882	Second Baron Belper
1883	Hon. Robert Grimston
1884	Fifth Earl Winterton
1885	Third Baron Wenlock
1886	Fifth Baron Lyttleton
1887	Hon. Edward Chandos Leigh
1888	Sixth Duke of Buccleuch
1889	Sir Henry James
1890	Twenty-second Baron Willoughby de Eresby
1891	V. E. Walker
1892	W. E. Denison
1893	Sixth Earl of Dartmouth
1894	Seventh Earl of Jersey
1895	Fourth Baron Harris
1896	Fourteenth Earl of Pembroke
1897	Third Earl of Lichfield
1898	Hon. Alfred Lyttleton
1899	Sir Archibald L. Smith
1900	Hon. Ivo Bligh
1901	Fourth Earl Howe
1902	A. G. Steel
1903	First Baron Alverstone
1904	Marquess of Granby
1905	C. E. Green
1906	W. H. Long
1907	First Baron Loreburn
1908	Third Earl Cawdor
1909	Tenth Earl of Chesterfield
1910	Second Earl of Londesborough
1911	First Baron Desborough
1912	Ninth Duke of Devonshire
1913	Earl of Dalkeith
1914-1918	Seventh Baron Hawke
1919	First Lord Forster
1920	Fourth Earl of Ellesmere
1921	Hon. Sir Stanley Jackson
1922	First Viscount Chelmsford
1923	First Viscount Ullswater
1924	First Baron Ernle
1935	Admiral of the Fleet Sir John de Robeck
1926	Third Viscount Hampden
1927	Third Baron Leconfield

LORD'S LANDMARKS 1787–1838

1787 Thomas Lord opens first ground in Dorset Fields, north-west London. Marylebone Cricket Club formed

1805 First Eton v. Harrow match

1806 First Gentlemen v. Players match

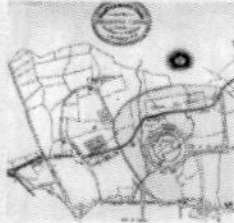

1811 Lord and MCC relocate to North Bank

1814 MCC move onto current site

1822 Benjamin Aislabie elected MCC secretary

1825 Fire destroys pavilion and all MCC records. Lord sells interest in ground to William Ward

1827 First Varsity match

1832 Thomas Lord dies

1835 James Dark buys out Ward

1837 MCC celebrate silver jubilee. Hot-air balloon ascent by Frenchman Garnerin

1838 Pavilion lit by gas

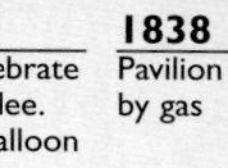

1928	Fifth Earl of Lucan
1929	Field-Marshal Baron Plumer
1930	Sir Kynaston Studd
1931	First Viscount Bridgeman
1932	Viscount Lewisham
1933	First Viscount Hailsham
1934	Second Earl of Cromer
1935	Ninth Viscount Cobham
1936	Sixth Baron Somers
1937	Colonel Hon. J. J. Astor
1938	First Earl Baldwin of Bewdley
1939-1945	S. Christopherson
1946	General Sir Ronald Adam
1947	Lord Cornwallis
1948	The Earl of Gowrie
1949	H. R. H. The Duke of Edinburgh
1950	Sir Pelham Warner
1951	W. Findlay
1952	The Duke of Beaufort
1953	The Earl of Rosebery
1954	Viscount Cobham
1955	Field Marshal Earl Alexander of Tunis
1956	Viscount Monckton of Brenchley
1957	The Duke of Norfolk
1958	Marshal of the R. A. F. Viscount Portal of Hungerford
1959	H. S. Altham
1960	Sir Hubert Ashton
1961	Col. Sir William Worlsey
1962	Lt. Col. Lord Nugent
1963	G. O. Allen
1964	R. H. Twining
1965	Lt. Gen. Sir Oliver Leese
1966	Sir Alec Douglas-Home
1967	A. E. R. Gilligan
1968	R. Aird
1969	M. J. C. Allom
1970	Sir Cyril Hawker
1971	F. R. Brown
1972	A. M. Crawley
1973	Lord Caccia
1974	H. R. H. The Duke of Edinburgh
1975	C. G. A. Paris
1976	W. H. Webster
1977	D. G. Clark
1978	C. H. Palmer
1979	S. C. Griffith
1980	P. B. H. May
1981	G. H. G. Doggart
1982	Sir Anthony Tuke
1983	A. H. A. Dibbs
1984	F. G. Mann
1985	J. G. W. Davies
1986	M. C. Cowdrey
1987	J. J. Warr
1988	Field Marshall Baron Bramall of Bushfield
1989	Sir Denys Roberts
1990	Baron Griffiths of Govilon
1991	M. E. L. Melluish
1992-1994	D. R. W. Silk
1994-1996	Sir Oliver Popplewell
1996-1998	A. C. D. Ingleby-Mackenzie
1998-2000	A. R. Lewis

SECRETARIES

1822-1842	B. Aislabie
1842-1858	R. Kynaston
1858-1863	A. Bailie
1863-1876	R. A. Fitzgerald
1876-1897	H. Perkins
1898-1926	Sir Francis Lacey
1926-1936	W. Findlay
1936-1952	Colonel R. S. Rait Kerr
1952-1962	R. Aird
1962-1974	S. C. Griffith
1974-1987	J. A. Bailey
1987-1993	Lt. Col. J. R. Stephenson
1994-	R. D. V. Knight

TREASURERS

1866-1879	T. Burgoyne
1879-1915	Sir Spencer Ponsonby-Fane
1916-1932	Lord Harris
1932-1938	Lord Hawke
1938-1949	Ninth Viscount Cobham
1950-1963	H. S. Altham
1963-1964	Tenth Viscount Cobham
1965-1976	G. O. Allen
1976-1980	J. G. W. Davies
1980-1987	D. G. Clark
1987-1992	G. H. G. Doggart
1992-	M. E. L. Melluish

LORD'S LANDMARKS 1844–1878

4
Indians
orm
bition

1846
First scoreboard installed. William Clarke founds All-England XI

1848
Dark sets up first print shop

1850
Lord Frederick Beauclerk dies

1860
Lord's freehold sold at auction

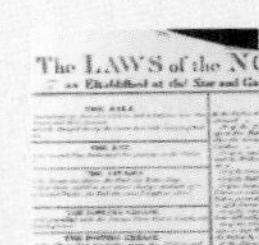

1864
Over-arm bowling legitimised. Lord's employs first groundsman

1866
MCC buy Lord's thanks to backing of William Nicholson. First Grand Stand erected

1867
Tavern pub is rebuilt

1868
Visit of touring Australian Aboriginals

1871
Turnstiles introduced

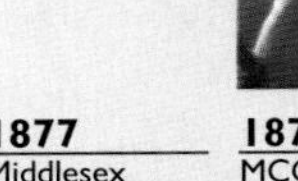

1877
Middlesex move to Lord's

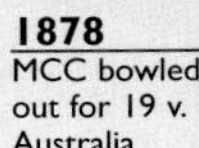

1878
MCC bowled out for 19 v. Australia

BIBLIOGRAPHY

The majority of my research for this book has come from contemporary newspapers and periodicals (mainly the *Daily Telegraph*, *The Times*, *The Guardian* and *Wisden*) and the books listed below. It would be perfectly possible to write several weighty volumes about Lord's and still not manage to give a complete picture of everything that has occurred in its long history. Anyone who wants to know more about Lord's or about the history of cricket should try to get hold of books from the following list.

Altham, H. S. (and Swanton, E. W.), *A History of Cricket*, George, Allen & Unwin Ltd, 1926-1962 (Swanton became co-author from 1938 onwards)

D'Oliveira, Basil, *The D'Oliveira Affair*, Collins, 1969

Frith, David, *The Golden Age of Cricket 1890-1914*, Lutterworth Press, 1978

Fry, C. B. ., *Life Worth Living*, Eyre & Spottiswoode, 1939

Grace, W. G. , *Cricket*, J. W. Arrowsmith, 1887

Green, Benny (Ed), *The Lord's Companion*, Pavilion, 1987

Harris, Lord G., and Ashley-Cooper, F. S. , *Lord's and the MCC*, The London & Counties Press Association Ltd, 1914

Hawke, Lord M. , *Recollections and Reminiscences*, Williams & Norgate Ltd, 1924

Heald, Tim (Ed), *My Lord's – A Celebration of the World's Greatest Cricket Ground*, Willow, 1990

Howat, Gerald, *Plum Warner*, Unwin Hyman, 1987

Hutchinson, Horace (Ed), *Cricket, Country Life Library of Sport*, 1903

Jessop, G. L. , *A Cricketer's Log*, Hodder & Stoughton, 1922

Lemman, David, *The History of Middlesex CCC*, Christopher Helm, 1988

Lewis, Tony, *Double Century*, Hodder & Stoughton, 1987

Lynch, Steven, *The Lord's Test*, Spellmount, 1990

Moorhouse, Geoffrey, *Lord's*, Hodder & Stoughton, 1983

Parker, Eric, *A History of Cricket*, Seeley Service and Co. Ltd, 1950

Plumptre, George, *The Golden Age of Cricket*, Queen Anne Press, 1990

Rippon, Anton, *The Story of Middlesex County Cricket Club*, Moorland, 1982

Ross, Alan *Ranji: Prince of Cricketers*, William Collins and Sons and Co. Ltd, 1883

Rutter, Edward, *Cricket Memories*, Williams & Norgate Ltd, 1925

Swanton, E. W. (Ed), *Barclays World of Cricket*, Collins, 1980

Taylor, Alfred D. , *Annals of Lord's and History of the MCC*, J. W. Arrowsmith, 1903

Warner, Pelham, *Lord's 1787-1945*, George G. Harrap & Co. Ltd, 1946

Wellings, E. M. , *A History of County Cricket: Middlesex*, Arthur Barker Ltd, 1972

Kerr, Diana Rait, *Lord's 1946-1970*, George G. Harrap & Co. Ltd, 1971

LORD'S LANDMARKS 1884–1910

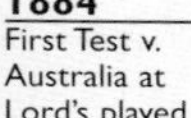

1884 First Test v. Australia at Lord's played

1887 MCC celebrates centenary

1888 MCC fight railway bill threatening Lord's

1890 New pavilion opened

1895 Lord's witnesses Grace become first man to reach 1,000 runs in May

1898 Testimonial match for Grace on his 50th birthday. New Test Match Board of Control meets at Lord's

1899 Mound Stand built on site of old tennis court. Albert Trott hits ball over pavilion

1903 Fry and MacLaren put on 309 for Gentlemen v. Players

1906 Press box built

1907 First Test against South Africa

1909 Imperial Cricket Conference established by England, Australia and South Africa

1910 Fowler's ma

INDEX

Page numbers in italics refer to illustrations.

LORD'S LANDMARKS 1914–1938

14
...break of ... Centenary ... of ground

1915
Death of Grace

1920
First-class cricket resumes. Warner captains Middlesex to win County Championships in his last season

1923
Grace Gates erected

1926
Jack Hobbs hits 316 not out for Surrey v. Middlesex, then the highest score at Lord's. New Grand Stand built

1928
Lord's stages first Test v. West Indies

1930
Australia make 729 for 6 v. England at Lord's. Bradman makes 254

1931
First Test v. New Zealand 1932-33 Bodyline controversy

1934
Verity takes 15 wickets v. Australia. Harris Gardens laid out

1935
Lord's sees England lose to South Africa for first time

1937
MCC celebrates 150th anniversary

1938
Last Ashes series for nine years

LORD'S LANDMARKS 1939–1968

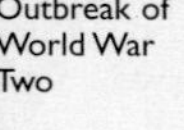

1939 Outbreak of World War Two

1945 Victory Tests v. Australia

1946 India first side to tour England after the war

1947 Compton and Edrich dazzle Lord's with record run-scoring

1948 England beaten by 409 runs by Bradman's 'Invincibles'

1950 West Indies win first Test in England at Lord's

1953 England regain Ashes. Duke of Edinburgh opens Memorial Gallery

1958 Warner Stand opened

1962 Amateur/professional distinction abolished. last Gentlemen v. Players fixture

1963 Cowdrey bats with arm in plaster in thrilling climax to Test v. West Indies. First season of Gillette Cup, Sussex win final at Lord's

1966 MCC members revolt over redevelopment plans

1967-68 South-west corner redeveloped. New Tavern Stand opens

LORD'S LANDMARKS 1968–1985

8
sfer of
er from
C to
ket
ncil,
prising
y formed
B, NCA
MCC

1969
D'Oliveira affair leads to cancellation of South Africa tour

1972
Australia's Bob Massie takes 16 wickets v. England at Lord's. First Benson and Hedges Cup final

1975
West Indies beat Australia in first World Cup final

1977
Packer controversy, MCC Indoor school opened

1978
Botham breaks records v. Pakistan

1979
West Indies retain World Cup

1980
Centenary Test at Lord's

1981
Botham inspires England to Ashes victory after resigning captaincy at end of Lord's Test

1983
India beat West Indies in World Cup final

1984
Greenidge hits 214 not out as West Indies stun England

1985
New library opened

LORD'S LANDMARKS 1987–1999

1987 MCC celebrates bicentenary. New Mound Stand opened by Duke of Edinburgh

1988 Electronic scoreboard installed

1989 Q Stand renamed the Allen Stand in memory of Sir George Allen

1990 Gooch hits 333 and 123 for England v. India. Centenary of Pavilion

1991 Opening of Compton and Edrich Stands

1992 Pakistan continue to torment England

1993 Renovation of museum, England crushed by Australia

1994 South Africa return to England after 29 years. Atherton's 'dirt-in-pocket' affair

1995 Duke of Edinburgh opens new Indoor school. England beat West Indies at Lord's

1996 Pakistan beat England in dramatic finish

1997 England and Wales Cricket Board becomes new governing body

1998 New Grand Stand officially opened, England lose to South Africa at Lord's but win series

1999 New Press centre opens